POPES
& BANKERS

Other books by Jack Cashill

Hoodwinked

Sucker Punch

Ron Brown's Body

What's the Matter with California?

POPES
& BANKERS

A CULTURAL HISTORY OF CREDIT AND
DEBIT FROM ARISTOTLE TO AIG

JACK CASHILL

THOMAS NELSON
Since 1798

NASHVILLE DALLAS MEXICO CITY RIO DE JANEIRO

Published in Nashville, Tennessee, by Thomas Nelson. Thomas Nelson is a trademark of Thomas Nelson, Inc.

Thomas Nelson, Inc., titles may be purchased in bulk for educational, business, fund-raising, or sales promotional use. For information, please e-mail SpecialMarkets@ThomasNelson.com.

Unless otherwise noted, all Scripture references are from the King James Version.

Library of Congress Cataloging-in-Publication Data

Cashill, Jack.
    Popes and bankers : a cultural history of credit and debit from Aristotle to AIG / Jack Cashill.
        p. cm.
    Includes bibliographical references.
    ISBN 978-1-59555-273-0
    1. Banks and banking—History. 2. Credit—History. 3. Usury—History. I. Title.
HG1551.C37 2010
332.09—dc22   2009047867

Printed in the United States of America

10 11 12 13 14 RRD 6 5 4 3 2 1

To my big brother, Bill.

Contents

Introduction

MICHAEL RADFORD'S 2004 FILM VERSION OF WILLIAM SHAKESPEARE'S
The Merchant of Venice opens as follows: A boatload of mean-looking monks
floats along a Venetian canal, holding crucifixes and chanting vile imprecations,
as monks in movies are wont to do. They pass a sophisticated group of Venetians
wearing funny masks with phallic noses and cavorting with half-naked floozies.
The floating monks now approach a bridge crowded with red-faced religious
fanatics. Egged on by the monks, the fanatics beat the red-capped Jewish "usurers" in their midst and casually chuck them into the eco-unfriendly canal below.

Just another day in Christian Venice.

Be assured, this is not Venice as Shakespeare imagined it. The Bard liked
his Venetian merchants and at least respected the usurer Shylock. Rather, this
is Venice as Radford sees it, and his view is not at all exceptional. How these
sophisticates, fanatics, and usurers would turn Christendom into the world's
freest, richest, and most enduring commercial civilization is a question Radford
and most of his peers could not begin to frame, let alone answer.

It is much remarked in the literature of credit that only Jews and Christians—of
all ancient people—held usury to be sinful. Yet they also collaborated almost
exclusively in the creation of the West's extraordinary economy. Is it possible that
monks and other Judeo-Christian moralists were useful, maybe even essential,

to the creation of this economy? If so, then is it possible that their dismissal from the marketplace has condemned us to our current economic purgatory?

These questions, one suspects, are also beyond Radford's grasp, beyond the grasp of most economists for that matter, but they deserve to be addressed. By tracing the history of credit and debt, or *usury*—as lending at interest was widely called until at least AD 1800—we can begin to answer them.

For the record, the word *usury* comes rather directly from the Latin *usura*, which means the charging of interest on loans, any interest. As we shall see, the larger history of credit and debt is in its essence a history of man's struggle to make sense of God's law. Given the limits of human nature, man never quite succeeds. And yet the creative tension between pious restraint on the one hand and economic ambition on the other has made us as prosperous as we are. The struggle continues.

one

The Seventh Circle

BOSTON IS THE HOME OF ONE MELONIE GRIFFITHS-EVANS. WERE SHE to die unrepentant, which seems likely, she might well find herself in the fourth circle of Dante's Inferno among the prodigals. A word used less today than it ought, *prodigal* simply means "given to excessive or impru-dent spending." The prodigals have long been with us. "For, as has been said," Aristotle writes in the *Nicomachean Ethics*, "he is liberal who spends according to his substance and on the right objects; and he who exceeds is prodigal."[1] Prodigals matter here because historically they have kept lenders in business. They still do.

The ethics surrounding credit and debit—or *debt*, for our purposes—find expression in the oldest written records, those of the Greeks and the Hebrews. But the real history predates that, as the Mesopotamians kept records of bor-rowing and lending on stone tablets. And yet even when the terms of a loan were literally "written in stone," people sought to evade them, most typically prodigals like the aforementioned Ms. Griffiths-Evans.

Fortunately for Griffiths-Evans, she has the sympathetic David Koeppel of *MSN Money* to chronicle her tale, not the judgmental Dante Alighieri. As Koeppel tells it, in 2004 Griffiths-Evans contracted to buy a $470,000 home in Boston's Dorchester section with no down payment. She claims to have been looking for an apartment, but those that suited her fancy cost about $5,000 to $6,000 a month. At that time, the amount was more than she could afford. Landlords, after all, demand rent. Lenders can be more flexible. Ambitious beyond her means, Griffiths-Evans heeded their siren song.

The first question the obliging Koeppel asks her in a recorded interview is, "Was your loan a predatory loan?" Griffiths-Evans answers without hesitation, "It definitely was."[2] To swing the deal, she took out a fairly standard 8.5 percent loan on 80 percent of the purchase price. Lacking the traditional 20 percent down payment, she took out a second loan at a whopping 12.5 percent. Her combined monthly payment ran roughly $3,500 a month to begin, increasing as the loan adjusted.

Historically, lenders would not have allowed that size of a payment for anyone making less than about $200,000 a year, presumably more than Griffiths-Evans earned as a part-time teacher. But lenders in the first years of this new century were encouraged to accommodate people like Griffiths-Evans. She got the money. Still, she claims her lender told her that she could soon refinance into a lower-cost, fixed-rate mortgage. "That is where it became predatory," she reassures herself and Koeppel.[3]

There is nothing unique about Griffiths-Evans. A million Americans just like her have unwittingly conspired to wreck the world's economy. Writing twenty-three centuries ago, Aristotle sniffed out their ambitions:

> They become apt to take because they wish to spend and cannot do this easily; for their possessions soon run short. Thus they are forced to provide means from some other source. At the same time, because they care nothing for honor, they take recklessly and from any source.

What changed over time, as shall be seen, was the nation's willingness to oblige its prodigals. To fix her innocence, Koeppel asks Griffiths-Evans no questions about her elusive husband, her income, her seeming inability to save money, her job prospects, the alleged cost of rental housing, or any potential plans she might have had to surf the rising tide of real estate prices and flip the house for a profit, plans possibly swallowed in the subprime morass.

Like most in the media, Koeppel thinks less harshly of prodigals than those who enable them. In this comprehensive article, the reader hears not a word from Griffiths-Evans's lenders or any other lenders. They remain as faceless and generic as the Jewish moneychangers in Radford's Venice. Koeppel gives the final word to one of the predatory lender's presumed prey: "If you're given fraudulent loans," says still another bamboozled woman, "someone needs to go to jail. Someone needs to be held accountable."[4]

Unlike Dante, Koeppel does not seem to think of prodigals as sinners, preferring instead to think of them as they think of themselves—as victims. Indeed, it could be argued that the real divide in America today is not between left and right, but between those who would sympathize with Griffiths-Evans and those who would not. The latter we will call traditionalists; the former, social puritans, shorthand for those secular moralists who confuse their local banker with the devil and Wall Street with hell.

Koeppel has no sympathy at all for lenders and no apparent interest in their motivation. And yet as offended as he seems to be by predatory lending and lenders, Koeppel, I suspect, would scoff at the whole concept of usury and usurers. To the modernist ear, the very words sound hopelessly papist and mired in medieval superstition.

When social puritans survey the moral landscape, they see aggregates of predators exploiting aggregates of victims, the goodness and badness of each fixed by little more than fashion. Koeppel, for instance, titled his article "Single women slammed by housing mess." A traditionalist might just title the article "Single women help cause housing mess" and, if feeling churlish, talk of Griffiths-Evans as a "predatory borrower."

Traditionalists like Dante and Shakespeare have a distinct artistic advantage: they believe in sin. When they survey that same moral landscape, they see a thousand different souls struggling with a thousand different demons. Nor do traditionalists attempt to exculpate sinners by downgrading their demons to disease, depression, addiction, or "circumstances beyond Melonie's control." Sin makes for much better drama. It might also make for a much better economy.

Dante, in particular, was a connoisseur of sin. He could divine its subtle gradations as finely as an Eskimo could snow. Indeed, the first part of his *Divina Commedia*, "Inferno," reads like a veritable taxonomy of sin.

Written in the first person, in vernacular Italian, almost exactly seven centuries ago, the *Divine Comedy* recounts Dante's guided tour through the three zones of the dead—*Inferno* or hell, *Purgatorio*, and *Paradiso*. He begins his journey on Holy Thursday of Easter Week in the year 1300 and ends the following Wednesday.

His tour guide through hell and purgatory is not a saint or even a fellow Christian, but the Roman poet Virgil. From Dante's perspective, sin transcended the priestly imagination. It was a universal, as was salvation, which "shows the road to everyone, whatever our journey."[5]

The opening of "Inferno" finds Dante in the full throes of a midlife crisis and on the verge of moral breakdown, perhaps even suicide. It is at this low moment that Virgil rescues the troubled Florentine, and the two begin their journey through hell. The condemned sinners occupy nine descending circles: the self-indulgent the first five, the violent the next two, and the treacherous the bottom eighth and ninth.

The first circle is reserved for those otherwise good souls who did not know or accept Christ, including Virgil himself. In this halfway agreeable Limbo-like state, Virgil and others live out an eternity deprived of a joy they cannot even fathom.

Eternity starts getting rough in the second circle. Here, just as they were torn by their own passions in life, the lustful are torn about forever in eternal storms. In the third circle gluttons are made to wallow in a nasty slush of freezing rain and black snow.

The fourth circle holds the miserly and the prodigal, now condemned to ram huge massive weights into each other for eternity. In the fifth circle the wrathful slug it out on the surface of the swamplike River Styx, while the grim and sullen get waterboarded, or something much like it, below. Things literally heat up in the sixth circle, where various and sundry heretics find themselves trapped in a flaming tomb from which they cannot escape.

Until this point in Dante's narrative, the modern reader would find little to disturb his or her finely tuned sensitivities. Dante gives the heathens a break in the first circle. He comes down relatively lightly on adulterers in the second, and since the greedy, the gluttonous, and the grim are always other people or their children, the reader would not particularly sweat their fates either.

It is with the seventh circle, and only in its innermost ring, that Dante begins to challenge modern presumptions. The outermost ring is the unhappy home of the murderous and tyrannical. They stew in a river of boiling blood while centaurs shoot arrows at those who would dare escape. Few today would object to this consignment. Some would like to see Congress so consigned.

In the middle ring dwell the suicides, now reduced to "stumps of wood,"[6] painfully sensitive to any touch, eternally plucked at by Harpies. The punishment might seem harsh to the modernist, but he would not be surprised that people once thought thusly or that many still do.

Condemned to the inner and most frightening ring of the seventh circle are those whose offenses run counter to "nature and her gifts"[7]: the blasphemers who defy God; the sodomites who defy their own nature; and, yes, the usurers who defy the right order of things. All are condemned to a half-life in a desert of flaming sand with fire raining upon them from the sky—Bakersfield as imagined by a San Franciscan.

The sodomy he gets, but Dante has a hard time understanding why usury is sinful. "Please," he asks Virgil, "could we retrace our path back to that place where you said usury offends celestial Goodness, and solve that knot."[8] Usury here means no more than the lending of money at interest, even at a moderate rate. Anyone today who has ever deposited money in a bank, which in turn lends that money at interest, has committed this sin as Dante understood it.

To make his case, not an obvious one even then, Virgil cites several esteemed sources, both secular and Christian, to the effect that "man should thrive and gain his bread"[9] either by nature or art, that is, either through working the land or working with one's hands. The usurer, however, "takes a different way,"[10] and in so doing defies God's plan for man. That much said, and it is frankly not much to go on, Virgil ploughs ahead with his student in tow.

Only two circles remain in the pair's descent, and they host the consciously fraudulent and treacherous. The eighth circle is subdivided into ten truly vile pits. Here suffer the pimps, the flatterers, the false prophets, the corrupt politicians, the hypocrites, the thieves, the alchemists, the counterfeiters, the perjurers, and the "fraudulent advisors"[11]—but more on Bernie Madoff later.

The icy hell of the ninth circle belongs to traitors, the most notorious of whom—Brutus, Cassius, and Judas Iscariot—hang from the bloody mouth of the greatest traitor of them all, Satan. As is fairly evident, the conscious act of betrayal—of one's friends, one's country, one's nature, one's God— troubles Dante more than the everyday vices that bedevil all of mankind.

Wiser for having seen the horrific fate of traitors and the other evildoers,

Dante follows Virgil down and out through an opening where he sees, on this glorious predawn Easter day, a sky brightly studded with stars, "some of the beautiful things that heaven bears."[12]

Dante did not write the *Divine Comedy* just to sell books. He wrote it to instruct his fellow man in the remarkably structured Christian cosmos and man's place within it. To be sure, all cultures have their gods, their cosmogonies, their system of rewards and punishments, but none have anything like medieval Christianity's intellectual order.

Even in 1300, that sense of order, a reflection of God's divine plan, shaped Dante's perception of the economy. After showing Dante the squalid materialists condemned to hell's fourth circle, Virgil instructs his pupil in the ways of Fortuna, the angelic regulator who oversees the economic sphere. God has assigned her the "invisible" role of distributing "goods of worldly splendor"[13]—not at all unlike the famed "invisible hand" that ruled Adam Smith's eighteenth-century economy. Try as he might, man proves incapable of fully grasping how the invisible hand works, how Fortuna "foresees, judges, and rules her appointed realm." Adds Virgil, "She is cursed too often by those who ought to sing her praises."[14] Dante has come to understand that those doing the cursing have likely violated God's good order.

Much to her misfortune, Melonie Griffiths-Evans had no Virgil in her life, no guide through Boston's unmapped moral terrain. And that has proved costly for all.

"Society cannot exist unless a controlling power upon will and appetite be placed somewhere," said the Anglo-Irish political philosopher Edmund Burke more than two centuries ago, "and the less of it there is within, the more there is without."[15] The denouement of the Griffiths-Evans case shows just how intrusive and expensive that controlling power can be when imposed from without.

If Griffiths-Evans lacked a guide, she did not lack for advocates in the streets or in the media. City Life/Vida Urbana, a Boston community activist group, organized noisy street protests to forestall two separate eviction attempts. "We're going to take back our cities! We're going to take back our neighborhoods! We're going to do what's right for families, not what's right for bankers!" Griffiths-Evans told the fifty or so protestors at a 2008 rally, four years after she bought the house.[16] For all of its rhetorical bluster, her call to political action would have left Fortuna's head spinning. It made no economic sense whatsoever. As amplified and ratified, her rallying cry has pushed Western civilization to the edge of an economic abyss.

In his benchmark book *The Spirit of Democratic Capitalism*, Michael Novak insists that to be successful, "the moral cultural system of democratic capitalism must resist hedonism and decadence with all its power, and not merely accommodate itself to fashion."[17] The moral cultural is one pillar out of three that Novak sees as sustaining the capitalist enterprise. A functioning democracy provides the other two: the freedom to take risks without undue interference, and a reliable system of laws to protect the rights of the risk takers.

The media covering the Griffiths-Evans saga knew little about the moral cultural history that brought them to this moment. The protestors knew less. Playing to their cameras, they embarrassed the lender into allowing Griffiths-Evans to stay in her home for three more months, presumably free of charge, while she tried to find a buyer. When she failed to find one, the lender gave her still more time to find an apartment. Through it all, this poster child for the subprime meltdown remained confident that she would not be evicted. As she confided to the *Boston Globe*, likely without consulting her source, "The Lord is on my side."[18]

two

Unto a Stranger

HIGH ON THE LIST OF HISTORICAL IRONIES IS THIS: JEWS WERE THE first people to prohibit usury and, in the pre-Christian era, the only people of consequence to do so. Hittites, Phoenicians, Egyptians, and Babylonians accepted usury as a matter of course. Future developments aside, the Jewish prohibition should not be surprising. Jews were the first people to divine a monotheistic God, one who cared deeply enough about his people to share with them a how-to guide to life.

As chronicled in the first five books of the Old Testament, God gave this law to the Israelites through Moses. The law begins with the Ten Commandments and includes many narrower rules of observance. These Jews call the Torah, or, as translated, "the Law." An atheist might challenge the source of the law, but he would be hard pressed to deny that it transformed human history.

By contrast, the Code of Hammurabi, developed during the eighteenth century BC, has all the inspiration and ethical punch of a set of government regulations. In this spirit, the Code treated usury as a matter of ordinary Babylonian commercial life. The relevant articles of the code, in fact, were niggling enough to have been written by an IRS lifer: "If a merchant lent grain or money at interest and when he lent [it] at interest he paid out the money by the small weight and the grain by the small measure, but when he got [it] back he got the money by the [large] weight (and) the grain by the large measure, [that merchant shall forfeit] whatever he lent."[1] Word to our political betters: enduring civilizations are not built on regulations.

In Mosaic law, violations had existential consequences: they offended God. Although not all of the law was transformative—"He that is wounded in the stones, or hath his privy member cut off, shall not enter into the congregation of the LORD" (Deuteronomy 23:1) comes to mind—much of it was. Like no other code before and few since, Mosaic law respected the individual and treated those under its sway more or less equally.

On the usury question, however, it should be noted that when Mosaic law was codified, Jews were a largely pastoral people, living less-settled lives than their contemporaries in Mesopotamia. They did not have complex systems of trade and the understandings those systems inspire. Thus when the law turned to the question of usury, it did so in the context of neighbors dealing with neighbors, not traders dealing with customers. That much said, the codifiers consistently and unequivocally scorned usury—at least among God's people, and there, alas, was the rub.

The first prohibitions appear in Exodus, in the second book of Moses, which likely dates back to the thirteenth century BC: "If thou lend money to any of my people that is poor by thee, thou shalt not be to him as an usurer, neither shalt thou lay upon him usury" (22:25). The Hebrew word for usury in this instance, *neshek*, literally means "something bitten of."

Calvin Elliott, who wrote the twentieth century's most spirited defense of the usury prohibition (albeit in 1902), traces the origin of the *neshek* to the biting of a serpent. To make his case, he cites the research of a contemporary with the intriguing name Dr. George Bush. Bush argues that a serpent's bite "is often so small as to be scarcely perceptible at first, yet the venom soon spreads and diffuses itself till it reaches the vitals, so the increase of usury, which at first is not perceived, at length grows so much as to devour a man's substance."[2] This whole notion of biting and slicing and infecting will resonate throughout the history of this subject up until the present. Elliott's take on the subject has had such sufficient staying power that his book was reprinted in 2007.

David, the second king of the united kingdom of Israel, reigned in the neighborhood of 1000 BC. A gifted musician as well as a warrior, he is believed to have authored many of the Psalms. In Psalm 15, he shares his take on the usurer's trade with his countrymen. "Lord," David asks, "who shall abide in thy tabernacle? who shall dwell in thy holy hill?" (v. 1). On the short list of those who just might hope to ascend that hill is "He that putteth not out his money to usury, nor taketh reward against the innocent" (v. 5). Recited in congregation, the Psalms had the effect of bringing community pressure to bear on the shaky resolve of the individual. Given that the composer was also the king, the sing-alongs must have been lively.

David's successor, King Solomon, understood that in his time and place the question of usury was one issue that could not be split down the middle. In Proverbs 28:8, he links usury directly with other financial scams. "He that by usury and unjust gain increaseth his substance," declares Solomon, "he shall gather it for him that will pity the poor." One implication, as in most of the Old Testament citations on the subject, is that usury hurts the poor. There are, to be sure, no references to commercial loans, let alone collateralized debt obligations or credit default swaps, in the Old Testament. A second implication here, one that shows Solomon at his wisest, is that usury will inevitably betray the usurer.

Going forward, the prophets were not too keen on usury either. In the days after Solomon's passing, corrupted perhaps by the wealth and power their kingdom had amassed, the people began to lose their moral vigor. Partly as a result, the unified Jewish nation split in two—Israel to the north and Judah to the south. The prophet Isaiah warned that if the Jews did not heed the laws handed down by Moses, if they continued, among other sins, to "beat my people to pieces, and grind the faces of the poor" (Isaiah 3:15), they would soon enough find themselves carried captive to an alien land.

In the immediate decades before the catastrophe that Isaiah prophesied, the gloomy Jeremiah took up the warning. Writing circa 600 BC and weighing in on the moral corruption then infecting Jerusalem, Jeremiah revealed the depth of hostility toward the usurer without even intending to. "Woe is me," he writes in a trademark burst of self-pity, "my mother, that thou hast borne me a man of strife and a man of contention to the whole earth! I have neither lent on usury, nor men have lent to me on usury; yet every one of them doth curse me" (Jeremiah 15:10). Were a prophet today to conjure up a universally despised sinner as a point of comparison, he would likely say "child molester" or "AIG exec" and would be hard pressed to get beyond that. Back in the day, "usurer" did the trick. The stigma was that severe.

As Jeremiah feared, the kingdom of Judah did indeed fall to Nebuchudnezzar. The temple was destroyed. And the people were carried off in captivity to a land that had been practicing usury for more than a millennium. Here the Lord instructed Ezekiel, a learned priest among the Jewish captives, in the ways they had gone awry in this corrupt and credit-happy land:

> And one hath committed abomination with his neighbour's wife; and another hath lewdly defiled his daughter in law; and another in thee hath humbled his sister, his father's daughter. In thee have they taken gifts to shed blood; thou hast taken usury and increase, and thou hast greedily gained of thy neighbours by extortion, and hast forgotten me. (Ezekial 22:11–12)

In exile, deprived of power and inspired by priests like Ezekiel, the Jews began to define themselves by their adherence to the Torah. Removed from their own temporal kingdom, no force except the force within could compel them to honor it. That force, to be sure, would need constant propping.

After the overthrow of Babylonia by the Persians fifty years into the captivity, the Persian ruler Cyrus the Great allowed the Jews to return to their homeland. Many thousands accepted the offer and made their way back. Some eighty years later, they were joined by a second group of returning exiles. Neither group prospered. When a third wave failed to pull the enclave together, a prosperous Jew named Nehemiah gave up a comfortable position in the Persian court and headed back to Jerusalem. As appointed governor, he hoped to stabilize Judea, now a struggling Persian province.

Upon arriving, Nehemiah saw for himself that all was not well in the promised land. Everywhere he went, he heard griping about the indifferent rich who were oppressing their poorer Jewish brethren. The combination of drought and taxes had pressed the people into bondage once again, this time to Jews who profited from their land and labor. "And I was very angry when I heard their cry and these words," Nehemiah recounts. "Then I consulted with myself, and I rebuked the nobles, and the rulers, and said unto them, Ye exact usury, every one of his brother" (Nehemiah 5:6–7).

Nehemiah organized protests against the nobles and rulers and brought the pressure of the people to bear upon them. "Restore, I pray you," Nehemiah insists, "to them, even this day, their lands, their vineyards, their oliveyards, and their houses, also the hundredth part of the money, and of the corn, the wine, and the oil, that ye exact of them" (v. 11).

"We will restore them, and will require nothing of them; so will we do as thou sayest," said the moneylenders (v. 12), cowed by the thought of thousands of ACORN-like protestors and perhaps even a little contrite about ignoring the law of their forefathers.

During the nearly thousand years that separated Nehemiah from Moses, the hatred of usury remained white-hot, and the law remained largely unchanged. The authors who recorded this history could not be clearer or more consistent in their denunciation of usury, here meaning no more than the charging of simple interest on a loan. The question that remains, then, is, whence Shylock? How is it that the people with the world's most thoroughly chronicled rejection of a particular act could, in a historic eyeblink, become the poster children for that same act?

Here, much depends on one other citation from Deuteronomy (23:19–20 to be exact), arguably the most critical citation in all of Jewish history. The maxim begins unremarkably enough: "Thou shalt not lend upon usury to thy brother; usury of money, usury of victuals, usury of any thing that is lent upon usury."

The intent of the law seems fairly straightforward. In a closed society where one historically lent money as a form of charity, charging for that money debased the very act. This understanding holds true today as well. If a friend or relative needs help, the one who lends the money looks like a total *schmuck* if he asks for a little *neshek* to make it worth his while.

It is the second half of these verses that has caused the Jewish people so much grief: "Unto a stranger thou mayest lend upon usury; but unto thy brother thou shalt not lend upon usury." Over the centuries there has been endless debate as to who, exactly, a stranger was. Champions of the usury prohibition, like the aforementioned Mr. Elliott, have argued for its narrowest interpretation. They would contend that only the avaricious among the Jews classed all Gentiles in the stranger category. This interpretation, Elliott insists, "set every Gentile Christian's hand against the Jews for fifteen hundred years."[3] From Elliott's perspective, *stranger* refers only to active enemies like Canaanites and others "accursed of God."

Elliott, however, overlooks the dispersal of the Jews, the famed Diaspora.

As threatened in Deuteronomy 28:25, a Lord whose laws were ignored could and would allow his people to be "removed into all the kingdoms of the earth." Whether deserved or not, such was the fate of the Jews. Beginning with the Babylonian captivity and ending with the ruthlessly suppressed Bar Kokhba revolt against Rome in AD 132, the Jews were removed, if not to all the kingdoms of the earth, at least to all of those that had been Hellenized, and from the Greek perspective, those were all the kingdoms that mattered.[4]

In those few centuries on either side of the birth of Christ, Greek culture and language dominated the Mediterranean littoral. At the time, given their dominance, the Greeks believed in the oneness of humanity. Not unlike today's champions of inclusiveness, they saw theirs as a multiracial, multinational cultural empire that embraced any people that accepted their hegemony.

The children of Abraham, however, saw themselves as a race apart. Their belief in monotheism, their dietary and hygienic standards, their insistence on the barbarous practice of circumcision all reinforced their difference in a world of presumed harmony. Everywhere Jews looked they saw people who were strangers, who were not their brothers. Their laws forbade dining with these people, let alone marrying them. This self-imposed alienation was reinforced by a growing hostility from indigenous peoples put off by the Jews' seeming aloofness. The phrase *anti-Semitism* had yet to be coined, but the sentiment was alive and well centuries before the birth of Christ.

Most of these strangers, however, could have cared less about the Jews' willingness to lend money at interest. They had been doing the same for millennia. Ironically, the growing Jewish trade in usury would only trouble those Gentiles who inherited Jewish law, namely, the Christians. "Nothing more clearly marked the line between Christian and Hebrew during fifteen centuries than this one thing," argues Elliott, "that the Hebrews exacted usury or interest of the Gentiles while the Christians were unanimous in its denunciation, and forbade its practice."[5]

three

Hoping for Nothing Again

THERE CAN BE LITTLE ARGUMENT, EVEN AMONG NONBELIEVERS, ABOUT the identity of history's most influential figure. As Christians see it, the prophet Isaiah predicted his coming six centuries before his birth: "Therefore the Lord himself shall give you a sign," Isaiah proclaimed. "Behold, a virgin shall conceive, and bear a son, and shall call his name Immanuel" (Isaiah 7:14).

Despite his extraordinary influence on just about every moral issue under the sun, Jesus Christ was nearly mum on the subject of usury. The two times he does weigh in, he does so indirectly and enigmatically, no more so than in the controversial parable of the talents and the pounds, which both Luke and Matthew recount at length.

As Luke tells the story, a certain nobleman gives each of his ten servants one pound and tells them to busy themselves trading while he ventures into a far country to take over a kingdom. The nobleman, however, proves no more popular in his new kingdom than Cromwell in Ireland. The citizens hate him and let him know it in no uncertain terms. He soon heads home and upon returning convenes his servants and asks how they have done with the money.

The first servant boasts, "Lord, thy pound hath gained ten pounds" (Luke 19:16). Pleased with the profit, the nobleman gives him authority over ten cities. The second servant has gained five pounds through trading and gets five

14

cities. But the third servant hid the money while his boss was gone and returns just the one pound he was given. More provocatively, he tells the boss that he feared him for his hard-hearted profiteering.

The boss challenges his answer. If the servant were really afraid of him, why did he not put "my money into the bank, that at my coming I might have required mine own with usury?" (v. 23). In Matthew, the nobleman phrases his complaint almost identically: "Thou oughtest therefore to have put my money to the exchangers, and then at my coming I should have received mine own with usury" (25:27). In both accounts, the nobleman then takes the remaining pound away from his underperforming servant and gives it to the fellow with ten pounds.

Matthew and Luke both use the Greek word *tokos*, meaning "offspring," for *usury*. *Tokos* comes with the lively understanding that money breeds money, that savvy investments should multiply, if not like rabbits, at least like derivatives. Of historical note, *tokos* is the word that evangelists used when they were translating the usury references in the Psalms and Ezekiel into Greek.[1]

It should be noted, too, that Matthew uses the Greek word *trapezetes* to describe exchangers, or as it often translated, *moneylenders*. Matthew, Mark, and John use a different word, *kollybistes*, to describe the money changers whom Jesus famously threw out of the temple. These were not practitioners of usury but of simony, the selling of sacred things. What upset Jesus was that they had commoditized their sacrificial offerings and turned the temple into a spiritual swap-and-shop.

Although not as notorious as the temple's money changers, the nobleman in question makes an unlikely protagonist. Jesus, however, tells this tale not to endorse his behavior but rather to chide the unprofitable servant for failing to benefit from the opportunity and dissembling about the reason why. Jesus, it seems, uses the parable to make the case that mortals should take advantage of God's gifts while they can. Those who put those gifts to good use will be rewarded. Those who don't, and then make lame excuses for their poor performance, will find themselves among the goats at the last judgment, not the sheep.

Defenders of the usury prohibition have obvious trouble with this parable. Martin Luther, for instance, would cite any number of quotations from Luke and Matthew to attack usury, but he chooses not to talk about this parable at all. Calvin Elliott cites it only to dismiss it. To use the parable as a defense of usury, he says, is a "flagrant perversion of the truth."[2] In fact, however, most Christian defenders of usury, John Calvin among them, were as reluctant to refer to this parable as were usury's foes. To make the case that Jesus actually favored *tokos* would imply that the admonitions against *tokos* by David and Ezekiel no longer held sway, an argument that, if waged in the wrong circles, could get the usury defender into hot water or even boiling oil.

Although not exactly endorsing usury, Jesus does not seem terribly upset by the practice. Lending at interest was apparently common enough in his time, despite Mosaic legal prohibitions, that his listeners understood its workings.

Just about every Christian foe of usury has put great stake in one other citation from Luke—chapter 6, verses 30 to 35. It begins, "Give to every man that asketh of thee; and of him that taketh away thy goods ask them not again." Says Luther of this passage, "Here no exception is made of enemies or opponents; nay, they are included, as the Lord Himself makes clear in the same passage."[3] Luther quotes the following lines from Jesus to that effect:

> And if ye lend to them of whom ye hope to receive, what thank have ye? for sinners also lend to sinners, to receive as much again. But love ye your enemies, and do good, and lend, hoping for nothing again; and your reward shall be great, and ye shall be the children of the Highest: for he is kind unto the unthankful and to the evil. (Luke 6:34–35)

In practical terms, it is hard to summon a single biblical passage upon which so much has hinged. As interpreted by Luther and virtually every church father through the sixteenth century, this passage, specifically the line "hoping for nothing again," not only laid down the Christian law on usury but also explicitly put Jews outside that law. From this perspective, there were no strangers. Everyone was worthy of a loan without expectation of return.

To buttress their argument, usury foes have cited any number of other New Testament passages that show Jesus as a prudent and practical man, one who rejected material excess and unjust profit of the sort that usurers gathered.

As many of these passages also show, Jesus had no gripe with the making of profit per se. He grew up, after all, in a small business that he inherited from his earthly father and ran himself. He does have a problem, however, with an undue fixation on the making of money and the hoarding of wealth. What is remarkable about Jesus' teaching on matters economic is that he could run for office on his record in any country in the Western world and not be embarrassed by it. Indeed, it would put him in good stead almost everywhere.

Christian socialists labor to make Jesus one of themselves. In fact, proto-socialists like Robert Owen, Charles Fourier, and the Duc de Saint-Simon grounded their theories in the Gospels. Many contemporary socialists, Christian and otherwise, still do. In addition to citing Christ's frequent pleas for charity and compassion, some theorists make a macro case for socialism based on one particular passage from Matthew (25:31–46): "And before him shall be gathered all nations: and he shall separate them one from another, as a shepherd divideth his sheep from the goats" (v. 32).

The key word quoted above is *nations*. The argument goes that Jesus will reward those nation states that have assumed as a matter of policy a redistributive role toward "the least of these my brethren" (v. 40). The problem with this reading is that nowhere else in the New Testament—or the Old Testament for that matter—do Jesus, his apostles, the prophets, Moses, or God the Father suggest that the children of God should yield their good-deed doing to a coercive state. This is a task assigned in every instance in the Bible to the individual, the family, or the church.

There is one other major problem with the Jesus-as-socialist argument: in both the New Testament and the Old, one gave alms not so much to redistribute the wealth as to manage one's own eternal wealth. The English word *creditor* derives from the Latin *credere*—"to believe." In a very real sense, to extend credit to the poor was to testify to one's belief in God. As Jesus famously said to the rich young man in Matthew 19:21, "If thou wilt be perfect, go and sell that thou hast, and give to the poor, and thou shalt have treasure in heaven: and come and follow me." The payoff was to be expected not on earth but in heaven. Usury debased the currency of exchange.

Writing in the fourth century after Christ, Augustine of Hippo, the most justly celebrated of early church philosophers, clarifies the Scriptures' meaning. No fan of usury, he nevertheless uses the usurer as model:

Study the money lender's methods. He wants to give modestly and get back with profit; you do the same. Give a little and receive on a grand scale. Look how your interest is mounting up! Give temporal wealth and claim eternal interest, give the earth and gain heaven.[4]

Augustine asks rhetorically to whom should the money be given. The answer is the same person who "forbade you to be a usurer," the Lord himself. He now "comes forward [in the form of the poor person] to ask you for a loan." Augustine insists that Scriptures are clear on this point: "Anyone who gives alms to the poor is lending to the Lord."[5] This is at the very heart of the Judeo-Christian objection to usury. It also explains why Jews and Christians were asked to lend and not worry about being repaid. The ROI (return on investment) would come in heaven.

In our ignorance of the Scriptures, and in our ability to influence public polity, observes Old Testament authority Gary Anderson, "We have developed a larger interest in redistributing income legislatively than in providing a rationale for sacrificial giving on the part of the laity."[6]

And yet the socialist attempt to co-opt Christ's message is not entirely cynical. There is something about what Jesus says and does that intrigues even the most godless communists. There are two nonexclusive reasons why this might be so. One is that Jesus is, in fact, transcendentally wise. The second and less subjective reason is that the Christian ethos has so deeply penetrated Western civilization for so long that no one, not even those at the local Ministry of Atheism or the Church of Satan, are immune to its power.

In the first few hundred years after Christ's birth, usury did not preoccupy many minds. The Romans, whose laws held sway over the Mediterranean world, had had a mixed history on the subject. According to the historian Tacitus, Rome had no usury laws at all for the first three centuries of its existence.[7]

Codification came only in 450 BC with the Law of Twelve Tables. This may have been the first attempt by any culture to set a legal interest rate, in this case in the 8 to 10 percent range, depending on how the law is read. Lawmakers have obviously not lost this urge. As I write, the president of the United States is jawboning America's credit card companies into capping their interest rates and threatening legislation if they don't.

More so than the Greeks and other contemporaries, the Romans had a lingering cultural distaste for the practice of usury, legal or otherwise. Tacitus, who was born fifty years after Christ, called it "the old curse of the city."[8] In the half millennium between the Twelve Tables and Tacitus's birth, Roman law swung back and forth on its legality at least a half dozen times. And even when the law permitted usury, which was most of the time, the philosophical class held its collective nose.

The Roman statesman Cato, writing in the second century before Christ, imagined usurers in a class with murderers. Argued Cato, as Cicero remembered, "Would you take interest?" "Would you kill a man?"[9] Fifteen hundred years later, his countryman Dante Alighieri would also equate usury with homicide and consign the practitioners of both to the Inferno's seventh circle, the usurers deeper in. Dante's guide to the *Inferno*, the Roman poet Virgil, spoke of usurers in real life as "drones, a slothful race."[10] Cicero was no friend of the usurer either. In *De Officiis*, he cautions his son to avoid both money lending and tax collecting, "In the first place, those callings are held in disesteem that come into collision with the ill will of men."[11]

In the first few hundred years after Christ's birth, no Roman citizen inveighed more heartily against usury than Plutarch, the Greek-born biographer and moralist. In his essay "Against Borrowing Money," he denounces moneylenders as "barbarous and wicked," a scourge to be avoided at all costs. His description of the borrower's fate still resonates, especially among those trying to pay their lenders off on sports bets gone bad: "At the very delivery of their money they immediately ask it back, taking it up at the same moment they lay it down, and letting out to interest that which they have received for the use of what they had lent."[12]

What particularly piqued Plutarch, though, was what has always piqued intellectuals: being mocked by those lesser mortals whose actual practice undermines their best theories. "They laugh at the philosophers," laments Plutarch, "who hold that nothing can be made out of nothing."[13] The moneylender may have started with nothing, but he was obviously making enough out of it to irritate his intellectual betters.

Christians, in these first few centuries after Christ, had enough to worry about—the lions in the Coliseum for instance—without worrying about usury. The first church manual of instruction, called the Didache, does not mention usury at all, at least not directly. It does, however, consider the conditions of a loan's repayment and makes a salient distinction between the poor who cannot pay and the rich who can: "Woe to him that receiveth; for if a man receiveth having need, he is guiltless; but he that hath no need shall give satisfaction . . . until he hath given back the last farthing."[14] This instruction suggests that some impulse other than charity motivated the loan to the wealthy man, but it stops well short of condoning loans as investments.

It was not until AD 313 that the emperor Constantine called off the lions, at least officially. Twelve years later, more than 250 bishops convened in the town of Nicea in what is now Turkey for the first churchwide convocation. There were some weighty issues on the table, most notably the relationship between Jesus and God the Father. Participants hammered out consensus on lesser issues as well, ranging from self-castration (prohibited) to standing in church (approved) to usury (discouraged). These rulings have come to be known collectively as the Nicene Creed.[15]

The canon on usury restricted itself to the role of certain clergy, "motivated by greed and a desire for gain,"[16] in the lending of money. The specificity of the ruling—it documents a routine monthly rate of return of 1 percent— suggests that more than a few clerics had turned loan shark. The council determined that in the future any cleric who tried to earn a little discretionary income as a usurer was "to be deposed and removed from his order." Of note, the council based its prohibition not on anything Jesus had said or done, but on David's description of the good man in Psalm 15: "He that putteth not out his money to usury, nor taketh reward against the innocent" (v. 5).

Twenty years later, the Council of Carthage extended the usury sanction, calling the practice reprehensible. That same council reinforced the outright prohibition on the clergy doing the same. A century after Carthage, the Council of Arles II upped the ante on usurious clergy to excommunication.

One of the first of the church fathers to pay serious attention to usury was St. Ambrose, a fourth-century bishop of Milan and one of four significant early church doctors. His election to the bishopric shows just how inchoate the Catholic Church was in these first few centuries. A student of the law and a consular prefect, Ambrose attended a meeting after the death of the reigning bishop at which the quasi-heretical Arians were contending with the Catholic hierarchy over the succession. So persuasive was his call to order at this turbulent meeting that the participants elected the reluctant Ambrose bishop by acclaim. In that he had never been baptized, let alone ordained a priest, the election took him rather by surprise.

Once elected, however, Ambrose made the best of his new position. He gave away his land and money to the poor, got himself baptized and ordained, and chose to not marry, the last still an option for Catholic clergy. A serious intellectual, he addressed himself to the hot theological issues of the day, including usury, which he defined as "whatever exceeds the amount loaned."

Although he condemned usury in general, Ambrose was the first known Christian intellectual to address the seeming double standard on display in Deuteronomy. In his *De Tobia*, written in AD 377, he confirmed that it was, in fact, appropriate to extract usury from strangers, presuming they were the enemy in a just war. *"Ubi jus belli, ibi etiam jus usuras,"* he wrote somewhat famously—"Therefore, where there is the right of war, there also is the right of usury."

Ambrose's interpretation of Deuteronomy may well have shaped his controversial role in the attacks on non-Christians in the second half of the fourth century. Flexing their muscles as the empire's increasingly dominant religious group, Christians began the work of tearing down pagan temples and, soon enough, turned their ire on the Jews as well.

Although the Jews as a group were relatively wealthy, and conspicuously so, there is little hard evidence that the Christians attacked them at this stage because of their role as moneylenders. There was enough lingering resentment about the Jews' presumed role in the empire's earlier Christian persecutions to stoke Christian rage—that and the Jews' continued denial of the divinity of Christ.[17]

And yet the usury question could not have been too far below the surface. As early as the first century AD, Jewish philosophers like Philo were warning about the potential blowback from a practice that could fairly be interpreted as hostile, an interpretation at which Ambrose had himself arrived. Whatever his motive, when the emperor Theodosius I ordered a mideastern bishop to rebuild a synagogue his congregants had burned down, Ambrose intervened on behalf of the bishop, ultimately convincing the emperor that religious fervor trumps civil law.[18] In response to the much-asked question "What would Jesus have done?" a safe answer would have been, "Something different."

four

Master of Those Who Know

TODAY, PERHAPS THE ONLY POSITIVE THING THAT SCHOOLCHILDREN ARE encouraged to believe about the otherwise genocidal Christopher Columbus is his insistence that the earth was round. This distinguished him from the flat-earth crowd who, the students learn, ruled Christendom in the benighted Middle Ages. At a putative higher level of education, students are told that the semibarbaric Christians had driven the enlightened Muslims out of their Andalusian paradise and sunk Iberia and the rest of Europe into another half millennium of darkness before the first rays of the Enlightenment began to pierce through the papist clouds.

This is scarcely an overstatement. Consider the following passage from mainstream historian Daniel Boorstin, then the librarian of the United States Congress, in his 1983 best seller, *The Discoverers*:

> A Europe-wide phenomenon of scholarly amnesia . . . afflicted the continent from AD 300 to at least 1300. During those centuries Christian faith and dogma suppressed the useful image of the world that had been so slowly, so painfully, and so scrupulously drawn by ancient geographers.[1]

Boorstin was merely advancing an orthodoxy that has been alive and well for the last four centuries and that has truly flourished in this, our glorious multicultural moment. The early philosophers of the modern era set the tone with a vengeance. Shakespeare's contemporary, the scientist Francis Bacon, placed the preceding European centuries among the "deserts and wastes in times as in countries." The Baconian brand of thinking has lead directly to the kind of creepy caricatures of the Middle Ages seen in the opening of Michael Radford's *Merchant of Venice*, discussed earlier. It also distorts our whole understanding of the eventual lifting of the usury ban, which is not nearly as simple as the enlightened escape from medieval shackles it is made out to be.

As commonly used, the noun *Middle Ages* or the adjective *medieval* describes the period from the fall of Rome to the birth of the modern, roughly AD 500 to AD 1500 or 1600. No period is as misunderstood. Yes, it did get off to a rough start. This sometimes happens when successive waves of savage tribes overrun a declining civilization. The first few centuries after Rome's demise saw a decline in scholarship, a general breakdown in the civic order, and a scramble to survive the tribal realignments that had unsettled Europe. The one stabilizing, centralizing force in these first few centuries was the church, but church fathers, the occasional edict notwithstanding, had more pressing matters than to establish and enforce usury laws.

More critical for the history of usury law, although indirectly so, was the fact that Islamic tribes had swept out of the Arabian Peninsula and were establishing hegemony over a broad sweep of the known world from Persia to Iberia. As the culture of Islam matured, its scholars discovered and sought to preserve the works of the great Greek philosophers housed in libraries in Egypt, Syria, Mesopotamia, and elsewhere. They translated these works into Arabic, commented upon them freely, and sometimes expanded on their findings. Said the revered ninth-century Muslim philosopher Al-Kindi of his respect for the Greek heritage, "It would have been impossible for us, despite all our zeal, during the whole of our lifetime, to assemble these principles of truth which form the basis of the final inferences of our research."[2]

Arabs had also ventured into India. There, while still in their culturally curious stage, they had come across the essential building block of modern commerce, the Indian numbering system, including the magical "zero." This system would have at least as much liberating power on the development of a credit-based culture as any shift in law or faith.

Yet for all the glories of the Islamic breakout, the culture had some inherent restraints that would become obvious soon enough. Until modern times, for instance, only its mathematicians used Arabic numerals. Muslim scientists used a Babylonian system, and merchants used still another system based on the Arabic alphabet. As was true for Greek science and philosophy as well as for Indian numbers, the Arabs did the preserving and transmitting; the Europeans would do the exploiting and transforming.

For any number of reasons, global warming high among them, trade and commerce had once again come alive in Europe. One trader's son, Leonardo Fibonacci of Pisa, would make so stunning a contribution to this commerce it is hard to believe he remains unsung. As a young man, Fibonacci traveled to North Africa to help his father work his trading post. There he first became acquainted with the Hindu-Arabic numbering system. Sensing its superiority over the clumsy Roman numerals the West was still using, Fibonacci began a serious study under some of the leading Arab mathematicians throughout the Mediterranean world.

In his 1202 treatise *Liber Abaci*, Fibonacci introduced what he accurately called the *modus Indorum* (method of the Indians) to Europe. Given his father's background, Fibonacci took pains to show the system's potential not just for higher math but for everyday business calculations. Indeed, the cool new numbers made calculating interest and the compounding thereof much easier. Merchants and scholars both embraced the new math. It helped expedite the commercial revolution already underway and launch the scientific revolution that was to come. It also, alas, helped to enable fraud. Turning a 0 into a 6 or a 1 into a 4 was as tempting in Florence as it is on Wall Street. In 1229, concerned about fraud, Florence prohibited bankers from using the "infidel" symbols, but commerce, as always, found a way around regressive regulation.[3]

A historic turning point on the scientific front, rarely given its due, had taken place a few years earlier in Toledo. The Christian knights of the *Reconquista* period had lately—and rather civilly—repossessed the city from its Islamic placeholders. There, in the city's cathedral, a polyglot crew of Muslim, Jewish, and Christian scholars labored away in surprising harmony, translating into Latin the works of the great Greek philosophers that had earlier been translated into Arabic.

Richard Rubenstein, author of the impressive *Aristotle's Children* and not likely a Catholic apologist, calls the eventual outcome of this gathering "an acute source of embarrassment" for many modernists.[4] As it happened, Jews and Muslims would turn their backs on this treasure trove of admittedly pagan scholarship, and "farsighted popes and bishops therefore took the fateful step that Islamic leaders had rejected."[5] Not without a few speed bumps en route, the Catholic Church rode away with the goods. Historian Edward Grant calls the medieval Christian renaissance that ensued "the best kept secret of Western civilization."[6]

One of the rediscovered scholars so loomed above all the others that his acolytes in the next few centuries would refer to him simply as "the Philosopher." Dante had come across the Philosopher in the first circle of the Inferno, the one reserved for those good souls who had never gotten to know Jesus. "I raised my eyes a little," writes Dante, "and there was he who is acknowledged Master of those who know, sitting in a philosophic family who look to him and do him honor."[7] Among a cast that included Plato, Socrates, Democritus, Zeno, Empedocles, Anaxagoras, Thales, Heraclitus, Diogenes, and other pagan wise men, it was Aristotle who held center stage. The reader does well to recall that Dante was a devout Christian writing in the first decade of the 1300s. He and his readers proved immune to the "Europe-wide phenomenon of scholarly amnesia."

Some three thousand pages of Aristotle's wisdom had been retrieved through the Islamic connection, not just philosophy as we understand it, but also his insights into biology, physics, logic, political science, and, yes, even usury. Give Jesus Christ his due as history's most influential figure, but the case could be made for Aristotle as number two. On the subject of usury, however, Aristotle may have had even more influence than Jesus.

Writing in the fourth century before Christ, Aristotle's empirical research has held up reasonably well over the centuries. In his treatise *On the Heavens*, for instance, Aristotle affirmed the correct shape of the earth more than eighteen hundred years before Columbus. "In eclipses the outline is always curved," he writes. "And since it is the interposition of the earth that makes the eclipse, the form of this line will be caused by the form of the earth's surface, which is therefore spherical."[8] This bit of wisdom, by the way, was not lost with the fall of Rome. Even in the early Middle Ages, the dominant textbooks supported the spherical nature of the earth. In the *Purgatario* section of his *Divine Comedy*, Dante casually alludes to the curvature of the earth with his discussion of time zones and his recognition of the Southern Hemisphere's distinct perspective on the sun and stars. The canard that these early Christians thought the earth flat did not emerge until the post-Darwinian nineteenth century and was employed then, as now, as a way of slandering Christian scholars.

To be sure, there were many points on which the views of Aristotle diverged from those of the monotheists gathered at Toledo. Where Christian scholars found common ground with Aristotle was in their shared belief in an ethical, perfectly ordered universe. What attracted them to Aristotle in particular was his ability to use reason to discern that order.[9] These scholars wondered whether they could marry Aristotelian reason to faith to help them locate a Christian God as the source of that order. What is more, unlike their Jewish and Islamic brethren, the Christian scholars worked within a monolithic church structure. If they could convince their superiors of Aristotle's value, that whole monolith just might embrace his work. In any case, they could not be easily marginalized.

One other new tool for educating ordinary citizens in the simple elegance of God's order was the clock. In the thirteenth century, mechanical clocks began to show up in Europe, most prominently on churches. Church fathers used them not only to get parishioners to church on time, but also to reinforce the rationality of God's universe. Although not obvious at the time, clocks would lead to the commoditization of time, and the understanding, most succinctly phrased by Ben Franklin, that "time is money."[10]

Clocks, of course, also added precision to the commercial revolution in progress, and commerce helped spread the word about Aristotle. Increased commerce, however, also renewed concerns about the practice of usury. At the second Lateran Council in 1139, Pope Innocent II did not exactly mince words in describing usury as "detestable and disgraceful rapacity condemned by human and divine law alike."[11] At the Council of Tours in 1163, Pope Alexander III expanded the definition of usury to include any sale on credit in which the accumulative price was higher than the cash price. In 1179, Alexander III argued that usurers should not only be excommunicated but also be denied a Christian burial. In 1187, Pope Urban III reaffirmed the position taken by his predecessors, this time basing his objection to usury on Christ's counsel in Luke 6:35, "lend, hoping for nothing again."

All the while these popes were weighing in on the usury question, Aristotle's wisdom was spreading about as quickly as it could in a world where even an "instant message" could take weeks to deliver. By the beginning of the thirteenth century, his books were being read and taught at the nascent European universities, particularly at that hotbed of radicalism, the University of Paris. Today's students could not begin to imagine the intellectual fervor of their medieval counterparts. If debate ranged within certain accepted Christian boundaries, those boundaries were at least as expansive and no more "correct" than those of the typical American university. The early modernist attempt to deny the intellectual progress of this period astounds. Indeed, Rubenstein compares it to "the rewriting of history that we associate with Stalinism in the Soviet Union—the 'airbrushing' out of figures and events embarrassing to the current regime."[12]

Then, as always in the Western world, push meant push back. Throughout Christendom, there was mounting pressure on church officials to ban the arguably heretical works of the inarguably pagan Aristotle, much as those works were already being censored in the Muslim world.

The issue moved front and center at the Fourth Lateran Council convened by Pope Innocent III in 1215 and died there. The founder of the order that bore his name, Domingo de Guzman (known to history as St. Dominic), argued successfully that the reasoning of Aristotle was essential in the fight against heresy. And so began the century of Aristotle's greatest ascendance, made possible in no small part due to the genius of Aristotle's most devoted follower, the Dominican scholar Thomas Aquinas.

In the way of background, Thomas had grown up in the hill country between Naples and Rome, the son of an ambitious nobleman. His father had sent Thomas to be educated by the monks with the expectation that his bright son would quickly ascend the church hierarchy and help accommodate family ambitions. At the University of Naples, however, Thomas encountered the fresh Aristotelian breeze blowing in from the Arab world and liked the feel of it. What Aquinas pulled from Aristotle was that reason ought to be embraced, not feared. He came to believe, as Aristotle did, that a rational man could make sense of the world through his experience. By reflecting upon that experience, man could discern the causes that shape existence. To find these first causes, Aristotle argued, and Aquinas agreed, should be the whole object of man's knowledge.[13]

The Dominicans' enthusiasm for intellectual exchange inspired Thomas to join this ascetic, unworldly order. This move so displeased his worldly father that he had Thomas's brothers kidnap the precocious lad and hold him under something like house arrest for two years while the family tried to break his will. When the father finally relented, Thomas fled directly to the Dominicans in Paris.

The stolid Thomas so kept his own counsel at the university that his fellow students took to calling him the Dumb Ox, but those who watched Thomas up close knew otherwise. His mentor, the Dominican scientist and philosopher Albertus Magnus, chastised Thomas's classmates, saying, "You call him a Dumb Ox; I tell you this Dumb Ox shall bellow so loud that his bellowings will fill the world."[14] If anything, Thomas exceeded Albert's expectations.

In Thomas's time, despite the papal edicts of the previous century, lending at interest remained, at the street level at least, a lively subject of debate. The best evidence for its still unsettled nature can be found in the usury chapter in Thomas's masterwork, the unfinished *Summa Theologica*. At the outset he poses the question of "whether it is a sin to take usury for money lent"[15] and then lays out a series of popular objections to that premise. Relentlessly fair, Thomas makes a good case for the opposition. Alluding to Deuteronomy, he wonders how it could be sinful to lend money to one's brother but not to a stranger, or how could it be wrong to follow a civil law if that law allows usury, or how one erred by accepting something that is freely given, or whether the Lord's counsel in Luke 6:35—"lend, hoping for nothing again"—was "binding" or merely just good advice.

The problem, as orthodox Catholic scholars like Thomas Woods and John Noonan concede, is that Thomas's response to his own objections is not particularly convincing. Here, his fondness for Aristotle seems to betray him. Rather critically for the history of Western commerce, Aristotle deeply disliked the whole practice of usury. But unlike the Jewish and Christian scholars before him who had objected to usury over social justice concerns, Aristotle objected largely on the issue of taste. In the *Nichomachean Ethics*, he compares usurers to "those who ply sordid trades, pimps and all such people" and scolds them all for the "sordid love of gain."[16] This sentiment, to be sure, has lost no currency.

For Aristotle, the charging of interest was not only unseemly but also unnatural. So he argues in his *Politics*: "Very much disliked also is the practice of charging interest; and the dislike is fully justified, for the gain arises out of the currency itself, not as a product of that for which the currency was provided."[17] He elaborates that the Greek word for usury, *tokos*, means "offspring," as we have previously noted. As each animal produces its like, so "interest is currency born of currency." This he finds "most contrary to nature."[18] In Dante's *Inferno*, it should be recalled, Virgil contends that it is usury's unnatural character that provokes God to place usurers in hell's seventh circle. He cites only two sources to make this argument: Genesis and Aristotle's *Physics*.

"Study your *Physics* well," Virgil tells Dante, "and you'll be shown in not too many pages that your art's good is to follow Nature insofar as it can."[19] In other words, work with your hands or work the land; don't let money work for you. Aristotle's works carried so much weight that smart Christians like Dante echoed his thoughts even when they did not fully understand them. Seventh circle or not, no sin in the *Inferno* has less moral resonance than usury. By subtracting issues of justice and morality and even fairness from the usury equation, Aristotle rested his thesis solely on the flouting of nature, and it did not add up.

In the twentieth century, the poet Ezra Pound tried to clarify Aristotle's objection in his poem "With Usura," but his cockeyed economics only distorted the picture. Not unlike Aristotle, Pound considers usury a "sin against nature," but he somehow comes to the conclusion that "with usura is no clear demarcation / and no man can find site for his dwelling."[20]

Pound almost perfectly misunderstood the consequences of credit unleashed. As shall be seen, too many people would find their way into too many dwellings.

Aquinas wrote his *Summa Theologica* just one generation before Dante wrote his *Divine Comedy* and proved at least as dependent on the economic wisdom of Aristotle as Dante had been:

> Now money, according to the Philosopher, was invented chiefly for the purpose of exchange: and consequently the proper and principal use of money is its consumption or alienation whereby it is sunk in exchange. Hence it is by its

very nature unlawful to take payment for the use of money lent, which payment is known as usury: and just as a man is bound to restore other ill-gotten goods, so is he bound to restore the money which he has taken in usury.[21]

Aquinas makes the labored argument that commodities such as wine and wheat are, like money itself, sold to be consumed. "Accordingly," he writes, "if a man wanted to sell wine separately from the use of the wine, he would be selling the same thing twice, or he would be selling what does not exist." This, Aquinas reasons unconvincingly, would be "a sin of injustice." A house, on the other hand, is not consumed in the use. "For this reason," says Aquinas, "a man may lawfully make a charge for the use of his house."[22]

In his thoughtful book *The Church and the Market*, Catholic historian Thomas Woods can make no more sense out of Aquinas than the reader likely has to this point. As an exasperated Woods asks, when in all of human history has someone attempted to sell wine or wheat a second time separately from its use?[23] Merchants have lent money at interest, however, since the invention of money.

John Noonan, an authority on scholasticism, applies a classic Catholic maxim to the usury ban: *Cessante ratione, cessat ipsa lex*, "When the reason for the law ceases, the law itself ceases."[24] By the thirteenth century, the reason for the ban had ceased making sense. An invigorated commerce and a newfound ability to calculate interest had made the prohibition on commercial credit obsolete.

Here is where Aristotle channeled the flow of history, especially as it relates to Jews. The Philosopher carried such intellectual weight among Christian scholars that if he had championed banking, the ban on usury would almost surely have faded away. Aquinas and his pals could have then put their intellects to work differentiating between predatory loans and reasonable business transactions and in the process built an integrated Christian business philosophy into which Jews could have been easily assimilated. Unfortunately, none of this happened.

In the era of Aristotle's ascendance, although not yet reaching the point of stereotype, the image of the Jew as usurer was firming up. This is evident in certain rulings of the Fourth Lateran Council. Convened by Pope Innocent III in 1215, this council may have given Aristotle a second life, but it dealt a near deathblow to the Jewish banking community.[25]

By this time, church leaders had figured out that the usury ban had the practical consequence of enriching Jews. "The more Christians are restrained from the practice of usury," reads the council's *Constitution 67*, "the more they are oppressed in this matter by the treachery of the Jews, so that in a short time they exhaust the resources of the Christians." As this language suggests, the ban was also driving a wedge between the two groups. Of note, this council ordered Christians not to boycott usurers per se, or even Jewish usurers, but those who practiced "grave and immoderate usury." Another reference in the same text objects to "oppressive and excessive interest." Although unspoken, there seemed to a growing sentiment that charging modest interest might not be all that sinful.

In Greece, it was another occupation altogether that irked the Jews' Christian neighbors. Benjamin of Tudela attests to this in his wonderfully wide-eyed *Book of Travels*, which recounts his journeys around the northern rim of the Mediterranean in the late twelfth century. Although Benjamin thought his fellow Jews "rich, kind, and charitable," he acknowledges that the Greeks thought them otherwise "because of the tanners who pour out their dirty water outside their houses and thus defile the Jewish quarter."[26] How Aristotle felt about tanning is lost to history, but his hatred of usury predated the Greek hatred of Jews.

In one other critical area, Christian scholars followed Aristotle's lead with unfortunate consequences, at least on the public relations front. Aristotle, as it happened, believed in an earth-centered cosmos. Not all Christian scholars yielded to Aristotle's wisdom, of course. By 1514, Nicolaus Copernicus was speculating about a heliocentric universe and was being encouraged in his research by key players in the Catholic hierarchy. More than a half century after Copernicus's death, and armed with a powerful new telescope, Galileo Galilei began to flesh out Copernicus's theory.

For the greater part of his career, Galileo enjoyed the Vatican's support and did most of his work at church-sponsored observatories and universities.[27] In 1616, after one of Galileo's rivals called in a complaint to the Inquisition, Cardinal Robert Bellarmine met with Galileo and reviewed with him the church's position. As Bellarmine explained, Scripture seemed to argue for an earth-centered universe. In that the Catholic Church was under attack for being too lax on Scripture in this post-Reformation era, Bellarmine asked to see hard proof before the church rethought its interpretation. Galileo could continue his research, but Bellarmine asked that he not promote new findings without the church's approval.

A practicing Catholic, Galileo agreed and honored his word for several years. In 1632, chafing at the restraints and with a friendly new pope at the helm, Galileo published his *Dialogue Concerning the Two Chief World Systems*. Although he could count the moons around Jupiter, Galileo could not read the handwriting on the Vatican wall. It was bad enough that he had gone back on his word, worse that some of his proofs were far from certain—he argued, for instance, that the sun's movements caused the tides—and worse still that he named the pope character in his *Dialogue* Simplicio, a name as demeaning as it sounds. As Salmon Rushdie might agree, Galileo's getting off with house arrest seventy years into his church-subsidized life is a testament to the evolved state of mercy in sixteenth-century Christendom.

If historians and dramatists have forgotten, Galileo well understood that the real resistance to his theorizing came from a fundamentalist reading not of Scripture but of Aristotle. He observed:

> If Aristotle should see the new discoveries in the sky, he would change his opinions and correct his books and embrace the most sensible doctrines, casting away from himself those people so weak-minded as to be induced to go on maintaining abjectly everything he had ever said.[28]

From the seventeenth century on, church and science, like church and commerce, would more and more go their separate ways, and the world would not necessarily benefit from the divergence. "Business is a morally serious enterprise," Catholic social philosopher Michael Novak reminds us. "By its own internal logic and inherent moral drive, business requires moral conduct; and, not always, but with high probability, violations of this logic lead to personal and business disgrace."[29] An inverted yield curve in logic, as history has shown, tracks all too neatly with long-term prospects for disgrace.

five

Prepared for the Crown

ON OR ABOUT THE YEAR 1119, SOME TWENTY YEARS AFTER THE WARRIORS OF the First Crusade had captured Jerusalem, a group of pious Christians ventured out from that fortified city "in joy and with a cheerful heart" on an Eastertime pilgrimage to the River Jordan.[1] They never got there. In the mountainous region between the city and the river, a merciless swarm of Saracens descended on the pilgrims, unarmed and weak from fasting, and slaughtered them. Three hundred were killed. Sixty were captured. And all of Christendom was outraged.

In 1120, in the town of Nablus, forty miles north of Jerusalem, church and secular leaders from throughout the region gathered to plan a response to this and other assaults. The most memorable result of that assembly was the formal recognition of a unique monastic order, the brainchild of two French knights, both veterans of the First Crusade. King Baldwin II of Jerusalem sanctioned the new order and ceded it use of headquarters space on the Temple Mount, so called because the ruins of the ancient Temple of Solomon were believed to lie buried beneath. From the location, the order took its name, Poor Knights of Christ and the Temple of Solomon, or as it has come to be known to history, the Knights Templar.

Over the course of the next two centuries, the Templars would create the first great international banking enterprise. In the seven centuries following their demise, they would serve as grist for all manner of conspiracy mills—anti-Catholic, Masonic, anti-Masonic, anticapitalist. Indeed, had there not been a real Knights Templar, the publishing world would have had to create one. Today, scores of recently published books on the Templars—from the serious to the ludicrous to the blasphemous—can be had at the local bookstore. In addition to books, a browser on Amazon can easily find Templar armor shields, swords, pewter resin skull displays, high-gloss ceramic doorknobs, even "a Knights Templar Logo Baby Ultrasoft Onesie."

The fascination with the Templars derives largely from their oxymoronic role as an order of warrior monks fighting on behalf of a pacifist religion. The Templars, acknowledges Malcolm Barber, the leading historian on this subject, were admittedly an "unnatural hybrid."[2] Unnatural or not, this was a serious order, and these were serious people. Under the early guidance of Saint Bernard of Clairvaux, the knights lived by a code strict even by medieval monk standards: "Since despising the light of the present life, being contemptuous of the torment which is your bodies, you have promised to hold cheap worldly matters for the love of God."[3] So reads in part the "Rule" that guided them through their life of silent meals, coarse clothing, daily prayers, and perpetual celibacy. In this regard, the Templars were in sync with a spirit of reform then sweeping Catholic Europe, particularly among the priestly classes. Tempted as they inevitably were by the eternal vices, clerics periodically realigned themselves with their Christian mission—or at least they tried to.

The Templars faced temptations beyond those of ordinary monks. They were, after all, knights, a position that historically came with a goodly share of perks. Each Templar, for instance, was allowed three horses and a squire. A horse conferred genuine power, and power spawned pride. That pride manifested itself in knightly fashions like long hair and pointed lace-up shoes. These and other earthly seductions Saint Bernard railed against on a regular basis. And yet there was no denying the Templars' distinctive mission, and this Bernard did not attempt to soft sell: "After the consumption of the divine mystery," the Rule continues, "no one should be afraid to fight, but be prepared for the crown."[4]

Despite the church's approval of the order, more than a few church leaders were uneasy about the multitasking Templars. As early as 1159, John of Salisbury was openly questioning the wisdom of it all. "Communities which had originally rejoiced in poverty," he writes, "are now favored with privileges which, ceasing to be necessary and snubbing charity, are deemed to be instruments of avarice rather than of religion."[5] John conceded the biblical precedent for men who "wage legitimate war," David most notably, but he saw in the group's knightly vocation a slippery slope to greed and pride, two of the most deadly sins of that time and place.

John had a hard time finding an audience. By mid-twelfth century, the Templars had already proved their worth, not so much on the battlefield as off it. In 1147, they had accompanied the Crusaders under French king Louis VII to the Holy Land. As often happens on these kinds of military adventures, the king had run out of money halfway to his destination. At Antioch, lacking options as well as cash, he turned to the Templars for help. They raised the needed funds out of their own resources and likely supplemented those resources by borrowing.[6] Although the massive loan to the king nearly bankrupted them, the Templars had saved the Crusade, and the king acknowledged as much. So was launched a new mission for the pious knights, one that would prove more valuable than the military one that inspired their creation.

The emergence of the Templars' banking empire flowed naturally from their role as fighting monks. Once experience had shown them that pitched battles against a merciless enemy take an unholy toll on a religious order, they turned more and more to logistical support. Traditionally, monastic houses had provided safe storage for all manner of goods and documents. (Locals felt that if they could not trust the monks, whom could they trust?) The Templars inherited the good reputation of the monks who preceded them and built on it.

The Templars emerged as Europe's principal banking order for several obvious reasons. For starters, they had the equivalent of branch offices stretching from one end of the Mediterranean to the other. They also had major complexes in Paris and London, cities in which decisions about war and peace were often made. Even more usefully, the Templars interacted with kings and popes, and they did so precisely when those leaders needed money, namely, on the way to the battlefield. And finally, the Templars did not need to hire security to protect their money transfers. In the rougher neighborhoods in which they operated, their reputation preceded them, and that helped.

A detailed analysis of the Templars' performance under thirteenth-century

French king Philip IV shows just how wide ranging were the services they provided. They raised taxes for the king, paid bills, minted money, collected tariffs, chased down deadbeats, provisioned the army, supported diplomatic missions, and advanced loans to the kings' friends and relatives—even Grandma, literally.[7] Although a not-for-profit organization whose employees lived on little, the Templars still had to generate enough revenue to cover their extensive overhead, horses and squires included.

The Templars were well placed, of course, to finesse exchange rates over distance, a practice that was becoming widespread in Christian banking circles. In addition, there exists hard evidence that the Templars, on occasion at least, charged interest. When, for instance, Edward I of England reimbursed the Templars a substantial sum he had borrowed for a recently completed crusade, he included an additional 18 percent for "administration, expenses, and interest."[8] This was in 1274. Less than forty years later, the Templars would be history.

Despite the interest charges, the demise of the Templars had almost nothing to do with usury. Their asceticism in the service of kings and popes seems to have eliminated the social justice concerns that drove the usury debate in medieval Europe. The Templars were not exploiting anyone, nor were they living conspicuously high on the hog. Plus, they were too well connected and too well armed to accuse without superior arms to make the accusation stick. Philip IV of France had arms enough and debt even more.

In 1306, after years of debasement, Philip had ordered the return of his treasury to the hard-money standards of 1266.[9] To pull this off, he would need an infusion of specie, specifically gold and silver for recoining. Like Willie Sutton, who robbed banks because that's where the money was, Philip went after the bankers—the Jews in 1306 and the Templars in 1307. He had already driven the Italians and those pesky Lombards out of the country.

Given the Templars' reputation for financial probity, Philip accused them not of usury but of heresy and sexual depravity, charges roughly comparable in severity at the time.[10] Even then, Paris life could rob a people of their fighting edge, the Templars included; when the king's men swooped down on their HQ, they chose not to resist. The French government, acting under the cloak of Inquisition, proceeded to "get medieval" on them. Confessions were quickly forthcoming.

All too indicative was the confession tortured out of John of Tour, the fifty-nine-year-old treasurer of the temple at Paris. According to the notary who recorded it, John recounted the details of his initiation into the Knights Templar, a tale of depravity that could have rung true only to those who lusted for Templar property or who read Dan Brown novels.

"On the order of the receptor, [John] denied Jesus Christ once only, and spat upon the cross once." John also confessed to kissing the receptor three times in three places, none of them good, and acknowledging that although prohibited from knowing women, "if any natural heat should move him, he could unite himself with his brothers."[11] At the time of his arrest, John, a long-time trusted advisor of the king, was on official royal business. He, like the other Templars, would have had to live extraordinarily well-concealed double lives if one were to believe their confessions.

Under pressure from Philip—known as Philip the Fair, presumably for his good looks and not for his sense of justice—Pope Clement V ordered the arrest of all the Templars throughout Europe for further investigation. Clement's insistence on due process further irritated Philip, who was hoping to confiscate the Templars' property as quickly as he had the Jews' the year before. Worse, from Philip's perspective, the Templars had begun to recant their confessions. To keep the Inquisitional ball rolling, Philip threatened to invade the Papal States and proceeded to execute some of the Templars while he waited for a papal commission to decide whether or not they deserved it. Not until 1312 did the decision come in.

The commission refused to condemn the Templars as Philip had demanded, but the scandal had reached such proportions that the commission thought it better to disband the order. Then the commission applied the salt: the Knights Hospitaller, a less bellicose knightly order, would receive the Templars' holdings, not Philip the Fair.[12] One can imagine the howling from the palace when Philip saw the verdict.

Dante was in the process of writing his *Purgatorio*, the second part of his *Divine Comedy*, during Philip's assault on the Templars. In purgatory, the narrator encounters Hugh Capet, the originator of the Capetian line. "From me were born the Louises and Philips," laments Hugh. He sees himself not as proud patriarch but rather as "the root of that malignant plant, which overshadows all the Christian world."[13] In describing the current representative of that line, otherwise unnamed, Hugh says:

I see the modern Pilate so relentless,
This does not sate him, but without decretal
He to the temple bears his sordid sails![14]

A decretal is a papal decree. The temple is that of the Knights Templar in Paris. Pilate is Philip. Dante goes beyond scolding Philip. He compares the sacrifice of the Templars to that of Christ. The comparison has resonated through the ages, especially in reference to the order's last Grand Master, Jacques de Molay, who was burned at the stake in Paris in 1314.

In a popular book called *The Second Messiah: Templars, the Turin Shroud, and the Great Secret of Freemasonry*, Masonic historians Christopher Knight and Robert Lomas insist that the image on the famed shroud of Turin is not Jesus, but Jacques himself.[15] As the story goes, the establishment executed de Molay to keep him from revealing the untold story of Christ's real intentions for the world. Today, de Molay's legacy lives on in DeMolay International, a Masonic-sponsored youth organization founded in Kansas City in 1919. The Masons, in fact, have done much to keep the mystique of the Templars alive, if not exactly their history. It will not surprise the reader to learn that Catholics are not too keen on the Masons.

Then, of course, there is the question of Masonic influence on the seal of the United States—especially that weird pyramid with an eye on the top and the call to *Novus Ordo Seculorum*, or "new world order," on the bottom. Even though the seal adorns the United States dollar, the subject of much discussion to come, this author will choose to leave this particular can of worms unopened.

One subject that does merit exposure is the systemic British anti-Catholicism that tainted the reputation not only of the Templars but also of the Crusades themselves. Instead of working itself out after the civil wars of the seventeenth century, this sentiment continued to fester into the nineteenth century and found its literary outlet in the novels of Sir Walter Scott. Scott was educated in the Church of Scotland, a fire-and-brimstone enterprise that had not quite yet embraced the ecumenical spirit. Indeed, its ministers had a habit of referring to the Roman Catholic Church as the "whore of Babylon" and the pope as the "antichrist."

In the most popular of Scott's novels, *Ivanhoe*, published in 1819, a Templar named Brian de Bois-Guilbert plays the heavy. "They say he is valiant as the bravest of his order," says one of Scott's humble Saxons, "but stained with their usual vices—pride, arrogance, cruelty, and voluptuousness."[16] Among the Templar's impressive range of character flaws, bigotry stands out. "It would seem the Templars love the Jews' inheritance better than they do their company," says one character speaking for the author.[17]

Humiliated in a tournament, the Templar subsequently plots to rob a kindly Jewish moneylender, succeeds in kidnapping the man's beautiful daughter Rebecca, and flees to the nearest temple outpost from which he hopes to exit the country, hostage in tow. The Grand Master of the Templars shows up unexpectedly and is shocked by Brian's behavior. He concludes that only a witch could have caused a Templar to violate so many vows in so many outsized ways. Being a devout Catholic, the Grand Master promptly tries the Jewess Rebecca for witchcraft and sentences her to burn at the stake. Just another day at the office for the Knights Templar.

To his credit, Scott draws a sympathetic portrait of his Jewish characters, even the moneylender Isaac. Not wanting to estrange his less progressive audience, he concedes that Jews had adopted "a national character in which there was much, to say the least, mean and unamiable." But this, he attributes to centuries of hounding. "There was no race existing on the earth, in the air, or the waters, who were the object of such an unintermitting, general and relentless persecution as the Jews of this period."[18]

Like so many other enlightened souls to follow, however, Scott compensated for his largesse toward one group with his comically crude stereotyping of another. In his 1825 novel *Talisman*, Scott expands his protected classes to include the romantically heroic Crusade-buster, Saladin, at the expense, of course, of the venal and treacherous Crusaders themselves.

Scott's novels were enormously influential. They propagated the first seeds of a caricature that would blossom in the late twentieth century. That the Crusades were no more than a blundering, plundering proto-imperialism is today a truism believed by just about everyone except for serious students of history. "Historians have long known that the image of the Crusader seeking his fortune is exactly backwards," says Thomas Madden, a leading historian of the period.[19] As Madden observes, the Crusades were pilgrimages, acts of penance. Crusaders gave up just about everything, often their lives, to right undeniable wrongs. Typically, the Crusaders returned as soon as they could and usually with nothing more than the cross on their tunic. Indeed, if giving alms to the poor was thought to be an investment in one's heavenly reward, fighting a crusade was a leveraged buyout of the same.

six

Aboveboard

BEFORE JEWS HAD ASSUMED THE REPUTATION AS THE WORLD'S GREAT usurers, that honor—or dishonor, depending on one's perspective—belonged to the Italians. Italians brought Arabic numerals to the Western world, introduced the revolutionary concept of double-entry bookkeeping, and gave us the very word *bank* from the old Italian *banco*, meaning "bench or board." In Florence, the epicenter of banking in fourteenth-century Europe, a money changer would set up his board each morning in a designated Florentine street, lay a green cloth over it, place the official ledger on top of that, and start doing deals. The Exchangers Guild, to which he had no choice but to belong, dictated that every transaction had to be recorded. Although the origin of the phrase *aboveboard* is uncertain, an Italian banking provenance would make perfect sense.

Even seven centuries ago, there was something wonderfully improvisational about Italian culture. Despite being denied the banker's most essential instrument—the ability to lend money at interest—Italians had managed to create the world's most progressive banking system. In the fifteenth century, the Medici family would raise the art of improvisation to a new level of sophistication and always aboveboard—more or less.

No one has better understood the Italian ability to improvise—or described it more amusingly—than the fourteenth-century Florentine author, poet, and banker's son, Giovanni Boccaccio. That he kept his sense of humor in the face of the Black Death that ravaged Europe in mid-century, killing at least a quarter of its citizens, is a testament to the culture's historic resilience.

Boccaccio started writing his masterwork, *The Decameron*, in 1350, at the peak of the plague. The very first of his tales so nicely captures the creative tension of Italian culture that it makes the Medici century that follows almost comprehendible.

As the story opens, a clan of godless Burgundians is cheating a wealthy and well-connected merchant out of his rightful investments. So the merchant contracts with an even more faithless and violent rapscallion by the name of Ser Ciappelletto to shake down the Burgundians. The diminutive Ciappelletto glories in having committed every sin known to Dante. He was a "profuse blasphemer of God and His saints," a glutton, a drunk, and "as fond of women as a dog is of the stick." When all was said and done, Ciappelletto was "perhaps, the worst man that ever was born."[1]

On the way to the shakedown, Ciappelletto stops near Florence at the home of two brothers, both usurers, and there he falls gravely ill. The brothers are in a quandary. If they turn this sick man out of their house, their lack of mercy will outrage the villagers, who will be all the more outraged when they discover just whom the brothers have been harboring.

On the other hand, if the brothers let Ciappelletto die at their house, this aggressively wicked man will surely refuse confession and provoke the church into denying him burial. When his unburied body is found and identified, the usurious brothers fear the worst:

> In which case the folk of these parts, who reprobate our trade as iniquitous and revile it all day long, and would fain rob us, will seize their opportunity, and raise a tumult, and make a raid upon our houses, crying: "Away with these Lombard dogs, whom the Church excludes from her pale."[2]

Evil to the end, Ciappelletto proposes to solve the brothers' problem by an act of profanely reckless cunning. He will confess to "the worthiest and most holy friar" in the neighborhood a series of teeny counterfeit sins. "I have committed so many offences against God in the course of my life," he tells the brothers, "that one more in the hour of my death will make no difference whatever to the account." When the friar is found, Ciappelletto unblushingly confesses a life so saintly that that friar spreads the word of his holiness far and wide. Once dead and buried, the scoundrel becomes an object of local veneration.

Boccaccio gives the modern reader a humbling look back at fourteenth-century Italian culture. The people disdain usurers regardless of ethnicity—Lombards especially—and not without some cause. Although informed by a Christian ethos, they are not oppressed by it. They take their faith seriously, sometimes too seriously perhaps, but not preposterously so. This is the kind of open, ambitious, unruly world in which the Medici would prosper. It is not that much different from our own.

The Medici served as something of a Beta test for the merchant banking families that would follow: moneylending 1.0. Whether Protestant, Catholic, or Jew, the dynastic arcs of these outsized families—Morgan, Medici, Rothschild—track closely with one another. The Medici story might profitably begin with the bank's founding father, Giovanni di Bicci, born in 1260 into a respectable Florentine family of moderate wealth.[3] Thanks to the dowry from an ambitious marriage, Giovanni was able to finesse a partnership in a cousin's bank in Rome, then the hub of international finance.

Rome had assumed this role for one reason: the Catholic Church was headquartered here. In another one of history's great ironies, it was the flow of tithes to Rome that inspired the infrastructure for a continentwide financial network. It was the church's presence that made Italians the world's bankers. It was the church's regulations that made them such creative bankers. And it was the fear of God that kept their activities aboveboard, more or less.

From 1385 to 1397, Giovanni worked at his cousin's bank in Rome. There he learned what it would take to set up a major international bank of his own. This would include sufficient capital, branches in all the major trade centers staffed by Italians he could trust, and, finally, a discreet understanding of how money could be made in banking without charging interest. In 1397, Cosimo and two partners headed back to Florence and opened their doors for business.

Although it had other profit centers—the Medici were merchants as well as bankers—the Medici bank made most of its money by mastering the art of exchange. Let us say, for instance, that a merchant in Florence wanted to borrow a thousand florins to send a silk shipment to London. Once the silk was delivered and paid for, the merchant's agent would repay the London Medici branch officer back for the loan—without interest, of course—based on the going rate of exchange.

This transaction would seem pointless for the Medici given that exchange rates between currencies can float up or down. Fortunately, however, some banking records still exist, and they verify what everyone suspected: exchanges among agents in London, Bruges, and Venice from that period show a profit for the bankers in sixty-six out of sixty-seven cases. The gains ranged from 7.7 to 28.8 percent. The method of assuring profit was inordinately complicated—manuals were written to help bankers and merchants understand—but everyone got it. "Basically," writes Tim Parks in *Medici Money*, "the trick is that the currency quoted as a unit is always worth more in the country of issue."[4]

The Medici gained their edge by staffing their branches with relatives, in-laws, and other *paisanos* who could be trusted with the "trick." Ironically again, the usury prohibition helped drive international trade and made banking an international business. Church fathers insisted on distance to legitimize exchanges. Bankers went awry when they tried to pull off exchange deals with only a nominal swapping of currencies. This kind of transaction church fathers called a *cambio secco*, or dry exchange.[5] The church forbade it, and Florence outlawed it in 1429.

For all of the obstacles, however, the Medici had formalized what the Templars and others had pioneered, namely, the banking industry. What international banking did, the third Lord Rothschild would say with his inherited precision, was "facilitate the movement of money from point A, where it is, to point B, where it is needed."[6] In the process of moving this money, the Medici and others like them laid the foundation for the further economic development of the Western world.

By 1429, Giovanni had retired, and his son Cosimo had taken over the bank, now organized into a vast holding company. Each branch director had a stake in the company and an obligation to honor the holding company's guidelines, chief among them, "Thou shalt not gamble."[7] This meant no loans of more than three hundred florins to cardinals and no loans to Germans under any terms. The Medici effectively redlined Germany not out of blind prejudice but from the hard experience of getting stiffed with the full approval of German courts. If the loans to cardinals were made without charging interest—the expected payback was in averted gazes—the commercial loans were fueled by roughly the same kind of subterfuges that make *sharia* banking possible today.

The pawnbrokers' trade in Florence testifies to the city's flexible standards for both crime and sin. Then as now, society held pawnbrokers in much less esteem than bankers. In that they openly charged interest, pawnbrokers bore the added fifteenth-century stigma of being "manifest usurers." As such, they could not belong to the Exchangers Guild. They could, however, be fined. And conveniently for everyone, they were fined en masse—two thousand florins—for the "detestable sin" of usury each year.[8] By paying their individual share of that fine, pawnbrokers could be assured of another year without punishment or outside competition. Today, we call this a license. It was not until 1437 that the church banned Christians from the trade altogether. Although this ban proved to be an economic boon for Jewish pawnbrokers, they would pay a high dividend in anti-Semitic resentment.

To navigate a safe path between the Scylla of church and the Charybidis of state, Cosimo got deeper into politics than the old man. Like the big-city bosses of the twentieth century, he preferred to work behind the scenes, pushing deals and pulling strings. In fact, east of Chicago, there may have been no more politically turbulent time and place than the Italian peninsula in the fifteenth century. It should surprise no one that Niccolò Machiavelli, the author of that classic in political cynicism, *The Prince*, was born in 1469, the same year that Cosimo's grandson, Lorenzo, assumed power, and in the same city, Florence.

In fifteenth-century Christendom, few, if any, sovereign rulers could match Cosimo's political clout and ecclesiastical connections. "He it is who decides peace and war and controls the laws," said Pope Pius II of Cosimo in 1458. "He is king in everything but name."[9] Despite Cosimo's power, the church did not change its usury laws to accommodate him. As Tim Parks assures us in a compliment so left-handed that it could get that hand lopped off in a less-tolerant religion—one comes immediately to mind—"The church was not entirely rotten."[10] Thank you, Tim.

Throughout the Middle Ages, in fact, orthodox reformers battled the bureaucrats for the church's soul. Antonio Pierozzi, a Dominican friar better known as Saint Antoninus, was writing the *Summa*, his major work on moral theology, in Florence during Cosimo's tenure. And although he worked with the Medici on the renovation of San Marco, he gave them no leeway on the moral questions of the day.

"Usury," Antoninus writes, "ever breaks and consumes the bones of the poor, night or day, on feasts and workdays, sleeping or waking its work never ceases."[11] He had no use for usury's subterfuges either. The pawnbroker trade he particularly disdained. Given his social justice perspective, he likened it to prostitution, a comparison that surely would have offended the ladies of the Florentine night.

For all of Antoninus's distaste for lending at interest, his writing on economics revealed an evolving sophistication. He understood profit and loss and the need to make the former. Like most Catholic theologians, he had no objection to the *societas*, a partnership in which one partner invests and runs the risk of losing that money if the project goes awry. He recognized the legality of what was called *lucrum cessans*, the loss of an assured profit in a safe enterprise as a result of money lent to another, riskier one.

Antoninus approved of the *census* as well. This was a popular form of annuity contract in which an investor provided the up-front cash, often to a city, and was paid back over a period of years by the revenue, often tax revenue, generated from the investment. As Ekelund et al. concede in their unflattering economic history of the medieval church, "Practically from its conception, the Christian Church defended private property and trading activity."[12] Although deformed by the flat-out ban on usury, the quality of the moral dialectic on the economy in the fifteenth century has not been rivaled since.[13]

The Medici, meanwhile, concentrated on getting by. After a brief period of exile, the result of a political gambit gone south, Cosimo returned to Florence more powerful than ever. Among his first acts was to lift the ban on so-called dry exchanges. He cracked down on his enemies, exiled some of them, and got himself elected head of government when it suited his purposes. His grandson Lorenzo would confirm some years later, "In Florence things can go badly for the rich if they don't run the state."[14]

As happens in dynastic banking families, the heirs lose the passion for making money but not for spending it. Cosimo's well-fed son Piero, the "Fredo Corleone" of the clan, had no gift for the business. He got to mismanage it for only eight years before gout liberated him from this mortal coil. Piero's son Lorenzo had more talent than his father but even less interest in banking.

Blame it on Plato. Shortly before Cosimo's death and under his patronage, he had a friar named Marsilio Ficino translate the entire works of Plato into Latin. Ficino Christianized Plato through his translation, but he did so in a way that elevated art and life in general. Nature, in this interpretation, centers around the human soul, which naturally strives heavenward. To reach the pure light of God, that soul has to transcend the impure and earthly, and for Plato there was little more impure or earthly than the making of money, especially through usury.[15]

Ideally, government played a role in encouraging the heavenly aspirations of its citizens. The "safe and happy" state, Plato writes in *Laws*, accorded the place of highest honor to the soul. To the lowest place the state assigned "money and property." Plato mentions that "interest was not to be taken on loans," but he does so almost as an aside, as though the impurity of such a transaction were generally understood.

The celebration of Plato that Cosimo launched—including extravagant birthday parties every November 7—all but licensed Lorenzo to ignore the family business, which he promptly did. Now, as Lorenzo saw it, whatever he did short of making money glorified God. So he spent most of his energies on patronizing art, plotting intrigue, and writing poetry, much of it pornographic. One typical poem begins with the unsubtle line, "Cucumbers we've got, and big ones,"[16] and goes quickly and predictably downhill from there. Lorenzo also dabbled in bad loans and embezzlement. He managed to escape one assassination attempt that his brother Guliano did not and died in bed in that momentous year of 1492, consoled by none other than his erstwhile scourge, the Dominican firebrand, Savonarola.

Savonarola deserves a sidebar. While the young Lorenzo was writing porn about tumescent cucumbers, the young Savonarola was writing poems titled "On the Decline of the Church." If proof be needed that not all Catholic clerics were rotten, Savonarola served it up in spades. A contemporary of Lorenzo, Savonarola joined the Dominican order as a young man, heaven-bent on reforming the church from within. Never shy about speaking his mind, he wrote his poem on church decline during his first year of monastic life.[17]

In 1489, three years before Lorenzo's death, Savonarola descended on Florence determined to purge city and church of their conspicuous consumption. He did so, the Catholic Encyclopedia says in something of an understatement, "without regard to consequences."[18] At San Marco, a church funded by the Medici, he preached against not only the lenders of money but also the spenders of money, the prodigals. The Medici were both. A hard-core ascetic and self-mortifier, Savonarola was among the first to understand the synergy between usury and prodigality.

After Lorenzo's death, Savonarola stepped up his assault on then–Pope Alexander VI and the Medici. Inspired by Savonarola's impassioned homilies, the Florentines rose up and drove Lorenzo's tyrannical son and heir, Pietro, out of town in 1494, the effective end of the Medici banking era. Backed by French king Charles VIII, Savonarola and his allies established a lively democratic theocracy in Florence.

The highlight of Savonarola's ascendancy was the 1497 "Bonfire of the Vanities"—a series of public burnings of what secular moralists would one day call "nonproductive items of consumption": fine clothing, cosmetics, playing cards, dice, mirrors, and more. The impassioned Florentines went after the lenders as well as the spenders. They stormed the Medici palace and burned very near all of the bank's records.

A Savonarola partisan, the painter Sandro Botticelli is reported to have fueled one of the bonfires with a few of his own less inspired doodlings. Had he felt a wee bit more repentant he might have tossed in his now-classic *Adoration of the Magi*. As Florentine art fans surely knew, the three wise men in the painting were all Medici—Cosimo and his two sons, Piero and Giovanni. Botticelli might more accurately have labeled the painting *Adoration of the Medici*. The Medici were, not surprisingly, among Botticelli's more generous patrons.

Historians have a hard time with Savonarola. The excesses of the official church may trouble them, but the reformers frighten them, especially fundamentalists like Savonarola. At the risk of generalization, they would likely have cheered the humanist counterreformers who hanged Savonarola in 1498, just four years after he had driven the Medici out of town. Forty years later, the Florentine elite summoned Cosimo the younger back to Florence where he would eventually become the grand Duke of Tuscany, a Medici bailiwick for the next two hundred years.

The Medici would exact their most enduring revenge on Savonarola and his ilk in the person of Lorenzo's second son, Giovanni. Born in 1475, the future Pope Leo X was invested as a cardinal at sixteen while Lorenzo was still around to stage-manage his ecclesiastical career. Unlike the Jane Fondas and Tori Spellings of the world, who swear their last name had nothing to do with their success, Leo harbored no such illusions. He would ascend to the papacy in 1513 on skids well-enough greased that he did not trouble himself to become a priest until after he became pope.

Today's media critics envision popes as extravagant and self-indulgent, always scheming and intriguing, more interested in the power and perks of the office than in the saving of souls. They ignore the extraordinary two-thousand-year continuity of the papacy and the sterling examples of papal piety in their own lifetimes—Benedict XVI, John Paul II, John XXIII. They prefer instead to confuse the occasional bad apple with the entire crop. It is as if, when they imagine the American presidency, they ignore Lincoln and Washington and fix on Warren G. Harding.

As it happens, Pope Leo X *was* the Warren G. Harding of Catholic popes—a little bit worse actually, much worse come to think of it. In truth, he makes a much too appropriate poster child for those inclined toward anti-Catholicism. Raphael, who flourished under Leo's patronage, actually provided that poster. To this day, his painting of Leo hangs in the Pitti Gallery in Florence, and Leo does, in fact, look like confirmed Catholic-bashers might have hoped he would: corpulent, effeminate, bandy-legged, shifty-eyed. Were it not for the fact that Leo helped launch the modern era of democratic capitalism—and that by accident—he would have little to recommend him.

For the record, Catholics do not impute infallibility to the character of their popes. In Leo's case, that would require faith beyond all understanding. As Dante made clear, Catholics, like all Christians, fully recognize the weaknesses of a fallen human nature, even among popes. Indeed, the first pope, Peter, the rock upon whom the church was built, proved more gelatinous than rocklike on the eve of Jesus' death, and yet Jesus did not hold that permanently against him.

In Catholic doctrine, infallibility is reserved only for solemn declarations on faith or morals as inspired by divine revelation. Church rulings on usury have never quite risen to that level. Indeed, Leo would rewrite the rule book on this issue as an administrative aside, much the way Jimmy Carter did the 401(k), each ushering in an era of investment and prosperity without quite meaning to.

The case upon which Leo ruled involved an institution called the *Monte di Pietà* (Piety Mountain), this one located at Perugia in modern-day Italy. The case had been kicking around for a half century without resolution. The *Monte di Pietà* was run by the Franciscan order to help the poor through times of peril. Hard-pressed locals would come to the *Monte di Pietà* and leave the sixteenth-century equivalent of an engagement ring or a chain saw in exchange for a loan. The term of the loan would typically last the course of a year and then, ideally, the borrower would repay the loan and regain the collateral.[19]

The Bishop of London had launched the first such institution in 1361. Backed by generous donors who provided the start-up capital, these institutions found particularly friendly soil in Italy the following century. In his memoirs, Franciscan Marco di Matteo Strozzi has left a record of his order's intentions, namely, to deny Jewish moneylenders their seemingly usurious rates by replacing them with this chain of Christian-themed pawnshops.[20]

What the Franciscans may have overlooked is that the managers of Jewish pawnshops, not having taken vows of chastity or poverty, had wives and kids to support, some of whom were likely very demanding. What the Franciscans did not overlook is that they, too, would have to charge borrowers a certain interest rate to cover the occasional default and their own humble overhead.

To understand the spirit of the Franciscan endeavor, one need look no further than recent Nobel Peace Prize winner Muhammad Yunus, a Bangladeshi banker with an American education. Some thirty years ago, as a well-fed economics professor in a starving country, Yunus felt the moral urge to experiment with what he calls "micro-lending."[21]

The first loan—for just twenty-seven dollars—came out of his pocket. Although traditional bankers thought he was daft, Yunus kept making loans to collateral-less poor people. He was convinced that folks who had the gumption to start cottage industries would have the honor to repay their loans, and this they did. Indeed, more than 98 percent of his 2.5 million loans have been repaid. In the process, Yunus and his Grameen Bank have transformed thousands of poor people into a productive class of entrepreneurs. Some one hundred different countries have since adapted the Grameen micro-credit program, including our own.

Like the Franciscans, Yunus understood that he would have to charge a modest interest if he were to run a business. By the twenty-first century, even the socialists on the Nobel committee had come to understand this. They awarded Yunus and the Grameen Bank in Bangladesh top honors in 2006, the first for-profit enterprise ever to be so distinguished, a refreshing turn of events.

In the sixteenth century, however, the issue of interest remained unsettled. The rival Dominican order was vexed because the Franciscans seemed to be cheating on church law. The Jewish moneylenders were equally vexed because the Franciscans were undercutting their market. Charges were brought, and in 1513, they came before the Lateran Council over which Leo was presiding.[22]

An original of Leo's "broadside bull" still exists. Called *Bulla concilii in decima sessione super materia Montis Pietatis*, it is for sale online for a mere 1750 British pounds with, one hopes, easy financing terms available. In a nutshell, Leo ruled that the *Monte di Pietà* was a valuable institution and that its policies only made sense. Never one to do things halfway, he then threatened with excommunication anyone who said otherwise. Covering Leo's back during his papacy was cousin Giulio, the son of Giuliano de Medici, the unlucky brother killed during the assassination attempt on Lorenzo. Two years after Leo's death in 1521, Giulio was named Pope Clement VII.

Before dying, Leo excommunicated an obstreperous German priest. That same decade, an aspiring French theologian left the Catholic Church. Had he been paying more attention, Pope Clement VII might have been troubled by the respective falling away of Martin Luther and John Calvin, but that anxiety he would leave to future popes.

seven

The Rules of Equity

IN THE EUROPE OF THE 1450S, WHILE THE PIOUS POPE NICHOLAS V held (relatively) gentle sway over the united colors of Christendom, a German craftsman was hard at work on a project that would, without his intending, forever disunite them. Unworried by the intentions of Johannes Gutenberg, and generally encouraging of his progress, the Vatican in 1454 helped him finance his new endeavor by contracting with him to print thousands of indulgences, formal papal decrees that one's sins had been forgiven. A year later Gutenberg produced his famous Bible, and the world has not been the same since.

Print had at least as much impact on the fifteenth and sixteenth centuries as the Internet did on the late twentieth and twenty-first. Each democratized the flow of information, but any gain in knowledge was offset by a loss in humility, a formula for trouble in either era. Despite their enhanced access to data, the humanists of the Gutenberg era chose to forget the accomplishments of the millennium that had just preceded them. In their retelling, a purifying gale had blown through the Europe of that epoch, sweeping away with it the dust and cobwebs of a cranky old papacy.

On the economic front, this story line received its imprimatur with the 1905 publication of Max Weber's *The Protestant Ethic and the Spirit of Capitalism.* Weber argued, in essence, that the Protestant Reformation inspired the capitalist revolution. Once a Christian had lost the safety net of authoritative Catholicism, he was thrown onto his own resources. Insecure and anxious about salvation, especially if he hewed to a Calvinist faith, he turned his energy to work and looked to his ensuing success as a sign of his place among the elect.[1]

For Weber, this psychic energy survived the erosion of faith and piety and became part of the culture, no greater exemplar of which was one of America's own founding fathers. "We shall nevertheless provisionally use the expression 'spirit of capitalism' for that attitude which, *in the pursuit of a calling*, strives systematically for profit for its own sake in the manner exemplified by Benjamin Franklin,"[2] writes Weber. He traces this rationalization, at least in part, to the fact that Luther—and other self-styled reformers who followed—paid more attention to the Old Testament than the Catholic hierarchy had, and so were more influenced by Jewish thought.

For all his insight, Weber generalized much too freely in linking Martin Luther and John Calvin as partners in economic progress. The progress needed no jump start. When Luther and Calvin surfaced, both within a hundred years of the introduction of the Gutenberg Bible, they inherited a commercial revolution that had been progressing—with few major reversals—for the last five hundred years. Their contemporaries in the Catholic Church were quietly yielding on the flat-out usury ban. In the early sixteenth century, Franciscan Juan de Medina emerged as the first scholastic writer to insist that risk should rightly be rewarded with interest.[3] Others would follow.

As a case study in progress, one need look no further than the rollout of Gutenberg's Bible. Only in this fully Catholic world (and nowhere else) would Gutenberg have been able to find the freedom, the capital, and the institutional stability to industrialize the art of movable type. Gutenberg had investors, a practice the church allowed as long as all investors shared the risk. He also received a loan, presumably interest free, which remains one of the few advantages of having in-laws.

Complicating the whole notion of reform was that these two theological rebels, Calvin and Luther, had largely divergent views on the direction of things economic. Calvin was bridging to the seventeenth century, Luther to the fifteenth. Nowhere was their divergence more evident than on the related subjects of usury and the Jews. Given the Reformation's elevation of the individual preacher over the institution, Calvin would have more impact on the subject of usury than any pope who preceded him, and Luther would have more impact on the fate of the Jews.

In the way of background, the thirteen-year-old Martin Luther headed off to a Latin school in Magdeburg, Germany, in 1497, the same year that Savonarola was scorching the vanities in Florence. At twenty-one, Luther dropped out of law school and became a monk, an intensely introspective one at that. Two years later, he was ordained a priest and turned to teaching to help break out of his own self-imposed gloom.[4] In 1517, Luther posted his famed ninety-five theses on the door of the Castle Church in Wittenberg, objecting, among other things, to the sale of indulgences by the Vatican. A century earlier this would likely have remained a local dustup, but the printing press changed all that. Within months, Luther's defiance was the talk of Christendom.

For the next three years, the Vatican walked the increasingly obstreperous Luther through a series of unfriendly administrative hearings. Although the potential punishment could be a bit more severe—burning at the stake, for instance—these hearings were, if anything, more forgiving than those college students face today should they run afoul of campus thought police. In 1520, Lorenzo's son, Pope Leo X, issued a formal decree threatening Luther with excommunication if he persisted. Luther persisted in spades, publicly burning the papal bull and irrevocably crossing the Rubicon that he had dug for himself. A year later, Luther was declared a heretic. He escaped with his freedom and, possibly, his life only through the intervention of certain sympathetic German nobles.

For the next twenty-five years, Luther would speak and write on any number of subjects, but few with more vigor than when speaking on usury, a subject he addressed in detail in 1524, just three years after his final break with the Catholic Church. Given that the ranks of the shy and diffident produce few heretics, it should not surprise that Luther spoke forcefully, even when merely defining a subject. "He who lends expecting to get back something more or something better than he has loaned," writes Luther, "is clearly a damned usurer."[5] His source was Christ himself. Here he cites the critical passage in Luke, "Lend, hoping for nothing again."

Luther then focuses his ire—and his irony—on those arguments used to justify this "tender business."[6] He had a particular distaste for semantic evasions. Just as today one man's interest-only, adjustable-rate mortgage is another man's predatory loan, so the neologism *interesse* was, for Luther, just another way of saying "damned usury."

Interesse derives from the Latin, meaning "that which is in between." Introduced by the Christian scholar Hispanus in the early thirteenth century (but far from universally accepted), *interesse* was originally used to describe the compensation awarded a lender for a loan not returned on time. It covered his theoretical loss of the use of that money from the date that the loan should have been repaid until the date it was repaid. In more opportunistic circles, *interesse* all but replaced the word *usury* to describe the opportunity cost of money lent during the entire cost of a commercial loan. In English, it would hold that meaning and evolve into *interest*.

Luther would have none of this. To him "this noble, precious, tender, little word" was simply usury by another name. "Here they say, now, that the purchase of the income is proper because, with these [100] gulden, I might perhaps have made more in a year, and the interest is just and sufficient," he observes. But, as Luther fairly argues, nowhere in the real world is there any guarantee that money would make money during a given time. "If I have a hundred gulden, and am to do business with it," says Luther, "I may run a hundred kinds of risk of making no profits at all, nay, of losing four times as much besides."[7]

Luther was more understanding of income invested in land, but here, too, he offered caveats. He objected to the lumping together of properties, as was common, and insisted on "specifying and defining the particular piece of ground from which the income is derived." In this way, the income would fluctuate with the value of the ground, "as is right." He also objected to the taking of "too much return" on the land. He defined "too much" as the 7 to 10 percent return that was then something of a norm. "The poor common people are secretly imposed upon and severely oppressed," he objected. In other words, there should be no bundling of mortgages, no subprime loans, and no predatory lending, even on land. "The rulers ought to look into this,"[8] says Luther, nearly five hundred years before his time.

Perhaps given his German background, Luther was not averse to using the state to enforce the comprehensive Christian business ethics that he lays out for his followers (and not just on the question of usury). Like almost all Christian philosophers, Luther accepted private property and enterprise. "It is not to be denied," he writes, "that buying and selling are necessary."[9] He believed, however, that a combination of internal and external restraints should shape the kind of trade that states and individuals transacted.

"Cattle, wool, grain, butter, milk and other goods," Luther writes, "these are gifts of God." He may have been the first person of consequence, however, to inveigh against "foreign trade," especially trade from points east like "Calcutta, India, and such places." The problem with this trade was not only that it "drain[ed] away the wealth of land and people," but that it also corrupted them, specifically those "costly silks, gold-work and spices, which minister only to luxury and serve no useful purpose."[10]

Luther's frustration with high prices moved him to favor government intervention. Much to his chagrin, the merchants of his acquaintance seemed to have only "one common rule," namely, to sell at whatever price the market would bear. If, on the upside, this practice was returning a good profit, on the downside it was "opening every door and window to hell."[11] In an ideal Christian world, as Luther saw it, the common rule would not have been, "I may sell my wares as dear as I can or will," but rather, "I may sell my wares as dear as I ought, or as is right and proper." Unfortunately, sixteenth-century Germany was not an ideal Christian world. Such a world has not yet existed.

Given the shortcomings of human nature, Luther recommended instead a practice that has been tried by any number of temporal rulers since (although it's always failed). The authorities, writes Luther, "should appoint over this matter wise and honest men who would appraise the cost of all sorts of wares and fix accordingly the outside price at which the merchant would get his due and have an honest living." Luther was savvy enough to know that Germans were too "busy with drinking and dancing"[12] to tolerate much regulation. The best he could hope for was that competition would force merchants to sell their wares in a common market at a customary price.

Luther wrote in detail about a wide range of commercial transactions—annuities, a just price, and usury among them. In this he was not unique. In pre-Enlightenment Christendom, Protestant and Catholic philosophers saw no reason to separate faith and finance. Many tried to craft an integrated Christian business ethic. But as international commerce became more uniform, and faith became less so, such efforts came to seem less and less relevant. If they chose to, and many did, leaders in the realm of commerce could ignore the whole history of Judeo-Christian business philosophy. As shall be seen, this has not necessarily been to the benefit of the world's economy.

French theologian John Calvin broke from the Catholic Church in the same turbulent decade that Luther did, but from his writing, especially on the subject of usury, one would think that he happened on the scene a century or so later. Environment mattered here. While Luther wrestled with his demons in the closed quarters of a German monastery, Calvin stuck with law school—and that under the influence of reform-minded French humanists.

In the France of the 1530s, reform was a pretty brutal business, and Calvin and friends found themselves on the run, first to Geneva and then to Strasbourg and then to Geneva again and then to Strasbourg again and then finally to Geneva. In 1536, still only twenty-six years old, Calvin published his theological masterwork, *Institutes of the Christian Religion*, and his reputation was established. Calvin would live and write for nearly thirty more tumultuous years and leave perhaps his greatest influence on Western culture through the portal of New England.

Although Weber and others have given Calvin, if anything, too much credit for the development of the capitalist spirit, Calvin deserves his due on the subject of usury. In this regard, he was something of a revolutionary. In his celebrated letter to his colleague Sachinus in 1545, he broke with the nearly three-millennia-old Judeo-Christian usury ban and adapted the spirit of the Gospels to the imperatives of sixteenth-century commerce.

In reading Calvin and Luther, one cannot help but be impressed by their super-sized certitude. Catholic church fathers like Aquinas and Antoninus moved forward but always probingly, with continual backward glances at the wise men who preceded them, Christian and classical. For Calvin and Luther, it was pedal to the metal, with no looking back until they got to Jesus. They may have respected their predecessors, but they trusted their own instincts and inspiration more.

"I am certain that by no testimony of Scripture is usury wholly condemned," writes Calvin. "For the sense of that saying of Christ, 'Lend hoping for nothing again' (Luke 6:35), has up to this time been perverted."[13] Perverted! One reason Calvin succeeded while so many other breakaway divines failed is the clarity of his thought and language. He may have spoken boldly, but he did not bluster. Nor was he at all intimidated by the cautious thinking on this subject of the church fathers, let alone Luther. Says Calvin of Jesus, "His words ought to be interpreted that while he would command loans to the poor without expectation of repayment or the receipt of interest, he did not mean at the same time to forbid loans to the rich with interest."[14] Touché!

Calvin strikes the contemporary reader as the first theologian to assess the usury question in the context of a highly evolved sixteenth-century commerce. "If all usury is condemned," he writes, "tighter fetters are imposed on the conscience than the Lord himself would wish."[15] He worried that an absolutist interpretation could lead to the abandonment not only of the usury ban but also of the spirit behind it. In this regard, he echoes traditional church canon, *Cessante ratione, cessat ipsa lex*: "When the reason for the law ceases, the law itself ceases."

The intrepid Calvin took on Aristotle as well: "It is said, 'Money does not beget money.' What does the sea beget?" Calvin walks the reader through the process by which money does, in fact, beget money; that is, through "the product that results from its use or employment." Why, he wonders, is it morally acceptable to squeeze a poor tenant farmer for a cut of his harvest, but not acceptable to ask a wealthy merchant for return on a commercial loan that has been put to use in some productive industry? "I therefore conclude that usury must be judged, not by a particular passage of Scripture," says Calvin in summary, "but simply by the rules of equity."[16]

Christian defenders of the usury ban in the centuries that followed—especially his namesake Calvin Elliott—had obvious problems with Calvin's stance. The one argument Elliott uses to undercut Calvin is to suggest that his writing on this subject "is wanting in that positive air of assured certainty" that one finds in his *Institutes*.[17] Wanting in what positive air? It is hard to imagine how Calvin could have written with more certainty. In truth, Calvin weighs into this subject with such jaw-dropping bravado that, seemingly overnight, he would help take usury off the table as a subject of any real controversy in Protestant domains, at least those forms of usury not "repugnant both to Justice and to Charity."[18]

Given his acceptance of lending at interest, Calvin did not share the epoch's widespread animus toward Jews. In his writings, he treated Jewish arguments respectfully and objectively, so much so that Lutheran antagonists would accuse him of being a "Judaizer" or even a Jew himself.[19]

No one ever accused Luther of being either. True, when he broke from the Catholic Church, he looked to the Jews to support his new interpretation of the Bible. They, in turn, were encouraged by his rejection of the papacy for no other reason than it seemed to divide and weaken their enemies. But this uneasy détente would not hold. In his 1523 pamphlet "Jesus Christ Is the Born Jew," Luther argued that since Christianity had been freed of its papal chains, there was no reason for Jews not to convert en masse. The Jews did not quite see it that way. They argued that the Talmud was a truer version of the Bible than Luther's and suggested that perhaps he might convert to Judaism.

Increasingly frustrated by their obstinacy, Luther turned on the Jews with a vengeance. In 1543, he published "On the Jews and Their Lies," a 65,000-word treatise more elaborately angry than anything any pope or church doctor had written in the last fifteen centuries. Fueling Luther's rage, although not explaining it, was his hostility toward usury. The pamphlet contains no fewer than twenty-five distinct attacks on the Jews for this one practice alone.

Luther does not tread gently. "Their breath stinks with lust for the Gentiles' gold and silver," he writes of his once almost-allies, "for no nation under the sun is greedier than they were, still are, and always will be, as is evident from their accursed usury."[20] Lending with interest was the least of their intergenerational failings. "They are steeped in greed, in usury," he warns, "they steal and murder where they can and ever teach their children to do likewise."[21] This language would resonate down the German centuries. Paul Johnson, author of the definitive *History of the Jews*, describes the treatise as "the first work of modern anti-Semitism, and a giant step forward on the road to the 'Holocaust.'"[22]

As Luther saw it, the Jews profaned the Bible by locating their justification for usury within its pages, specifically the "stranger" exemption in Deuteronomy 23:20. "They not only practice usury—not to mention the other vices—but they teach that it is a right which God conferred on them through Moses. Thereby, as in all the other matters, they slander God most infamously."[23]

As keen as Luther was on government intervention, he saw no hope of the state solving his Jewish problem. "Our princes and rulers sit there and snore with mouths hanging open," he writes of the compromised German authorities, "and permit the Jews to take, steal, and rob from their open money bags and treasures whatever they want."[24] Meanwhile in England, still another Protestant split-off, rulers were doing a good deal more than snoring. The

most notable of them, Henry the VIII, was on the verge of passing into law
the "Act 'In restraint of usury.'"[25]Although its intent is not easily fathomed in
the name, this bill represented the first time a major Christian state gave the
green light to usury, albeit with a 10 percent annual limit.

In the Muslims' continued defense of usury, the educational site *Mission
Islam* declares of this time and place in Christian history, "It was now possible
for anyone to decide whether something was right or wrong."[26] One can hardly
fault our Muslim friends for thinking so.

eight

I Stand Here for Law

NOT LUTHER, NOT CALVIN, NOT BOCCACCIO, NOT DANTE, NOT AQUINAS, not Aristotle, not all of them together have shaped the popular perception of the usurer as much as has a glover's son from small-town England. William Shakespeare was not yet thirty-five when he wrote *The Merchant of Venice*, and although he surely knew a moneylender or two—his father dabbled—he may not have known a Jew.

When Shakespeare was coming of age in the late sixteenth century, there were officially no Jews in all of England. They had been expelled some three centuries earlier after two hundred uneasy years on the island. The first Jews in any number to reach England came in the wake of William's incursion in 1066. By this time, their identity as the world's usurers had become more or less fixed. Ironically, as usury laws eased in England during the next two centuries, Jews became less essential and more expendable. In 1278, according to one report, some members of the community stood accused of "coin clipping,"[1] a subtle shaving of a coin that allowed the shaver to pocket some percentage of the precious metal and still exchange the coin at face value. This was obviously not appreciated by the locals. They reportedly hanged three hundred of the offenders. In 1290, they drove the entire Jewish population from the island.

The English Jews dispersed throughout Europe and some found safe harbor in the Iberian peninsula. This did not last. Little did for Europe's Jews. By the late fifteenth century, the Spanish Inquisition, a state-sponsored affair, made life untenable for Spain's Jewish population, even those who had converted to Christianity. In 1482 Pope Sixtus IV attempted to intervene in this royal witch hunt, but without success. His demands that those accused of heresy receive due process fell on Ferdinand's willfully deaf ears, and by century's end the Jews of Spain had been exterminated or expelled.

For most of the sixteenth century, Europe's Jews were buffeted about by the winds of the Reformation and Counter-Reformation. They had to feel as lost and luckless as they had in the desert circa 1200 BC. Toward century's end, as the reformers' zeal exhausted itself, pressures eased, even in England. True, in AD 1552, Parliament had reinstated the usury ban lifted seven years earlier, calling the practice "a vyce most odious and detestable,"[2] but in 1571, under Elizabeth, the usury ban was rescinded once and for all.

That lending at interest was now legal in England did not mean that it was popular everywhere. Puritan divines would rail against usury and usurers for decades to come, if not centuries, and the prejudice against Jews faded no more quickly than did the stigma against money lending. Young Shakespeare had to absorb a good deal of the controversy, which was now millennia old and continent wide. This cultural bias finds its most storied expression in *Hamlet*, when Polonius advises his son Laertes of the seductions that await a student in Paris:

> *Neither a borrower nor a lender be;*
> *For loan oft loses both itself and friend,*
> *And borrowing dulls the edge of husbandry.*[3]

Shakespeare pulled the plot for *Merchant* from an Italian collection called *Il Pecorone*, meaning "The Simpleton," written two centuries prior.[4] As to the sensibility, however, that was fresh, bold, and uniquely his own. The action of the play unfolds in contemporary Venice, a city that Shakespeare had never visited. Englishmen thought of Venice in those days much as Henry James and Thomas Mann would three centuries later—dark, decadent, exotic. For all of the city's storied darkness, however, Shakespeare portrays its citizens as brightly as if they were Englishmen—honorable, upright, and loyal to a fault.

Young Bassanio needs money to woo the fair and seriously affluent Portia, whom he dearly loves. The title character, Antonio, is eager to lend his friend Bassanio the money he needs. Although confident that the ships he has commissioned will soon return to Venice with profits many times the requested loan, Antonio lacks the up-front cash. To get the money, Antonio turns to literature's most well-known usurer and one of its most memorable characters, the Jew, Shylock. He may be cold and cruel, but Shylock is nobody's fool. In an aside, upon being introduced to Antonio, he sums up fifteen hundred years' worth of growing enmity:

> How like a fawning publican he looks. I hate him for he is a Christian, but more
> for that in low simplicity he lends out money gratis and brings down the rate
> of usance here with us in Venice. If I catch him once upon the hip, I will feed
> fat the ancient grudge I bear him. He hates our sacred nation, and he rails, even
> there where merchants must do congregate, on me, my bargains and my well-
> won thrift, which he calls interest. Cursed be my tribe, if I forgive him.[5]

The quarter of the city where merchants "must do congregate" lies beyond the walls of the consigned Jewish quarter. That quarter took its name from the Venetian word for *slag*, a material found in abundance in this, the old foundry area of Venice.[6] That word was *getto* or *gheto*. The ghetto system spread to other cities in the Italian peninsula, as did the word itself. Its purpose was to allow Jews to participate in the city's commercial life, where they were useful, but to exclude them from its social life, where they were not. For all its implicit indignity, the ghetto provided Jews something of a refuge and one that enabled them to sustain their culture. Although Shakespeare erred in a few details about the life of a Jewish moneylender, he gave Shylock an arresting and authentic personality, the first multidimensional one for a Jew in Western literature.

Elizabethan playgoers would surely have identified with Antonio, but even the folks in the cheap seats could have understood the Jew's grudge against him. The merchant does not deny that he has spit on Shylock and called him a dog. He does not ask for Shylock's friendship, just his money. In the spirit of Deuteronomy, he expects Shylock to lend it as though to "thine enemy" and to exact a penalty beyond the interest if he does not meet his obligation.

Loan or no loan, Antonio has no intention of changing his ways toward this Jew or any other. Shylock gets the message, as is evident in the penalty that he demands of this "prodigal Christian," namely, "an equal pound of your fair flesh" [Act 1, Scene 3]. Overconfident Antonio readily consents to this demand over Bassanio's heated objection.

Not surprisingly, some Shakespeare scholars have imputed a barely latent homosexuality to Antonio's sacrificial affection for Bassanio. Except for one wrinkle, this would not be noteworthy, as academic critics have attempted to "out" just about every character in world literature up to and including Felix and Oscar in Neil Simon's *The Odd Couple*. What makes this assertion interesting, as famed homosexual poet W. H. Auden was quick to notice, is that Shakespeare "must have been familiar with the association of usury with sodomy of which Dante speaks in the Eleventh (sic) Circle of the Inferno."[7] The two are thought to be sins against nature. Antonio, perhaps like his creator, has flirted with both.

In one of the play's subplots, Bassanio's friend Lorenzo has struck up a serious relationship with Shylock's daughter Jessica. Few critics note the most basic message implicit in their affair, namely, that Jews are part of the family. They are not the usurious swine that later generations of Europeans, Germans in particular, would portray them.

In Elizabethan England, for all of the discrimination against them, Jews moved through the world with more respect and more rights than blacks did in America just fifty years ago. At least they did in Shakespeare's world. As the plot works itself out, all of Antonio's ships are lost, and he defaults on his obligation. Shylock, the nightmare usurer, seeks literal satisfaction of his bond. A lesser playwright would have given him the snarling silliness of a Silas Barnaby, the *Babes in Toyland* villain who tried to foreclose on the little old woman who lived in the shoe. Shakespeare instead allows Shylock to establish his shared humanity through a passage of sufficient power that it would forever subvert the urge to anti-Semitism in the English-speaking world.

Hath not a Jew eyes? Hath not a Jew hands, organs, dimensions, senses, affections, passions? Fed with same food, hurt with the same weapons, subject to the same diseases, healed by the same means, warmed and cooled by the same winter and summer, as a Christian is? If you prick us, do we not bleed? If you tickle us, do we not laugh? If you poison us, do we not die? And if you wrong us, shall we not revenge." [Act 3, Scene 1]

The courtroom scene that follows suggests why the English-speaking countries would eventually dominate the world's economy and why Jews would prosper in those countries as nowhere else. To succeed, the capitalist enterprise hinges on the rule of law. Its entrepreneurs, minorities included, must be able to depend on the efficacy and fairness of that law. This under-standing originated in Mosaic law and was transmitted to Europe through the active agency of Christianity. Although usury laws were still imperfect and evolving in mid-millennium Europe, the attention paid to those laws by both secular and ecclesiastical authorities testified to the moral seriousness of the commercial enterprise.

Shylock understands this, and he fully expects Christian courts to honor his contract. "The duke shall grant me justice," he assures Antonio. "I'll have my bond" [Act 3, Scene 3]. Noble Antonio accepts the imperatives of the system as well. Even though it means his death, he is prepared to fulfill the contract into which he willingly entered. "Make no more offers, use no farther means," he tells the duke. "But with all brief and plain conveniency let me have judgment and the Jew his will" [Act 4, Scene 1]. In that *Merchant of Venice* is a comedy, the audience understands that Antonio will not die, and Shylock will not have his revenge. As the plot turns, Bassanio's beloved Portia shows up in court dis-guised as an esteemed young "doctor of the law" by the name of Balthasar (a curious turn, as men played women's parts in Shakespearean theater). "I stand here for law," Shylock assures the young jurist there to offer his authoritative opinion on the difficult case at hand [Act 4, Scene 1].

Although acknowledging that the law is on Shylock's side, Balthasar makes a distinctly Christian plea: "Therefore, Jew, though justice be thy plea, consider this, that, in the course of justice, none of us should see salvation: we do pray for mercy." Shylock will have none of it. "I crave the law," he insists.

Bassanio, now flush after his marriage to Portia, offers Shylock twice his investment and much more if he will spare Antonio's life. When Shylock refuses, Bassanio begs Balthasar to put the law aside. Balthasar denies the request, arguing that it would set a dangerous precedent to do so. "A Daniel come to judgment! Yea, a Daniel!" Shylock gushes about the "wise young judge." It is at this point that Balthasar serves up more justice than Shylock desires. Yes, he can have the pound of flesh, but not a drop of blood with it. Balthasar also reminds Shylock and the audience that the law, although executed precisely, is not without its inequalities as written. An "alien" who attempts to take the life of a "citizen," even if done legally, forfeits his entire estate, half to the intended victim and half to the state.

The modern audience watches the denouement uncomfortably. In his mercy, Antonio allows Shylock to keep half of his estate on two conditions: one is that he bequeath the estate to Jessica, now married and converted to Christianity; the second is that he, too, become a Christian. The Elizabethan audience, however, would feel no such discomfort. They would interpret Antonio's gift as he intended it, a token of mercy: the great Christian gift of redemption, Shylock's one chance for salvation.

For a century after its initial performance, no one thought to revive *The Merchant of Venice*. In 1701 George Granville brought a mutilated version to stage called *The Jew of Venice*. Although Granville gave Shylock top billing, he stripped him of his soul and turned him into the stock Jewish villain that audiences of that era expected. In one telling scene, after Bassanio and friends offer toasts at dinner to eternals like friendship and love, this Shylock toasts the glories of compound interest: "My money is my mistress! Here's to Interest Upon Interest."[8]

It was not until 1741 that *The Merchant of Venice* had a serious revival. The person responsible was an Irishman from Donegal named Charles Macklin. That the English thought even less of the Irish than they did of Jews may have helped Macklin get in character. If that affinity were not enough, Macklin immersed himself in Jewish history and culture, even visiting the coffee houses in London where "the unforeskinned race"[9] held forth, stock-jobbing and exchanging money. By all accounts, Macklin returned the power to Shylock and wiped away all traces of comic villainy from his character. The Shylock Macklin portrayed was malignant, menacing, and dark, and he played that part for the next forty years, until he could no longer remember the lines.

Another century would pass before British actors began to portray Shylock sympathetically. This had much to do with the growth of nineteenth-century liberalism, not just cultural but economic. By this time, lending money at interest was a given. A sophisticated audience would have had a hard time grasping the Venetian anxiety about the same. Nineteenth-century America witnessed no fewer than one hundred productions of *Merchant*—some of them sympathetic, some less so.

The most celebrated of the American Shylocks that century was Edwin Booth. His father of the same name had been a successful actor in London before abandoning his family and absconding to America with a Covent Garden flower girl—think Eliza Dolittle—with whom he would have ten children. Edwin was the fourth of their six sons.[10] His little brother, John, would have his greatest fame on the stage of the Ford Theater in Washington. It was there he uttered his memorable line in Latin, *"Sic semper tyrannis."* Twelve days later an unappreciative audience of Union soldiers shot and killed brother John.

Just two years after the assassination of Lincoln, Edwin debuted at the Winter Garden in a sumptuous presentation of *The Merchant of Venice.* Booth played Shylock not as a tragic Jewish figure but as a greedy capitalist, an increasingly common target in theatrical New York. Writes critic John Gross of Booth's perspective, "There was no reason not to believe the moneylender when he said that Antonio's chief offense in his eyes was bringing down the rate of interest 'here with us in Venice.'"[11]

Among those who saw Booth at the Winter Garden was the venerable American poet and literary critic William Cullen Bryant. He wrote a review of the performance under the title "Shylock Not a Jew." Observed Bryant, "It is true that money-changers once spat on in the ghetto are now hugged in the palace." Bryant cites here the Rothschilds, who were, in fact, Jewish, and the Goulds, who were decidedly not. "But it is not so much that the prejudice against the Jews has ceased but that the love of money has increased—not that the Jews have become as Christians, but that the Christians have become as Jews."[12] That same year, a continent away, Karl Marx released the first volume of his comprehensive masterwork, *Das Kapital,* a work rooted in almost exactly the sentiment that inspired Bryant's unease, but with a rather different solution.

nine

Prodigals and Projectors

IF KARL MARX HAD AN URGE TO UPEND THE ESTABLISHED ORDER, ADAM Smith had the urge to establish exactly what that order was. As the fellow who hammered out the concept of a new economic man, his name was almost too perfect. A smith was someone who forged something refined out of something raw. Adam was, of course, the first man. In 1723, when young Adam came howling into existence, "Smith" was no longer just a profession, but a name. In England, thanks to the advance of democratic capitalism, even the humblest citizens had distinct identities and names of their own, first and last. Smith got his name from the old man. A Scottish attorney, the senior Adam Smith died before his son was born. Beyond the name, Smith the elder and the Smiths before him had bequeathed young Adam a keen sense of self and an economic system that encouraged its exercise.

Smith put his genius on full display in his masterwork, *An Inquiry into the Nature and Causes of the Wealth of Nations*, published in the milestone year of 1776. He was the first political philosopher to establish that free individuals making independent decisions in their own self-interest constituted a viable economic system, one that produced better outcomes than any system any planner could hope to design. A champion of *laissez-faire*—a concept the French introduced but subsequently ignored—Smith rejected prohibitions against usury.

This was not surprising. What was surprising, inexplicable really, was that he waxed wobbly on one key point in the usury debate. For reasons equally unclear, upstart Jeremy Bentham zeroed in on this inconsistency in his memorable and occasionally hilarious attack on the good "Dr. Smith," one of the more entertaining philosophical spitting matches of the era.

In *Wealth of Nations*, Smith provides a quick history on English usury laws from the time of Henry VIII. As mentioned, the much-married Henry removed the ban and declared all interest above 10 percent unlawful. His son, Edward VI, in a spate of what Smith calls "religious zeal," put the ban back in place. His half sister Elizabeth revoked the ban and set the legal rate of interest once again at 10 percent. James I lowered the rate to 8 percent, which was then reduced to 6 percent soon after the Restoration and to 5 percent by Queen Anne. Smith observes that all of these rate changes "seem to have been made with great propriety"[1] and followed market rates. As a result, they tended to not retard economic growth in England, which Smith saw as trending upward since the time of Henry VIII.

By Smith's era, the great majority of loans at interest were made in money, which Smith saw not as "barren," as Aristotle famously did, or idle but as potentially bountiful. What the borrower received was not so much money as "money's worth," the ability to put that money to work in some productive endeavor. Of course, not everyone did. Smith makes the by then well-understood distinction between those who used the borrowed money to consume and those who used it to invest.

From the lender's perspective, all loans at interest were made as though to an investor. The lender expected to get the principal back along with "a certain annual rent for the use of it"[2] regardless of what the borrower did with the money. The borrower who used the loan for consumption, alas, acted "the part of a prodigal, and dissipates in the maintenance of the idle what was destined for the support of the industrious." Smith was confident, however, that the industrious outnumbered the prodigals. Pre-Darwinian logic dictated as much. "The man who borrows in order to spend will soon be ruined," Smith explains, "and he who lends to him will generally have occasion to repent of his folly."[3]

As coherent and as finely reasoned as *Wealth of Nations* is, Smith makes an oddly illiberal argument on the subject of government-set interest rates.

Bottom line—he has no problem with them. In fact, he argues that the authorities should keep those rates as restrictively low as possible, just slightly above the lowest market rate. If the legal interest rate in Great Britain were to be set much higher, Smith feared that lenders would look to those borrowers willing to pay high rates, namely, the "prodigals and projectors."[4]

As Smith explains, a projector is someone who undertakes new projects. Bentham describes them as those who "strike out into any new channel, and more especially into any channel of invention."[5] For us, they are venture capitalists. Prodigal is well enough understood. The ledger on their historic performance runs long, lively, and consistently in the red. Dante knowingly puts them in the *Inferno*'s fourth circle. And yet as keen a judge of sin as Dante was, he would not have known in which circle to put a projector. In fact, he would have had no reason to put them in the *Inferno* at all. Smith, however, thought of projectors much as he did prodigals—reckless souls who would soak up whatever capital was available.

If the legal interest rate were to be kept low, Smith reasons, projectors and prodigals would have to compete with "sober people."[6] Unlike the prodigals and projectors, the sober were not "likely to waste and destroy" what they had been given. If the return on investment were even close to comparable—and restrictive interest rates would insure they were—bankers would invest in the tried and true endeavors of the dependably sober. "A great part of the capital of the country," argues Smith, would be "thus thrown into the hands in which it is most likely to be employed with advantage."[7]

In his bold and often funny *Defence of Usury*, written a decade after *Wealth of Nations*, the irreverent Bentham all but gags on this defection from orthodoxy by the high priest of classical liberal economics. A generation younger than Smith, and a class or two above him by birth, Bentham was never wanting in self-confidence. A whiz kid from the get-go, he had started his study of Latin at the age of three and while still in his twenties was commissioned to write the British government's official rebuttal to the Declaration of Independence, penned by fellow prodigy Thomas Jefferson, five years Bentham's senior.

A philosopher and reformer, Bentham is often credited with fathering utilitarianism, a school of thought that traces its roots back to Epicurus but that blossomed in nineteenth-century England.[8] In his treatise *Introduction to the Principles of Morals*, Bentham laid down the principle of "utility." He judged an action's value by its capacity to generate happiness, which he thought of as the presence of pleasure and the absence of pain. The idea of an act being right or wrong had no purchase with Bentham. To distinguish between the two would require a moral legislator, presumably a supernatural one, and Bentham had moved beyond that hypothesis. Like Smith, but through different eyes, Bentham saw the inarguable utility of free-market economics, but he went well beyond Smith in highlighting the utter futility of a usury prohibition. Indeed, after Bentham got through trashing it, no serious intellectual would take up its defense again.

Bentham had a problem with the very word *usury*, which he thought capable, through sheer connotation, of stirring the passions in unpleasant ways. "Usury is a bad thing," he teases, "and as such ought to be prevented: usurers are a bad sort of men, a very bad sort of men, and as such ought to be punished and suppressed."[9] This was the supposition that even sophisticated eighteenth-century Englishmen took for granted, having inherited it from their progenitors, and they from theirs. It pained him that this ancient grudge against usury and usurers, real and fictional—Shylock comes to mind here—had wormed its way into the national pysche:

> Now, I question, whether, among all the instances in which a borrower and a lender of money have been brought together upon the stage, from the days of Thespis to the present, there ever was one, in which the former was not recommended to favour in some shape or other, either to admiration, or to love, or to pity, or to all three; and the other, the man of thrift, consigned to infamy.[10]

Bentham concedes that in no time or place has money lending been a popular profession. The psychology behind the resentment he puts in the simplest of terms: "The children who have eat [sic] their cake are the natural enemies of the children who have theirs."[11] Writ large, Bentham elaborates, those who have sacrificed the future to the present envy those who have sacrificed the present for the future. This envy is sublimated at the time of the loan, of course, but as the due date approaches the lender morphs in the borrower's eyes from benefactor to tyrant. "It is an oppression for a man to reclaim his own money," Bentham observes wryly. "It is none to keep it from him."[12] Were

Bentham alive today, this is precisely the kind of takeaway message he would draw from just about any home foreclosure story on the six o'clock news.

Only among Christians, and in Christian times, however, was money lending proscribed. So Bentham argues, conveniently overlooking the original proscription against usury in Deuteronomy. His anti-Christian bias showing, he wonders how it was that his forebears had labored so long under so transparently flawed an idea. Here he is at his most amusingly acerbic, if not exactly his most accurate. He observes that when Christianity broke away from Judaism, "it came to be discovered that the distance between the mother and the daughter church could not be too wide." As to money-lending in particular, "this Jewish way of getting it was too odious to be endured." As a consequence Christians left the Jews to gather money any way they could, and when Christians needed to raise revenue, the "method pretty much in vogue" was simply "to squeeze it out of them."[13]

As rough as Bentham was on his Christian ancestors, he was rougher still on Aristotle, "that celebrated heathen, who, in all matters wherein heathenism did not destroy his competence, had established a despotic empire over the Christian world." Despite all the money that passed through Aristotle's hands, "more perhaps than through the hands of any philosopher before or since,"[14] Aristotle had failed in his most essential quest:

> [He] had never been able to discover, in any one piece of money, any organs for generating any other such piece. Emboldened by so strong a body of negative proof, he ventured at last to usher into the world the result of his observations, in the form of an universal proposition, that all money is in its nature barren.[15]

In a single comic paragraph, Bentham undermines the anti-usury infrastructure of the last six centuries. No one before or since has given any classical philosopher such a public spanking and, in this case, such a well-deserved one. Bentham, however, follows his wit a bit too far afield. Where he strays—a routine error among the Enlightenment's best and brightest—is in imputing the basest of motives to those who have come before him, especially Christians. He declares, and he seems to mean it, that the acceptance of Aristotle's usury position was driven by the anti-Jewish faction among Christian philosophers. This is nonsense. In his airy dismissal of the Christian-Aristotelian fusion, the bedrock of the Enlightenment that followed, his prejudice trumps his perception.

When he turns to the details of usury law, Bentham does not trouble himself with the question of whether lending money at interest was right or wrong. In England, at least, that question had not been on the table since "a suppurating tumour"[16] dispatched teenage king Edward VI heavenward more than two centuries earlier. Usury, in fact, no longer even meant lending at interest. The contemporary meaning was much more arbitrary, namely, the attempt to charge more interest on a loan than the government had decided was either moral or proper. Bentham wasn't buying that definition either.

"There can be no such thing as usury," Bentham reasons, "for what rate of interest is there that can naturally be more proper than another."[17] He cites the wide-ranging experience of different countries and different times. Official interest rate maximums varied dramatically from era to era and place to place. There was nothing proper about any of these limits, nothing moral either. Other than a lingering prejudice against moneylenders, Bentham could see no reason why, in adjusting the relative interests of lenders and borrowers, the government always favored the borrower. Even in England, he observes, "The lender's advantage is for ever to be clipped, and pared down, as low as it will bear. First it was to be confined to ten per cent, then to eight, then to six, then to five, and now lately there was a report of its being to be brought down to four."[18]

Bentham saw the same prejudice at work in the prohibition of compound interest "as a sort of usury." He failed to see the logic of a law that protected a creditor's right to collect on a loan but that denied him any relief if the debtor failed to pay on time. "The gain, which the law in its tenderness thus bestows on the defaulter," writes Bentham, "is an encouragement, a reward, which it holds out for breach of faith, for iniquity, for indolence, for negligence."[19]

The illogic of British usury law manifested itself even more clearly in the case of the pawnbroker. Despite the fact that the pawnbroker had the borrower's collateral firmly in hand, he could legally charge interest as high as 12 percent. And his customers were those whom usury laws were designed to protect—the indigent and the simpleminded—active subsets of the genus prodigal.

Even here, Bentham could see no need to regulate. As long as a prodigal had something to pledge, even if he could find "none of those monsters called usurers to deal with him," Bentham was confident that he would not lie quiet.

Instead, he would do what he had to do to get money, occasionally activities more injurious to himself and to society than borrowing. "The tacking of leading-strings upon the backs of grown persons, in order to prevent their doing themselves a mischief," writes Bentham in unaccented libertarian, "is not necessary either to the being or tranquillity of society."[20] The best protection for prodigals and the indigent alike he saw as an open competition among lenders, bankers, and pawnbrokers that would at least keep the rates down.

Writing in 1787, another momentous year in America history, Bentham thought the official effort to stem the natural flow of money from lender to borrower as futile as King Canute's effort to stem the flow of the tides. In Russia, where he was living at the time, evasion of the law had become normative. Although the legal limit was 5 percent, the people who wanted money paid what the market demanded—in that time and place roughly 8 to 10 percent. No sooner would the lender draw up a legal contract for 5 percent than he and the borrower would cut a side deal for the 3 or 4 percent differential. Writes Bentham, "The whole system of laws on this subject is perfectly, and very happily, inefficacious."[21] In Russia, as elsewhere, money found its natural level.

The futility of regulating interest rates seemed such a given, especially from a free-market perspective, that Adam Smith's waffling struck him as borderline heretical. In his uniquely comic style, Bentham tries to account for how "so great a master" could have fallen into so obvious an error. He writes, in seeming irony, "You heard the public voice, strengthened by that of law, proclaiming all round you, that usury was a sad thing, and usurers a wicked and pernicious set of men."[22] In fact, however, this is likely what had happened: Smith had so deeply absorbed society's prejudice against usurers that he could not find it within himself to purge it.

Smith's support of rate regulation was irritating enough, but it was his distrust of "projectors" that inspired Bentham to new heights of pique. "You heard from one at least of those quarters," Bentham adds, "that projectors were either a foolish and contemptible race, or a knavish and destructive one." Bentham analyzes what it is that projectors do and why lenders should expect a higher rate of return when investing in their projects: "No new trade, no trade carried on in any new channel, can afford a security equal to that which may be afforded by a trade carried on in any of the old ones."[23]

Bentham makes a compelling case that none of Britain's great industrial breakthroughs "could have existed at first but in the shape of a project." Today's everyday convenience was yesterday's innovation, Bentham continues. These were all the result not of some rash speculation but of some "rare endowment of genius." The notion that some legislator "of the most perfect ignorance"[24] would be granted the power to pass judgment on the credit-worthiness of a project about which he knew nothing appalled Bentham, who did well to die before the 111th U.S. Congress was seated. As he saw it, if such legislators had had their way, the British would still be eating acorns and wearing animal hides. Smith's refusal to agree astonished Bentham:

> "No," I think I hear you saying, "I will not thank projectors for it, I will rather thank the laws, which by fixing the rates of interest have been exercising their vigilance in repressing the temerity of projectors, and preventing their impru- dence from making those defalcations from the sum of national prosperity which it would not have failed to make, had it been left free."[25]

Having taken Smith to the philosophical woodshed, Bentham claims that he did so as a form of tough love. The ever-cocky young scholar expresses the marvelously presumptuous hope that in his next edition the master would make the corrections that he has recommended. Smith never would. Although rumors circulated that Smith had come around to Bentham's view, there was never any proof of it. Given the sharp edge of Bentham's wit and his eager- ness to draw blood, Smith had better sense than to engage in a public spat.

No doubt, this round went to Bentham. Logic was clearly on his side. But history has been kinder to Smith. More than two hundred years later he is still being studied and taught, while Bentham has slipped into obscurity. In lesser hands, utilitarianism devolved into pretty much whatever the utilitarian-in- chief thought was the common good. Bentham's heirs include Robert Owen, who gave us the word *socialism*, and the still-extant Peter Singer, who has made "animal liberation" intellectually respectable, at least at Princeton.

The reason for Smith's intellectual endurance can be found in his first major work, *The Theory of Moral Sentiments*, published in 1759. Unlike Bentham, Smith built his economic philosophy the old-fashioned way—on a comprehensive moral and ethical foundation. Although theologically adventurous—his work was a mix of stoicism and Christianity—Smith saw morality as much more than a mere calculus of pleasure and pain. On the contrary, he stood firm for a natural law, one that had been given to mankind "for the direction of our conduct in this life."[26] As to the source of that law, he did not hedge: "Those important rules of morality are the commands and laws of the Deity, who will finally reward the obedient, and punish the transgressors of their duty."[27]

Given his grounding, Smith was much more likely than Bentham to err on the side of mercy. He also understood something fundamental about free enterprise that Bentham did not: namely, that the "self-command" essential to its success had to be rooted in a larger ethic. Michael Novak, who contributed the highly useful phrase *democratic capitalism* to our vocabulary, summarizes Smith's and his own take on this ungainly but extraordinary system: "Precisely because rational self-interest does not always result in moral outcomes, religious (and other) values are indispensable to democratic capitalism."[28] Although Smith would not live to see the day in which there were insufficient "values" to sustain the system, Novak would, and Bentham would be at least partly to blame.

ten

Tulips

THE YEAR THAT ADAM SMITH SR. MARRIED MARGARET F. DOUGLAS in Kircaldy, Scotland—1720—was quite possibly the most economically unstable in Western Europe since the Norman invasion in 1066. Both France and England were swept up in parallel mania. The French one, called the "Mississippi Bubble," had almost nothing to do with Mississippi. The English one, called the "South Sea Bubble," had even less to do with the South Seas. Both, however, were genuine bubbles. When they burst, as bubbles inevitably do, the thousands of people left holding soap and air would never forgive the dastardly projectors who launched these bubbles skyward. Young Adam must have gotten an earful.

Although much more consequential, the Mississippi and South Sea Bubbles have attracted less popular attention than a bubble-like mania that gripped the northern Netherlands nearly a century before the French and English agitation. To understand that phenomenon, it is helpful to understand the republic that created it and the financial instruments that helped create that republic. The most essential of those instruments was the bond. The market that developed for the sale of those bonds, built on the international banking infrastructure, empowered Europe's nation-states and widened the divide between commerce in the West and commerce in the rest of the world.

As with banking, the bond market traces its origins to the city-states of northern Italy. In an increasingly complex marketplace, there is a refreshing simplicity about the way bonds work. In Italy, the city-states would issue bonds to pay their debts, typically the debts attendant on waging war. In today's terms, a citizen might buy a 100,000-*lira* bond at a fixed rate, or "coupon," of 3 percent. This investment promised a payback of 3,000 *lira* per year. In Florence, the government more or less forced citizens to buy these bonds.[1] Happily for everyone, the obligatory nature of the purchase excused the citizens from the usury ban. Better still, the government—and the church—allowed them to sell the bonds to their fellow citizens if they needed liquidity, meaning cash.

If Florence had been successfully smashing its enemies and seemed to be marching toward peace and prosperity, citizens would see these bonds as good long-term investments. Bondholders would have little trouble finding buyers if they chose to sell. The ensuing excess of demand over supply would push the market price of the bond above its "par" value. The coupon, however, would remain fixed. So if an investor paid 120,000 *lira* for the bond, his annual return of 3,000 *lira* would yield 2.5 percent.

If, on the other hand, the war were going badly, and Florence's survival seemed at risk, bondholders would be inclined to sell their bonds. There would not be many takers. One selling point would be higher yield. A 100,000-*lira* par-value bond bought at 60,000 *lira* still promised a 3,000-*lira* annual return. The purchaser would have to weigh this 5 percent return against the likelihood of default. What might prompt the purchase is what we call today *asymmetrical information*. In other words, the buyer had the inside skinny on the war's outcome and invested accordingly. In an era when information could move no faster than a pigeon, the ability to transmit that information more swiftly and surely than the competitors could make a huge difference.

It should be noted that all of these financial instruments came online in a fully Catholic Europe. Likewise in 1500, all of the world's great commercial centers—Venice, Florence, Bruges, Antwerp, London—paid fealty to Rome. The Protestant Reformation—*pace* Max Weber—did not create capitalism. It only seemed that way when, after the split, the Catholic Church identified its interests with the old-world mercantilism of the Spanish Empire.

Spain and France did, in fact, mimic the Italian model to finance their wars but with less success. The problem was that an authoritarian nation had less incentive to honor its bond obligations than a competitive, commercial city-state. Throughout the sixteenth and seventeenth centuries, Spain periodically defaulted on its bonds, and this understandably scared investors away. Investors had more consistent success with Spain's principal antagonist throughout this period, the provinces of the northern Netherlands. In 1581, seven of these provinces unified to create the Republic of the Seven United Provinces.

To finance its on-again, off-again wars of liberation against Spain, the United Provinces adapted the Italian financial models and expanded on them. Among the most significant Dutch innovation was the limited-liability joint stock company. The first of these, the United Dutch Chartered East India Company (the Dutch shorthand for which was VOC), attracted more than a thousand investors upon its chartering in 1602. Government sponsorship and monopoly status gave investors confidence in the firm's eventual success, and "limited liability" assured them that they could lose no more than they had invested.

The mission of the VOC was legitimate: to consolidate Dutch trading operations in the East Indies and exploit the opportunities the islands offered.[2] Given the sizable start-up costs, initial returns were less than stellar. The VOC, in fact, paid no dividends at all until 1610, and those were paid in the form of spices. In 1609, frustrated by the VOC's failure to deliver, prominent Dutch businessman Isaac le Maire and his pals formed a secret cabal to squeeze what money could be had out of this stasis. What they did was quietly borrow shares from other shareholders for a fee, with the promise to return the shares at a future date. They then sold those shares at market value and stealthily talked down the company's future prospects, scaring others into selling their shares and driving down the share price 12 percent over the next months. Le Maire and his coconspirators then bought shares at the lower market price, returned them to the lenders, and pocketed the difference.

In essence, Le Maire and his fellow "bears" had "shorted" the market. This took the VOC shareholders by surprise, as they had no prior experience with shorting or bears. As one might suspect, the strategy, once revealed, did not particularly amuse them. In fact, they took Le Maire to court and tied him up there for the rest of his career.

By 1612, it had dawned on just about everyone that the VOC was not about to buy back anyone's shares in the near future. As with bonds in Florence, those seeking liquidity had no choice but to sell shares of their stock to other would-be investors. And so was born the world's first stock market. Among its first regulations was to ban selling short. The state, however, did not exactly outlaw futures trading. Rather, it declared all futures contracts legally unenforceable. This understanding helped incite the mania in question.

In between founding the first joint stock company and the first stock market, the resourceful Dutch introduced the world's first modern central bank, the Amsterdam Exchange Bank, or *Wisselbank*.[3] The United Provinces, like other small European countries, lacked the muscle and the square mileage to establish and enforce a dominant currency. As a result, the currencies of no fewer than fourteen other countries circulated throughout the new republic. The Dutch cleared up the confusion by creating a central clearinghouse to store their depositors' money, in whatever currency, and standardize exchange rates. A buyer with his money on deposit could purchase an item from a seller simply by having his account debited at the *Wisselbank* and the seller's credited the same amount.

Unlike most central banks that would follow, the *Wisselbank* kept enough metallic reserve, or specie, on hand to honor its depositors' demands, should they all have chosen to liquidate at once. This prevented any potential runs on the bank and helped make the bonds of the United Provinces the most secure in Europe throughout the seventeenth and eighteenth centuries. Soft-money advocates might complain that such "full reserve" banking did not allow for credit creation, now seen as the defining characteristic of a bank. Hard-money advocates might respond that it created credit enough that this tiny republic would dominate world commerce for two hundred years after the bank's founding. Along the way, the Dutch pioneered the various credit instruments—futures, options, selling short, and the like—that helped make the Amsterdam market the center of the financial world.

The dynamics of the Dutch system encouraged the kind of active citizen participation in markets seen nowhere before. By the early 1600s, the Netherlands had become a nation of day traders. One reason for this development, usually overlooked by economists, is a cultural one, namely, that the majority of the republic's churchgoers embraced Calvinism, the first major Christian movement to accept usury as normative. Soon enough, the Calvinist Dutch Reformed Church would attain privileged status, meaning that to be a public official one first had to be a communicant in the church; not necessarily a pious one, but a communicant nonetheless.[4]

In cities like Amsterdam and Haarlem, the everyday seductions of urban life—Amsterdam's famed red-light district, *De Wallen*, dates back to the fourteenth century—worked to keep piety to a minimum. Urban moral fiber was further frayed by an outbreak of bubonic plague that ripped through the United Provinces in 1634, wiping out some 15 percent of the populous before subsiding three years later. A giddy fatalism set in behind the plague, and the survivors seemed eager to embrace the here and now, especially at the clusters of taverns, called colleges, where the traders met to make their deals. "In the midst of all this misery," a Dutch historian would later write, "people were caught by a special fever, by a particular anxiety to get rich in a very short period of time."

If international trade exposed the citizens to deadly new viruses, it also exposed them to more benign life forms, none more amiable than the tulip. Fifty years earlier the average Dutch citizen could not have told a tulip from a tomato, both sixteenth-century imports—the tulip from Turkey and the tomato from South America.[5] Blame what happens next on the French. In the 1630s or thereabouts, French women, fashion-mad even then, had begun to adorn the tops of their gowns with fresh flowers. Their wealthier beaus competed to woo the eligible among them with the most exotic plants on the market, tulips here having an aesthetic edge over tomatoes.

True to form, once a modest demand began to develop, the Dutch managed to commoditize tulip sales.[6] Common bulbs were sold in standard units of a pound. Contracts for "pound" goods did not distinguish among individual bulbs any more than a wheat contract distinguished among shafts of wheat. Since the bulbs could be safely delivered only in a three-month period beginning in June—after the bulbs' brief photo-op flowering in April or May—a purchase after September and before the following June was by necessity a futures contract. By 1636, the peak year of the plague, an informal tulip futures market had grown up in the Amsterdam colleges.

The futures market in tulip bulbs functioned much the way futures markets function today. The buyer of the bulbs and the seller agreed to a contract, one that bound them to exchange bulbs for money on a specified settlement date at a settlement price—the official price bulbs were selling for at the end of the day on the settlement date. The difference between this spontaneous futures market and contemporary ones is the absence of controls. Sales were between individuals. The individuals did not require margin deposits to assure compliance. Nor were the contracts continuously "marked to market" as they are today—that is, repriced daily to capture day-to-day fluctuations. And deep down, the traders knew that if things really went awry, the courts would not enforce the contracts. The rules, in fact, were few and rough-hewn. As economist Peter Garber observes, "Typically the buyer did not currently possess the cash to be delivered on the settlement date, and the seller did not currently possess the bulb."[7]

What happened next is long on myth and short on documentation. The price spike began with a particularly beautiful and rare form of mutated tulip and spread to common tulips soon thereafter.[8] That there were no actual tulips to be bought or sold only seemed to feed the mania. This all took place before there were any sporting events to bet on in the otherwise dreary, plague-ridden winter months of 1636–1637. Prices mounted steadily from November through February, flattened for a moment, and then suddenly, inexplicably, plunged. Think roller coaster. The tulip mania was over before anyone could figure out how it began.

On February 24, 1637, florists meeting in Amsterdam proposed that would-be buyers who entered contracts after November 30, 1636, be allowed to opt out on payment of 10 percent of the sale price to the seller. By April, provincial and city governments were stepping in, enabling buyers to get out of contracts by paying some small fraction of the contract price. This would not be the last time overly protective governments bailed out imprudent investors.

Curiously, the tale of Dutch tulip mania slipped into history's fog for the next two centuries, until the 1841 publication of a book by British journalist Charles Mackay, *Extraordinary Popular Delusions and the Madness of Crowds*. Mackay's account of ruined tulip investors and severe nationwide shock found a receptive audience among those who did not much like capitalism and/or the Dutch, a pool large enough to assure the book best-seller status.[9]

Mackay was not the first author to let the facts stand in the way of a good story. His retelling simply does not track with contemporary Dutch accounts or with transaction records. Tales of woe are conspicuously absent from period literature, and the tulip business rebounded nicely. The tulip unblushingly emerged not as a symbol of folly but as the nation's iconic flower. As Garber observes, the players had no equity, less sense, and an abiding belief that the state would rescue them from their folly, which it did. "This was no more than a meaningless winter drinking game," says Garber, "played by a plague-ridden population that made use of the vibrant tulip market."[10]

What kept the tulip mania at the game level was the absence of an expansive monetary policy by the state. The various local governments may have bailed the players out, but they did not put their money in the game. The same can definitely *not* be said of the governments in early eighteenth-century France and England. Their participation assured that the ensuing bubbles would be huge and their fallout toxic.

eleven

Bubbles

THE LONDON OF THE EIGHTEENTH CENTURY WOULD HAVE CHALLENGED even Dante's imagination. The visitor did not have to go far to find a lively cockfight. Bearbaiting and bullbaiting spectacles were as casually attended—and bet on—as NFL and NBA games are today. For the adventurous, there were more imaginative contests involving donkeys, monkeys, and dogs (don't ask). The stock-jobbers and projectors in 'change alley felt right at home in this kind of environment. For those weary of betting on bears, bulls, and monkeys there was always a new project to invest in, like a perpetual-motion machine or a new gizmo to extract lead from silver.[1]

As in Amsterdam a century earlier, speculators did not hesitate to hawk goods they did not yet possess. The trick was "to sell the bearskin before catching the bear." Those who sold short were thus known as "bearskin jobbers," which very likely gave us "bears" and "bear markets." In the baiting contests, the opposite of bears, who fought cagily, were the bulls, who just plowed right ahead. Staged animal fights have long since been banned—ask Michael Vick—but the language endures.

Although born into an aboveboard Scottish banking family, John Law found his true calling in London's seamy underground. One contemporary described him "as nicely expert in all manners of debaucheries."[2] In April 1694, this twenty-three-year-old gambler and ladies' man extraordinaire strode angrily out of a Bloomsbury tavern, followed by one Edward Wilson. Having had serious words about a woman they both professed to love, the pair had decided, in classic barroom fashion, to take it outside. There, in Bloomsbury Square, the two drew their swords. The fight did not last but a minute. Law lunged forward and, so said the court brief, "inflicted one mortal wound of the breadth of two inches and depth of five inches, of which said wound the said Edward Wilson then and here instantly died."[3]

Law was arrested in a day and within two weeks was prosecuted and sentenced. As he rotted in the Newgate jail, just days away from his own public hanging, even Law, ever the optimist, could not have foreseen a future in which he would one day almost single-handedly transform France's economic system into the most powerful in the world and would himself stand astride that system—at least for a moment—as its Bernanke, its Geithner, its Buffet, all in one.

First, Law had to escape from Newgate, and this he did with a little bit of help from his friends. They spirited him out of England and into Amsterdam, a congenial climate for an unrepentant rake like the young Law. There he took up gambling once again, but not at all recklessly. A mathematics prodigy, he studied the odds and played accordingly. Within a few years, he had a small fortune. By the time he made his way to France, twenty years after the Bloomsbury incident, he had amassed a serious fortune.

During his years in exile, Law found his ambition as well and studied the Amsterdam bank and its markets with the same zeal and skill as he did dice odds.[4] Ten years after his escape, he penned his thoughts on the benefits of a credit-based economy in a forty-thousand-word treatise that established his reputation as a first-rate theorist. In 1705, he used the treatise as leverage to grease his return to Scotland, where he hoped to implement the system of his design. At the time, however, Scotland was negotiating a union with England, which was not yet ready to write off the murder of Wilson as a youthful indiscretion.

After another ten years of exile and rejection, Law finally found a country willing to experiment with his capital-S system. France had little left to lose. Knee-deep in debt, its economy slogged forward with little hope of extrication. Law charmed the Duke of Orleans—who was running the country until child king Louis XV came of age—into letting him launch a national bank, the *Banque Generale*. Even better for Law, the duke obliged his request to issue paper money, the first in French history.[5] At this time, Law merely proposed to add fluidity to the system. The bank notes could be exchanged for coin at any time. To improve confidence in the new paper currency, the duke declared counterfeiting a capital—from the Latin *caput*, meaning "head"—offense. He also instructed his tax collectors to send their money to Law in paper. Law was in business.

This was all well and good to a point, but Law, ever the adventurer, wanted more. His goal was to create wealth, not just move it around more easily. Inspired by the Dutch experience, he decided to merge his bank with a nearly bankrupt overseas trading company, the French Mississippi Company, which had a mission comparable to the Dutch East India Company's. What it did not have was a chance of pulling a dime's worth of profit out of pestilential swamps of Louisiana, even if its principal city had been named after Law's patron, the Duke of Orleans.

Still, the Louisiana territory was so vast and so far away that a high-powered salesman like Law could imbue the new *Compagnie D'Occident* with the smell of potential riches. Having a government-issued monopoly status helped in the credibility department. No one could doubt Law's pull. If this were not enough, and initially it wasn't, Law promised investors that they could return bonds at par value in six months if they chose to redeem them.[6] This was an incredible bargain, given that eighteen months after launch, bonds were selling at only half of par. The French had never dealt in futures before, and they found the concept irresistible. Everyone wanted in.

To raise even more capital, the French government allowed Law to issue fifty thousand more shares in this international venture at an affordable par value of only 500 *livres*. To make the shares more attractive, Law introduced a new wrinkle that would haunt markets for the next three centuries: investors could buy "on margin."[7] In other words, they only had to put 75 of the 500 *livres*' par value down. The rest they could borrow, not from a bank or a brokerage house, but from the company itself—and on E-Z terms, twelve monthly installments, adding up to a total of 550 *livres*. No one complained about the 10 percent nut. Two centuries earlier Martin Luther had thought that the worst a nation's princes could do in the face of a usurious epidemic was to "sit there and snore with mouths hanging open," but the French princes did the Germans one better. They weren't snoring; they were investing. The preteen king was a major shareholder in Law's operation.

The year 1719 was a big one for Law. In January, the duke absorbed the *Banque Generale* and renamed it the *Banque Royale* with Law at the helm and its notes guaranteed by the Crown. In May, Law acquired the East India Company and the China Company and reorganized the whole overseas megillah as the *Compagnie des Indes* with a monopoly on all French trade outside Europe. In July, the *Compagnie* purchased from the Crown the right to mint its coins. By October, the *Compagnie* had assumed the power to collect all taxes.[8]

With the money from the shares pouring in, Law made an unprecedented and utterly implausible move that same year: he decided to buy all of France's debt, making him, in effect, the nation's only creditor. To sweeten the deal for the Crown he lowered the interest rate from 4 percent to 3. On the upside, payments on the debt provided Law's company a steady cash flow. On the down side, it was close to the only cash flow the company had.

Investors were happily oblivious to where Law's money was coming from. By the beginning of 1720, Law had issued more than 600,000 *Compagnie D'Occident* shares, worth 300 million *livres* at their par value. Only now, shares were selling for more than thirty times par and rising.[9] To describe the wealth of these charmed shareholders, a new word entered the world's vocabulary: *millionaire*. Unbeknownst to the millionaires, however, the company's revenues from overseas, including those from its dabbling in slavery and tobacco, could not begin to justify the share prices.

On January 5, 1720, Law was named Controller-General of Finances, with a power equivalent to prime minister.[10] He was already collecting the nation's taxes, minting its coins, printing its paper money, managing its central bank, directing all of its overseas trade, and overseeing the affairs of Louisiana, a territory half the size of the present-day United States. These were heady accomplishments for any man, let alone an illegal immigrant on the lam for murder.

Across the English Channel, the British looked on anxiously as their most feared rival boomed, or at least seemed to. The *Weekly Journal's* Paris correspondent shared Law's accomplishments with his no-doubt envious audience back in England: "By his wise management, in a very short time, the national debts have been paid, taxes removed, art encouraged, commerce improved, and credit restored: in one word, the nation rescued from ruin."[11] The British would not sit by idly and watch France surpass them. They would launch a bubble of their own.

On April 14, 1720, in London, John Blunt, a chubby shoemaker's son from Rochester, England, offered two million pounds' worth of new stock in his South Seas Company at the market price of three hundred pounds. Following Law's example, he, too, offered easy financing, 20 percent down and the rest payable in bimonthly installments.[12]

The South Seas Company had been formed a decade earlier with an avowed intention of opening South America to British trade. The fact that the Spanish and the Portuguese had carved this territory up between them two centuries earlier did not discourage the company's projectors. Ignorance helped. The less Blunt knew about the actual state of South American trade, the better he could sell it. Among the early investors to this company were Isaac Newton, Jonathan Swift, and King George I.

In its first decade as a trading company, the South Seas Company managed to do little more than ship a few slaves from Africa to South America and see its profits eaten up by Spanish taxes. By 1715, Blunt had managed to persuade the Prince of Wales to name him governor of the company. He quietly reoriented its mission toward his own strengths, namely, bribery and market manipulation. Like Law, he saw opportunity where others only saw problems: specifically in England's crushing debt. Daniel Defoe, the author of *Robinson Crusoe* and the company's chief pamphleteer, laid the blame for the debt on twenty years of bloody war. "Now we see our treasures lost," he wrote, "our funds exhausted, all our public revenues sold, mortgaged and anticipated, the whole kingdom sold to usury."[13] It would not be until the late twentieth century that "entitlements" supplanted war as the great debt generator.

By 1720 that debt had reached the then-astonishing sum of thirty-one million pounds. Blunt's plan was to raise money, as Law had done, to purchase that debt. Among the targeted shareholders were the government's creditors. They would exchange their annuities for shares in the South Sea Company at a higher market rate. To make the plan attractive to the government, he would reduce its creditors to one, his company, and its interest rate from 5 percent to 4. To make the plan attractive to the people who ran the government, the peers and MPs, he would sell them "notional" stock—no money down and criminally easy terms—that they could cash in if the share price rose.

Even with Parliament in his pocket, Blunt had to outbid the wary Bank of England for the contract, among the dumber auctions in the history of finance. This challenge was made all the more difficult because Blunt had no money. He could raise it only by selling the shares prepurchase and using the equity to buy the debt. As a contemporary historian wrote, "'Twas his avowed maxim, a thousand times repeated, that the advancing by all means of the price of the stock, was the only way to promote the good of the company."[14] Blunt had one other advantage over the bank. He had no legal or political limits on his ability to offer shares. He could sell as many as he chose or give them away. Indeed, he showered the Houses of Lords and Commons with shares. His enemies in the House of Lords warned against "the pernicious practice of stock-jobbing which produced irreparable mischief in diverting the genius of the people from trade and industry"[15] but to no avail. Blunt prevailed, and the deal was sealed.

As with the *Compagnie D'Occident*, the South Sea Company could prosper only as long as there were more people willing to buy more shares. To expand the pool, Blunt offered the eighteenth-century equivalent of subprime loans: 10 percent down and the rest in 10 percent installments spread over four years. Now, everyone wanted in. "I have enquired of some that have come from London, what is the religion there?" Jonathan Swift wrote from abroad. "They tell me it is South Sea stock."[16]

In France, meanwhile, Law had come across a problem he did not antici-pate. Surprised at the size of their profits, the newly minted millionaires were cashing out and buying precious metals. They failed to consider, rued Law, that "the stocks actually surpassed in value all the gold and silver which will ever be in the Kingdom."[17] To protect his fragile system, Law waxed tyrannical. He outlawed the wearing of diamonds without permission, the making or sell-ing of gold objects, and the storing of gold or silver beyond a bare minimum. To enforce the law, he recruited informers and authorized the *gendarmes* to search people's homes for booty beyond the government limit. Enlightenment wit Voltaire, then just in his twenties, called this crackdown "the most unjust edict ever rendered" and the "final limit of a tyrannical absurdity."[18] It did not exactly instill confidence in the investor class. Nor would it when FDR did much the same, some two hundred years later.

When the share prices began to falter, Law offered to buy the shares back at a price fixed above market, a promise he could not begin to honor if people took the offer seriously. They did, and he couldn't, but then again he did control the printing presses. He ordered nine of them to start rolling overtime to print the billions in *livres* necessary to meet the shareholder demand for cash.[19] This whole system was spinning madly out of control, and there was nothing sane that Law could do to stop it.

As night follows day, hyperinflation followed the infusion of excessive paper money. And as day follows night, bad behavior followed hard on heels of hyperinflation. Nothing seemed grounded anymore. So why not gamble, why not carouse? Why not sell your body if you have already sold your soul? And if you have run out of money of your own, why not take it from others? The French had never seen such highway robbery, and not just figuratively. Almost on a daily basis, the robbers' victims were being fished from the Seine.[20]

The violence, in turn, led to a rise in vigilantism and public justice. The Count of Horn, a distant, dilettantish young cousin of the Duke of Orleans, got to see justice up close. Having squandered his fortune on the stock market, he and two buddies robbed and murdered a broker. The young count got caught.

The wheels of justice turned swiftly in those days—and in this case, literally. In a week of eleven murders, the court decided to set an example. No hanging for the count, no beheading—he would be broken on the wheel. "Do you suffer much on the wheel?" asked the naïve young count. The answer to that question was a resoundingly painful yes. The count was stripped, stretched out on a huge barrel, and rolled to death slowly, all before a large and appreciative crowd. For entertainment, this beat bearbaiting any day. "I have often wished that these banknotes were consigned to hell-fire," a contemporary wrote. "It is impossible to describe all the evil that has resulted from them."[21] One wonders if Aristotle and Aquinas and Luther saw this kind of spectacle at the end of usury's road.

Following the count's grisly execution, Law began to crack down on speculation and its attendant sins. It was, of course, way too late. It was too late for any remedy. Before 1720 had come to an end, the duke and his council had pulled Law's notes from circulation, returned the country to gold and silver, and sent Law whence he came—into exile. As if in punishment for the nation's year of living prodigally, France was struck hard by a plague that had come from the Middle East. In January 1721, the bug shipped out aboard a convoy bound for New Orleans. Of the one thousand would-be colonists, two hundred survived. On both sides of the Atlantic, the French made the connection: at the end of the day, God trumps mammon.

Some good portion of fleeing French money found its way to England as Law's bubble was imploding, but there is never enough money in the universe to keep a bubble afloat for long. Blunt overreached much as Law had done and only a month or two behind him. He had his friends in government ban rival joint-stock companies. The move had the opposite effect from what was intended. It projected weakness, not strength. It shook public confidence, and that was all it took to puncture the illusion.

Jonathan Swift worked out his anxiety in his classic *Gulliver's Travels*, which he started writing as the bubble was bursting.[22] In the book, Gulliver is on the way to the South Seas when he is overtaken by a violent storm that leaves him stranded, exhausted, and numb from shock. No doubt but that the British investing class could identify. "There never was such distraction and undoing in any country," one contemporary wrote. "Not a penny stirring."[23]

Given the unchanging nature of the human condition, the shareholders blamed the directors of the South Sea Company—not, of course, their own cupidity—and turned to the government for relief, never mind that the government had been in the tank from the get-go. Although the majority of Parliament members had owned shares in 1720 (many of these outright bribes), that did not stop this august body from looking for a scapegoat—but, of course, never too hard. As to Blunt, he, too, was kicked out of town, his head, luckily, still on his shoulders. If this weren't bad enough, the plague struck England too. An editorial in the newspaper *Post Boy* may have gotten it right:

> The public calamities, which men naturally look upon as proceeding wholly from natural causes, ought to be considered by those who hold the faith as decrees of the providence of a just and merciful God . . . licentiousness and corruption, the fatal fruits of irreligion, reign everywhere; men give themselves up to insatiable avarice; usury and fraud are openly practiced; there is no longer any curb strong enough to restrain covetousness.[24]

As easy it is to blame Law or Blunt, they merely directed the mania along a given path. As economic historian Thomas Woods observes, "Only expansionary monetary policy can account for these phenomena."[25] And only the government can expand the supply of money. Once that supply is liberated, the resulting inflationary pressure deforms not only the economy of a society but also the psychology. Swift chose his words carefully. In the fervor they inspired, these manias mimicked the superficial trappings of a religion. In both England and France, given that fervor, it made a certain amount of sense to participate at least cautiously in a government-endorsed scheme seemingly modeled on the successful Dutch East India Company. As has been shown in these last few years, government-endorsed schemes still have the power to enthuse the ungrounded.

twelve

The Family Business

ANY NUMBER OF FAMILIES HAD A STAKE IN THE OUTCOME OF EVENTS ON the lush, green fields of Belgium that June day in 1815, the eighteenth. Nearly seventy thousand families from England, Prussia, and the Netherlands had sent their sons to fight under the various banners of the Seventh Coalition. An equal number or more sent their sons off to fight under the revived standard of the French Empire. But no family was paying closer attention to the battle that was about to be waged than a little-known clan that hailed from Germany. Although the paterfamilias, Mayer, had died three years earlier, his five grown sons had made this battle possible. If Napoleon kept his French army in the field the old-fashioned way—by plunder—Wellington kept his allied troops fed and armed the modern way, through debt. Debt prevailed. The Battle of Waterloo would make the reputation of the brothers who arranged it, and their astonishing work would forever change the way wars were financed and fought.[1]

Mayer Amschel Rothschild was born in 1744 in the city that Martin Luther hated above all others, Frankfurt. "Frankfurt is the golden and silver hole through which everything that springs and grows, is minted or coined here, flows out of Germany," he had written two centuries earlier. "If that hole were stopped up we should not now have to listen to the complaint that there are debts everywhere and no money; that all lands and cities are burdened with taxes and ruined with interest payments."[2] If anything, Luther would have had more to grouse about in the eighteenth century.

Mayer was not too keen on Frankfurt either. Although born just four years before Jeremy Bentham, Mayer came of age in a largely Lutheran city that seemed centuries removed from Bentham's London. Among the city's more memorable public displays was a mural called the *Judensau*, "the Jew's sow." The mural depicted a group of Jews subjecting a pig to various acts lewd even by today's standards. Above that unlovely image was one of a dead baby, his body punctured by countless knife wounds. Its caption told how "in the year 1475" Jews allegedly killed two-year-old Simon of Trent in a ritual murder,[3] except, of course, it did not use the word *allegedly*. Welcome to Frankfurt! The city's most celebrated native son and a contemporary of Mayer's, the writer Johann Wolfgang von Goethe, thought it entirely telling that the murals "were not the product of private hostility, but erected as a public monument."[4]

Mayer Rothschild inhabited a world of unpleasant surprises. He and his sons would tread as lightly through it as Shylock did through his. Even after the family had accumulated more than forty stately homes throughout Europe and wealth beyond counting, the Rothschilds trod lightly. "They begrudge us Jews the eyes in our heads," Mayer's son Amschel would write well after the family had grown rich, "[and want] to drink our blood."[5] The derangement in their native Germany two centuries after Mayer's birth would prove even the most anxious among them something other than paranoid.

Stacked deck or not, the Rothschilds played a damned shrewd hand. The governing classes of the surrounding region—princes, archdukes, electors—served the Rothschilds the way savings and loan execs would the Salomon Brothers two centuries hence. They were the market's fools, the ones whose ignorance and prodigality made wiser men rich. The fact that the region's affluent often spent more than they made served up opportunities for those who made more than they spent. The fact that they did much of their business in Frankfurt opened doors for the Rothschilds.

By this time, even in Luther's Germany, usury was no longer an issue. German bankers routinely lent at interest, and almost no one felt the need to repent.[6] For all of Germany's progress, however, Jews retained a widespread reputation for being more astute at the business of money changing and money lending than their Christian peers. This reputation cut both ways.

Writing well after the Rothschilds had come to dominate European finance, Max Weber could describe the "politically and speculatively oriented" Jewish approach to business as "pariah capitalism" and compare it unfavorably to the hearty "Protestant ethic" of his fellow Germans.

For sure, Mayer Rothschild knew his way around money. He had lifted his family from its pious and humble roots by acquiring an expertise in rare coins and medals. The people who collected what Mayer dealt were inevitably well heeled and occasionally deeply in debt. Mayer expanded his business to meet their needs. The neediest of this clientele was Crown Prince Wilhelm of Hesse, later Wilhelm IX, for whom Mayer served as court Jew in all but official title. Wilhelm's leading exports, as American schoolchildren once knew, were those dread Hessian soldiers. By arranging financing for Wilhelm, Mayer helped put the soldiers in the field. As the eighteenth century neared its end, his service to Wilhelm and fellow travelers helped make Mayer one of the wealthiest Jews in Frankfurt, a status his sons would quickly render trivial.

For all his good fortune, Mayer had no greater bounty than these five sons. His dutiful wife Gutle bore him a child very nearly every year from 1771 to 1992. Of the nineteen or so children they brought into the world, ten lived to adulthood, a depressingly typical survival rate in the eighteenth century. Of the ten, five were boys—Amschel, Salomon, Nathan, Carl, and James. In the relentlessly male-oriented Rothschild household, those five sons would learn the rules from the old man—and repeat them among themselves—until they became gospel. No rule was more important or more nearly prophetic than the one Mayer shared with Amschel on his deathbed: "Keep your brothers together, and you will become the richest people in Germany."[7] In honoring this request, the boys would surpass even Mayer's grandiose ambitions.

While still healthy, Mayer was not above hectoring the lads, especially Nathan, the borderline black sheep who would one day become the most powerful of all Rothschilds, his father included. "To begin with, all our correspondents complain about you, Dear Nathan," he wrote to his third son, recently decamped to England, "and say that you are so disorganized when sending consignments." This he followed with a more universal axiom: "They say that without good order a millionaire can go broke the more business he does, because the whole world is not, or not very, honest."[8]

On another occasion, Mayer chided Nathan for absorbing too many unproductive loans and not disclosing them. "If you have many bad debts, which God forbid, and enter them as if they are good, that is simply to pretend that you are rich."[9] Had Wall Street heeded this advice in the twenty-first century, there would have been no subprime crisis.

Some of the advice Mayer gave, however, mined the darker shafts of the Jewish consciousness. These words of wisdom were singular in their focus: "Our late father taught us," Salomon reminded Nathan, "that if a high-placed person enters into a partnership with a Jew, he belongs to the Jew."[10] Harsher still was Mayer's oft-repeated survival dictum, "If you can't make yourself loved, make yourself feared."[11] The Rothschilds did just that, but before they could hope to intimidate Europe, they first had to win the Battle of Waterloo.

By the time Napoleon broke out of exile on St. Helena for his final surge, the brothers Rothschild had positioned themselves all across Europe. Amschel had taken over the Frankfurt Bank. Salomon had launched his operation in Vienna. Nathan had moved to London. Carl set up shop in Naples, and James had made Paris home. Nathan had proved the cleverest of them all. Historians still puzzle over how this obscure merchant banker, not yet forty, who had only recently been a minor textile exporter, came to be the man who rescued Europe from Napoleon. "My brother in London is the commanding general," Salomon would write at the time, "I am his field marshal."[12]

The Duke of Wellington needed help. Although Britain had the soundest and most transparent finances in the world, the seemingly endless wars against a foe who could throw his whole people's army into battle had drained its treasury. In February 1813, Wellington was reporting that he could "scarcely stir out of my house on account of the public creditors waiting to demand payment of what is due to them."[13] Appointed official financier in 1814, Nathan had much to offer besides good connections and industrial strength *chutzpah*. A recovering smuggler, he and his brothers knew how to gather specie from all over the continent and get it to Wellington in spendable form. The brothers' trust in each other and their ability to communicate quickly and securely among themselves made all the difference. More so than the Medici or any family that preceded them, the Rothschilds *frères* formed the first real multinational corporation.

In regard to the battle's outcome, at least as it affected the Rothschilds, a sea of myth surrounds an almost imperceptible outcropping of truth. The story was widely believed, and may still be, that Nathan quit the battlefield as soon as victory was assured, braved the stormy English channel in his frantic trip home, and commenced to buy stocks on a depressed English market, knowing that the good news to come would elevate their price. He is alleged to have pocketed as much as 135 million pounds by his cunning.

The real story has none of the drama or the profits. In fact, the Rothschilds felt about Wellington's quick and decisive victory much the way Halliburton must have after Schwartzkopf's unexpectedly quick and decisive victory in the Gulf War. The months, maybe years, of steady work to come had been shortened to days. Even worse for the Rothschilds, they had bought up all that specie when it was scarce and the prices high. Unloading it postwar would be difficult and expensive. Offsetting the losses were Nathan's very real purchases in the London bond market at war's end, but the profits from these deals were nowhere near those of myth.[14] The tensions during this period tested the brothers' legendary synergy.

If their finances suffered at Waterloo, the brothers' reputation did not. The battle had transformed them from an obscure clan of ghetto Jews to the Bonapartes of the banking world, Nathan in particular. The payoff came three years after Waterloo, when one of the still-broke allies, namely, Prussia, turned to the newly famous Rothschilds to dig them out of their hole. It was not the size of the subsequent bond offering that made history but the conditions. Nathan had the nerve to demand of the Prussian government "some security beyond the mere good faith of government."[15]

Mere good faith? How those words from an upstart Jew must have rankled in Berlin, and Nathan was just warming up. He insisted that any loan be secured by a mortgage on Prussian royal domains, that the loan originate in London, that bonds be issued not just in London but also in Frankfurt, Berlin, Amsterdam, Hamburg, and Vienna—and all in sterling. These demands were as revolutionary as they were insulting, but the impoverished Prussians had little choice. As Mayer used to remind the lads, "It is better to deal with a government in difficulty than one that has luck on its side."[16]

Yes, Virginia, conspiracy theories predated the Internet, and in the nineteenth century no people attracted more conspiracy chatter than the Rothschilds. They were Jewish by origin, international by design, and richer than Croesus, three triggers then and now. They were the Bilderbergs, the CFR, the Jekyll Island crowd, the neocons, all in one family. That they married largely among themselves—cousins, nothing too kinky here—and entrusted only male heirs with positions of power heightened the intrigue surrounding them. "The Rothschilds are the wonders of modern banking," an American observer wrote in 1835. "We see the descendants of Judah, after a persecution of two thousand years, peering above kings, rising higher than emperors, and holding a whole continent in the hollow of their hands. The Rothschilds govern a Christian world."[17]

Writing his fiction four years after Waterloo, Sir Walter Scott projected the Rothschilds six centuries back into history. "These Gentiles, cruel and oppressive as they are, are in some sort dependent on the dispersed children of Zion," explains *Ivanhoe*'s fair Rebecca to her money-lending father. "Without the aid of our wealth they could neither furnish forth their hosts in war nor their triumphs in peace; and the gold which we lend them returns with increase to our coffers."[18]

Given their pivotal role at Waterloo, some sizable cohort of otherwise smart people would accuse the Rothschilds of inciting every military adventure up to and including Pearl Harbor. What the conspiracy-minded overlooked, however, was the Rothschilds' business model. Waterloo had changed it. They were no longer traders but fund managers, tending to a large and growing portfolio of government bonds. They did not need war. They did not want it. War puts bondholders in jeopardy. If the originator of the bond ended up in the shape, say, of Italy or Germany circa 1945, a whole lot of people were going to be left with a whole lot of useless paper. By mid-century, the Rothschilds had become peacemongers, and this the Confederate States of America would learn the hard way.

At the American Civil War's commencement, the Confederates had good reason to believe that the Rothschilds would put their financial muscle behind the Southern cause. August Belmont, the Rothschilds' man in New York, served as the Democratic Party's national chairman. He had strenuously opposed Abraham Lincoln's candidacy in 1860 and his "fatal policy of confiscation and forcible emancipation."[19] So outspoken was Belmont that Union sympathizers naturally assumed that the Rothschilds would back the South. Not surprisingly given the time and place, some were less than PC in their response. "Belmont, the Rothschilds and the whole tribe of Jews . . . have been buying up confederate bonds," warned the *Chicago Tribune*.[20] Others envisioned their enemy as an unholy trinity of "Jews, Jeff Davis, and the devil."[21] The fact that the South had tasked its Jewish secretary of state, Judah Benjamin, with recruiting Britain to the cause did little for interfaith harmony north of the Mason-Dixon Line.

If politics makes strange bedfellows, war makes stranger ones. When the Rothschilds first staked out a position in American finance in the 1830s, a surprisingly tenuous position at that, Southern pols did not exactly set up the folding chairs and pass out the lemonade. The governor of Mississippi was quick to denounce Nathan, the "Baron Rothschild," with all the cultural clichés at his disposal. Said the governor, "The blood of Judas and Shylock flows in his veins . . . and unites the qualities of both his countrymen."[22]

The Rothschilds proved coy in this unlikely courtship. Whether they had qualms about slavery is unknown, but they most certainly had qualms about underwriting a nation unlikely to meet its debt obligations. The South had money problems from Fort Sumter on. Although its citizens responded eagerly to the Confederacy's first two bond offerings, foreign investors balked. Without an international assist, there were very real limits to the South's ability to finance itself. The semifeudal nature of southern society did not do wonders for regional liquidity.

To compensate, the Confederates collaborated with a French merchant banking house on a scheme that was almost very clever. The firm floated a bond on the South's behalf that was redeemable not in specie—there was precious little of that—but in cotton, which was abundant. The terms were generous. The bonds had a 7 percent coupon and a maturity of twenty years.[23] Better still, or so it seemed, the purchaser could redeem the bond in cotton at the prewar price of six pence a pound. The British textile industry depended on southern cotton. By withholding supply, the South could drive up the price of cotton and make the cotton-backed bonds attractive to investors.

This was all going swimmingly until the Union seized the port of New Orleans just one year into the war. Now, to cash in the bonds for the cotton collateral, a British merchant would have to run a formidable Union blockade. The only thing heading south at this point was the value of the bonds. With foreign capital drying up, the Confederates decided to print their way into liquidity. Before the war was through, they would distribute 1.7 billion increasingly worthless Confederate dollars. Although the Union was also printing money generously, the South was setting a standard of fiscal promiscuity that would not see its equal until Weimar, Germany. As inevitably happens in these circumstances, inflation shot through the roof. A loaf of bread that cost ten cents at war's beginning would have cost *four hundred* Confederate dollars at war's end. People were going hungry.

The Rothschilds "would help decide the outcome of the American Civil War," writes the clan's definitive historian, Niall Ferguson, "by choosing to sit on the sidelines."[24] That choice proved prescient. Those loyal enough or reckless enough to invest in Confederate bonds paid for their loyalty and/or their imprudence with their life savings. The North refused to honor the South's debts. And its banks were not about to redeem the "greybacks" with anything, even cotton. As the Rothschilds well understood, and would come to experience firsthand, a lost cause inevitably results in lost fortunes.

thirteen

The Socialism of Fools

HEINRICH HEINE WAS BORN JEWISH IN DUSSELDORF FIVE YEARS AFTER the birth of James, the youngest of Mayer Rothschild's five surviving sons. In 1811, James, not yet twenty, moved to Paris to stake out a position there. Six years later, he opened a merchant banking house, de Rothschild Frères, and soon enough, predictably enough, alchemized himself from teenage dross into the most powerful banker in France.

Heine, too, found his way to Paris. For a German Jew in the nineteenth century, his was, if anything, the road more traveled by, the revolutionary road. He dabbled in banking under the watchful eye of Uncle Salomon in Hamburg and then dallied a while studying law in Bonn and Berlin, but the City of Light beckoned. Along the way, Heine underwent a total cultural makeover. He took to writing poetry, shucked his Judaism, changed his name from Hayyim to Heinrich, got himself baptized a Lutheran, and started flirting with socialism.[1]

Fueling his animus toward the capitalist enterprise was its identification with Judaism, a faith he had come to loathe as much as he loathed his old unhip self. The Gentile French Left had been pushing this identification for a generation before Heine arrived. In an 1808 treatise, Francois Fourier described commerce as "the source of all evil" and Jews as "the incarnation of commerce."[2] Pierre-Joseph Proudhon, the world's first self-labeled anarchist, a man who bequeathed the world the axiom "Property is theft," accused the Jews of transforming the European bourgeoisie into a likeness of themselves, "obstinate, infernal . . . the enemy of mankind."[3] A Fourier disciple, Alphonse Toussenel, wrote the first book-length exposé of Jews as usurious conspirators against humanity.

A lyric poet of growing reputation, Heine discovered that his cultural self-hatred played well in Paris's aptly named Left Bank, and he was not shy about expressing it. In 1822, he described the three great evils plaguing the world as "poverty, pain, and Jewishness."[4] As he saw it, the incarnation of the Jewish malady was the Rothschild family. Being close at hand, James, now a baron, caught most of the abuse. Heine called him "Herr von Shylock in Paris" and claimed, with a straight face, that he had once seen a stockbroker bow to James's chamber pot. He argued, only half in jest, that the Vatican had eased up on Jews because the pope was in hock to the Baron James. Said Heine most famously, "There is only one God—Mammon. And Rothschild is his prophet."[5] This much said, loud and often, Heine did not shy from cozying up to the Rothschilds for their patronage and to his uncle Salomon for an allowance. Even then, at the peak of its popularity, poetry did not pay well.

As influential as Heine was in his day, he would serve as warm-up act for a young man he befriended in Paris, one whose confused sense of self would transform the world, and not necessarily in a happy way. "What the two men had in common," historian Paul Johnson notes, "was their extraordinary capacity for hatred."[6] Johnson traces this dubious talent to their status as apostate Jews driven by unresolved self-doubt. Of the two, Heine's young friend Karl Marx was the more driven, the more hateful. About one hundred million corpses later, the world is still paying for his identity issues.

Like Hazel Motes, the confused protagonist of Flannery O'Connor's 1952 novel *Wise Blood*, Marx ended up recreating the structures of his parents' religion but without Yahweh at the center. Motes started the Church Without Christ. Marx went further. He started the Church Without God. As this bearded messianic German envisioned the future, an elite priesthood would interpret the iron laws of his secular Torah, while his self-created society moved dynamically and inexorably toward its apocalyptic end. As Dostoevsky said by way of Sartre, "In a world without God anything is permitted."

In the way of background, it was Marx's father who converted to Lutheranism largely as a way to improve his career chances. As it happens, he, too, changed his name to Heinrich, in his case from Herschel. The last name he changed from Mordechai to Marx. Karl Heinrich Marx was born to Heinrich and Henriette in Trier, in 1818, the third of seven children. Although his father was something of a deist, Marx grew up Christian. Upon graduation from the equivalent of high school, his diploma noted that Marx's "knowledge of Christian teachings and principles is clear and properly based. He also knows the history of Christian church to a great extent."[7]

After graduating, Marx was expected to study law, his father's profession. He proved to have as little interest in law as Heine and preferred, like his older friend, to try his hand at poetry, though without comparable success. Where he did succeed, like many college students before and since, was in discarding his fragile Christian faith. Reads one indicative verse, "I have lost heaven/ And know that for sure/ My soul, once faithful to God/ Now is destined for hell."[8] Unless God proves merciful beyond the call of duty, Marx likely foresaw his future.

While still in his twenties, this newly minted atheist and aspiring socialist turned his fury on the faith of his fathers. Marx did so in response to an essay written by one Bruno Bauer, a prominent leftist and unblushing anti-Semite, in which Bauer insisted that Jews abandon Judaism for the human liberation movement. Marx compressed his thoughts into two essays published in 1844 under the title "On the Jewish Question." He did not reject Bauer so much as transcend him. According to the respectful Marx, Bauer had packaged his biases "audaciously, trenchantly, wittily, and with profundity, in a style of writing what is as precise as it is pithy and vigorous."[9] The problem with Bauer, as Marx saw it, was that he transformed the question of Jewish emancipation into a purely religious question.

Marx believed the problem to be more fundamental. "For us," writes Marx, "the question of the Jew's capacity for emancipation becomes the question: What particular social element has to be overcome in order to abolish Judaism?"[10] To answer this question, Marx insisted on looking beyond the "Sabbath Jew," Bauer's target, to the "everyday Jew." According to Marx, ego and self-interest were what motivated the nine-to-five Jew, guided as he was by the Mosaic law, a document created largely to solve practical problems. Marx had not studied the Torah as a lad, but that did not stop him from reading between its lines. He dismissed the monotheism of Judaism and described the religion instead as "the polytheism of the many needs, a polytheism which makes even the lavatory an object of divine law."[11]

"What is the worldly religion of the Jew?" he asks. "Huckstering. What is his worldly God? Money." The way to "make the Jew impossible" would be to abolish the preconditions for huckstering. Without huckstering, Marx argues, the Jew's "religious consciousness would be dissipated like a thin haze in the real, vital air of society."[12]

Marx saw in Judaism an egotistic, antisocial strain that had infected society at large. Time and again, he interprets Judaism not as a theological movement but as a financial one. "The practical Jewish spirit has become the practical spirit of the Christian nations," he claims. "The Jews have emancipated themselves insofar as the Christians have become Jews."[13] This is an argument that would not have troubled Martin Luther, still another German law school drop out. Acceptance of Jews, Marx argues, comes to the degree that Christians mimic their usurious ways: "The god of the Jews has become secularized and has become the god of the world."[14]

Marx does not mention John Calvin. As a twenty-six-year-old, he may not yet have been aware of the split between Luther and Calvin on the usury question—Calvin, of course, being much more tolerant. That makes all the more impressive Marx's citation of the world's most aggressively Calvinist region as the one where "the practical domination of Judaism over the Christian world"[15] has become most evident. That region just happened to be New England.

Marx saw salvation for Jews and for society at large only after society had "succeeded in abolishing the empirical essence of Judaism—huckstering and its preconditions."[16] This would be no easy task. By his lights, huckstering was short-hand for the entire capitalist enterprise, and capitalism was code for Judaism. "The social emancipation of the Jew," he concludes wryly, "is the emancipation of society from Judaism."[17]

Marx had arrived in Paris only a year before he published these essays. His political philosophy was still in its larval stage. It would be another four years before he cowrote *The Communist Manifesto* and another twenty before he published his masterwork, *Das Kapital*. But one can see the wheels turning here. He dedicated three times as many words to "On the Jewish Question" as he did to the *Manifesto*. In the latter, he mostly just replaced the word *Jew*—which does not appear at all—with *bourgoisie*.

By 1848, a revolutionary year that shook the Rothschild houses to their foundations, Marx may well have absorbed a sentiment then current in the radical community, namely, that "anti-Semitism is the socialism of fools."[18] Lenin himself would repeat this phrase often, but it was not nearly as liberal as it sounded. Savvy leftists did not suddenly reject the stereotyping of Jew as exploitive hucksters. Rather, they came to believe that such hucksterism was epidemic and had to be treated systematically.

And yet Marx could never quite purge the image of the stereotypic Jewish moneylender from his rhetorical bag of tricks. His description of the capitalist in *Das Kapital* reads like the stage direction for Shylock in a Third Reich production of *The Merchant of Venice*: "Fanatically bent upon the exploitation of capital, he relentlessly drives human beings to production for production's sake."[19] Tellingly, Marx appends a footnote to the above passage, in which he refers to the "usurer" as "the perennially renewed form of capitalist."[20] Writing in the late–nineteenth-century London, where *Merchant* had become a West End staple, "usurer" had one very specific meaning, and Marx exploited it.

As Paul Johnson observes, "It is true to say that Marx's theory of communism was the end-product of his theoretical anti-Semitism."[21] In truth, his anti-Semitism reads like a toxic mix of cultural self-hatred and warmed-over Luther. One senses here a passing of the torch. Having transcended their animus against usury, the popes had passed it on to Luther, and his followers bequeathed it to Marx. From *Das Kapital* onward, Marx's disciples would wage the most relentless attack on the larger usurious enterprise and, when it served their purposes, the "fanatically bent" usurers themselves.

fourteen

The Country of Religiosity

KARL MARX HAD LITTLE USE FOR AMERICA. FROM WHAT HE KNEW IT was "pre-eminently the country of religiosity,"[1] and yet it seemed to be the one nation that had been most thoroughly corrupted by the Judaic spirit. Two strikes against America right there. The "free inhabitant" of New England, Marx writes in "On the Jewish Question," is convinced "that he has no other destiny here below than to become richer than his neighbor." When he travels, he worries "only of interest and profit." The world for the New England Yankee is "no more than a Stock Exchange."[2] As to idols, he has but one, and that is, of course, mammon. One sees in Marx's rant a precocious anti-Americanism that would deform the thinking of the international Left for the next 165 years and counting.

What Marx almost assuredly did not know is that two hundred years earlier, the very first New Englanders had taken a serious stab at the social scheme he was in the process of formulating. Plymouth Plantation governor William Bradford describes here the outcome of the colony's ambitious "from each according to his ability, to each according to his needs" experiment:

> The experience that was had in this common course and condition, tried sundry
> years and that amongst godly and sober men, may well evince the vanity of that

conceit of Plato's and other ancients applauded by some of later times; that the taking away of property and bringing in community into a commonwealth would make them happy and flourishing; as if they were wiser than God. For this community (so far as it was) was found to breed much confusion and discontent and retard much employment that would have been to their benefit and comfort. For the young men, that were most able and fit for labour and service, did repine that they should spend their time and strength to work for other men's wives and children without any recompense. The strong, or man of parts, had no more in division of victuals and clothes than he that was weak and not able to do a quarter the other could; this was thought injustice. The aged and graver men to be ranked and equalized in labours and victuals, clothes, etc., with the meaner and younger sort, thought it some indignity and disrespect unto them. And for men's wives to be commanded to do service for other men, as dressing their meat, washing their clothes, etc., they deemed it a kind of slavery, neither could many husbands well brook it. Upon the point all being to have alike, and all to do alike, they thought themselves in the like condition, and one as good as another; and so, if it did not cut off those relations that God hath set amongst men, yet it did at least much diminish and take off the mutual respects that should be preserved amongst them. And would have been worse if they had been men of another condition. Let none object this is men's corruption, and nothing to the course itself. I answer, seeing all men have this corruption in them, God in His wisdom saw another course fitter for them.[3]

Freed from the theoretical, Americans set about creating a distinctive and largely spontaneous commercial culture. Self-interest would drive it and self-control would restrain it. The Judeo-Christian legacy would inform that self-control and inspire it, but always imperfectly, given the fallen nature of man. The relative absence of external control would allow this dynamic to work itself out and, in the process, forge the most productive industrial enterprise in world history, but the balance between forces would always be a delicate one.

fifteen

Time Is Money

IN HIS WORTHY BOOK *FINANCING THE AMERICAN DREAM*, LENDOL CALDER nicely debunks the "myth of lost economic virtue."[1] Calder argues persuasively that each generation believes that its own is uniquely corrupt and looks to the generation before it as a debt-free Eden. Not so. "From Plymouth Rock to the present," writes Calder, "American dreams have usually required a lien on the future."[2] Even the Pilgrims lamented that debt was a "heavy burthen"[3] upon them.

What has changed is the way that Americans have financed that future. In the beginning of the American experiment there was very little of what we would think of as money. The early settlers rarely saw gold or silver and did not even know what paper money was. Much commerce relied on barter, the exchange of one good for another.

A strictly barter economy is limited by what economists call "a double coincidence of wants."[4] A colonist who wanted to buy corn but had only an old draft horse to trade would have to find someone with a surplus of corn who needed an old draft horse. The emergence of a commodity that almost everyone saw as valuable had the power to liberate commerce. In the northern colonies, beaver fur and seashells served as media of exchange with the Indians, as did fish and corn, but none had full acceptance as "commodity money." In the southern colonies, tobacco came close to filling that role. Tobacco, however, was an imperfect medium. If it had the advantage of being divisible, portable, and intrinsically useful, it had the disadvantage of being bulky, seasonal, and susceptible to the elements.[5]

As the economy grew, it became evident that even the most capacious fanny pack could not hold a tobacco bale. The two commodities that had passed all tests over the centuries were silver and gold, and in time gold and silver coins from foreign countries began to make their way into circulation in America. The most popular of these was the Spanish silver dollar. The word *dollar* derived from *thaler* (pronounced *TAHL-er*), the name given to coins first mined nearby and minted in Joachimsthal in Bohemia and originally known as Joachimsthalers. The milled Spanish dollars were easily cut into "bits," or pieces of eight. Thus *two bits* became standard lingo for a quarter of a dollar. In that gold and silver were internationally recognized commodities, foreign coins served perfectly well as a medium of exchange. In fact, it was not until 1857 that Congress outlawed the commercial use of foreign coins.[6]

The Western world had not seen government-issued paper money until colonial Massachusetts decided to improvise with it in 1690. After a military expedition to Quebec failed to pay for itself with the anticipated plunder, a government anxious to placate the disgruntled soldiers printed seven thousand pounds in paper notes. Future tax revenues would presumably allow the soldiers to redeem the notes within a few years in gold or silver. To bolster confidence in the notes, the government also promised to print no more paper money.[7] Not surprisingly, at least in retrospect, the government failed to redeem the soldiers' notes and printed considerably more notes the following year. One sees the beginning of a national habit here.

British financier Sir Thomas Gresham could have foretold what happened next. In 1558, he sent a letter to young Queen Elizabeth as she was taking the throne, cautioning her that "good and bad coin cannot circulate together."[8] Under her father, Henry VIII, and her half brother, Edward VI, England had allowed its coinage to be debased by minting coins whose gold and silver content had been reduced but whose face value remained the same. Citizens knew enough to trade with the debased coins and hoard the good ones, those whose face value reflected their real value in gold or silver. From this letter came Gresham's Law: "Bad money drives out good."

Although Gresham was granted naming rights three centuries after his famed letter, the concept is much older still. Consider the following from Aristophanes's *The Frogs*, written nearly two millennia before Gresham was born:

> *The course our city runs is the same towards men and money.*
> *She has true and worthy sons.*
> *She has fine new gold and ancient silver,*
> *Coins untouched with alloys, gold or silver,*
> *Each well minted, tested each and ringing clear.*
> *Yet we never use them!*
> *Others pass from hand to hand,*
> *Sorry brass just struck last week and branded with a wretched brand.*
> *So with men we know for upright, blameless lives and noble names.*
> *These we spurn for men of brass . . .*

Economists would eventually settle on the term *fiat money* to describe currency issues like that of Massachusetts. The term refers to money issued by government fiat—Latin *fiat*, "let it be done"—that is, either not fully backed by a specific commodity or not backed at all. All fiat money is "bad money" according to Gresham's Law. For the next several centuries, the progressive champions of fiat money would do battle with the stubborn dissidents who held out for commodity money, typically silver, gold, or both. As the dissidents came to learn, resisting the people who own the printing presses is likely to be a losing battle, especially when what they are printing is money.

In America going forward, credit and the attitude toward it would evolve on two distinct fronts, micro and macro, personal and institutional. The inherited Christian distaste for usury would forever color our attitudes about credit, debt, and related issues, both small and large. At the same time, the promise of the American dream and good old-fashioned prodigality would continue to undermine both personal and national resolve up to the present. This historic duality can be traced through the lives of two of America's most distinctive founding fathers, Benjamin Franklin and Thomas Jefferson.

Born in Boston in 1706 and educated in Calvinist-oriented Presbyterianism, Benjamin Franklin ran away to Philadelphia as a seventeen-year-old and there emerged as the apotheosis of the commercial American citizen. Even though his easy living in Paris would unnerve the literally Puritanical John Adams, Franklin was no prodigal. He deserved his rewards after seventy years of playing by the rules—rules that he did more to codify than anyone since Matthew, Mark, Luke, and John.

Franklin called his primary medium of instruction *Poor Richard's Almanack*, after the book's fictional author, Richard Saunders. Franklin began publishing the almanac in 1732 when he was just twenty-six years old and continued for the next quarter century, selling as many as ten thousand copies a year. Each edition contained the basics that one would expect in any almanac— a calendar, weather data, astrological and astronomical information, even demographics—but what distinguished it were Franklin's insights into the life well lived, many of which dealt with debt and credit.

It was Franklin who introduced into our common language the wonderfully succinct equation "Time is money."[9] This concept has at least as much power now as it did then.

As a case in point, in the 2005 Academy Award–winning film *Crash*, director Paul Haggis gives the film's critical punch line to young thug Anthony, played by rapper Ludacris. After a van full of Thai stowaways have fallen into his lap, Anthony chooses to not sell them into servitude. Instead, in his moment of personal redemption, he sets them free in Chinatown. "Come on now!" he yells as he hustles them out of the van. "This is America. Time is money. Chop, chop!" Only after the 2005 "immigrant" riots in France did at least some European intellectuals begin to appreciate the cohesive power of this understanding, the core virtue of what their peers deride as America's money culture.

Franklin's understanding of this equation was double-edged. "Waste neither time nor money," he urges, "but make the best use of both."[10] The notion of wasting time is obvious enough. Franklin considered such waste "the greatest prodigality." He observes that a worker who can earn ten shillings a day throws away five shillings if he sits idly half the day.

In that same essay, "Advice to a Young Tradesman," he makes the more intriguing point that "credit is money." He explains that a lender whose money sits idly loses the time value of that money. Without mentioning Aristotle by name, he undermined the Aristotelian theory that money is barren years before Jeremy Bentham would. "Remember that money is of the prolific, generating nature," Franklin writes. "Money can beget money, and its offspring can beget more, and so on."[11]

It is likely that Franklin knew his Shakespeare better than he knew Aristotle. If so, he would have certainly been aware of Polonius's well-worn advice to "neither a borrower nor a lender be," but that doesn't mean he abided by it. In *Poor Richard*, as seen, he endorses the lending of money, and his feelings about borrowing are mixed to the point of incoherence.

Time and again, Franklin warns the reader of the perils of borrowing money: "He that goes a-borrowing goes a-sorrowing"; "Rather go to bed supperless than rise in debt"; and even more emphatically, "The second vice is lying, the first is running into debt."[12] And yet, improbably enough, Franklin also instructs the reader in the value of borrowing money. "The use is all the advantage there is in having money," he wrote in 1736. "For six pounds a year you may have the use of one hundred pounds, provided you are a man of known prudence and honesty."[13]

Franklin goes so far as to develop an ethic around the borrowing of money. "Never keep borrowed money an hour beyond the time you promised," he insists, timeless advice for all users of credit cards. Always the pragmatist, he worries that a late payment will "shut up your friend's purse for ever."[14] He frets too that the very appearance of idleness or self-indulgence will make lenders wary and the borrower less credit worthy. Although not a churchgoer, he retained an active belief in a Christian God, one who would reward or punish him based on how he lived that life. And yet Franklin seems more concerned about what his fellow citizens will think about him than what God does, God being less likely to lend money at 6 percent per annum.

During the years Franklin was publishing *Poor Richard*, entrepreneurs were experimenting with deposit banking in the colonies. There had, in fact, been no banks of deposit in England until mid-seventeenth century. Prior to that, merchants tended to deposit their surplus gold in the king's mint. In 1638, Charles I broke them of that habit when he "borrowed" 200,000 pounds of the merchants' gold to finance an impending civil war.[15] The merchants eventually got their money back, but they had lost their confidence. They began instead to store their gold with private goldsmiths and would use the receipts as a convenient means of exchange. By the end of the civil war, some goldsmiths were issuing receipts for gold they did not have in store. Critics of what is called "fractional reserve banking" consider this the model for what was to come. Today, essentially all banks practice fractional reserve banking. In other words, they owe more money to their depositors than they have in reserve in their vaults. This sometimes causes problems.

The most prominent of the few private banks in the colonies was the Massachusetts Land Bank. Founded in 1740, it issued bank notes with land as the commodity in reserve. Given the illiquidity of land, people did not put a great deal of confidence in their ability to redeem the notes. This anxiety led to the creation of a rival silver bank whose notes were, allegedly at least, redeemable in silver.[16] The proliferation of these notes worried creditors who inevitably lost out in inflationary times. At the behest of Boston's merchants and governor, Parliament quickly stepped in and shut both banks down.

For a moment at least, these banks satisfied the public clamoring to have more money in circulation, a clamoring that never quite goes away. A hard-money advocate, Franklin suggested a half-serious solution to the problem. "If you will not be angry with me for giving it," he advises his readers, "I promise you not to be offended if you do not take it."[17] Franklin observes that his fellow citizens spend roughly 200,000 pounds a year on imported goods, money that is thus lost to local circulation. If half of that is spent on necessities, another half, Franklin argues, goes to "superfluities." He then offers a series of tips on how his readers might avoid those superfluous imports, most no more serious than "when you incline to drink rum, fill the glass half with water." This strategy would put an additional 100,000 pounds in circulation much more honestly than by printing money. "Then," he adds in all seriousness, "the merchants' old and doubtful debts may be honestly paid off, and trading becomes surer thereafter, if not so extensive."[18]

The Revolutionary War, like all wars, tested everyone's resolve to stick to hard money. To finance it, the Continental Congress issued fiat money with only the faintest resolve to redeem it in specie within seven years. As the war progressed, the Congress proceeded to print more and more "Continentals," which became more and more worthless as each year went by. By the sixth year of war, Continentals were trading at 168 paper dollars to one dollar of specie, which gave rise to the expression "not worth a Continental."[19]

Stung by the experience, and fiscally conservative by nature, the founding fathers moved back to a hard-money standard in drafting the Constitution.

Article I, section 8 gives Congress the power "to coin money, regulate the value thereof, and of foreign coin." Article I, section 10, meanwhile, forbids the states from coining money or making anything but gold and silver coin "a Tender in Payment of Debts." Importantly, however, Article I, section 8 also grants Congress the power "to borrow money on the credit of the United States."

In line with its constitutional powers, Congress passed the Coinage Act of 1792, which established a bimetallic standard for the United States. The two metals were silver and gold, with a fixed ratio of fifteen grains of silver to one of gold. This ratio reflected the market reality of 1792.[20] As happens with a bimetallic standard, though, market values change. And as the real value of gold gradually increased against silver, people began to stash their gold or melt it down, proving the truth of Gresham's Law once again. By 1810, silver coins, foreign and domestic, were just about the only legal tender in circulation.

A precocious holder of high public office, Thomas Jefferson anxiously watched the new republic find its financial footing. In 1776, when he had submitted the Declaration of Independence for Franklin's review, he was less than half the Philadelphian's age. Still, the difference in age had less of an effect on their respective characters than the difference in the environments that nurtured them. In the land-rich, cash-poor, morally ambiguous clime of antebellum Virginia, debt was something of a given for country gentlemen. And the older Jefferson got, the deeper he sank into it.

Yet, curiously, the more mired he became in personal debt, the more philosophically opposed Jefferson grew to national debt. As a young man, he kept an open mind on the subject. "The existence of a nation having no credit is always precarious,"[21] he wrote to James Madison in 1788, the year before the nation officially kicked into gear. "Were we without credit," he confided to George Washington that same year, "we might be crushed by a nation of much inferior resources, but possessing higher credit." To the Commissioners of the Treasury, again in 1788, he made a more compelling case: "I feel strongly the necessity of preserving the power to borrow."[22]

In each of these communications, Jefferson tried to overcome his peers' resistance to the borrowing of money. Still, he expressed reservations about using the nation's credit, save for "absolute necessity," and his experience in federal government would only fortify those reservations. In George Washington's first term, Jefferson, as secretary of state, went head to head

114

with Alexander Hamilton and his Federalist allies over the size and shape of government. In the process, he grew increasingly more wary of the aggrandizing and centralizing tendency of federal government. He saw money as the fuel for Federalist ambitions and pulled in the reins, or at least tried to.

In 1798, while serving as vice president under John Adams, he argued that the surest way to reduce the scope of national government would be to pass a constitutional amendment "taking from the Federal Government the power of borrowing."[23] If he'd had his way, he would also have denied the government the power of printing money or any other ungrounded legal tender. This would make waging war difficult, but he was beginning to wonder whether the power to borrow money or print it might actually lead to war. In a letter written fifteen years later, he made exactly that claim, arguing that the perpetuation of debt "has drenched the earth with blood." On the other hand, a government that honored the natural right to be free of debts offered "a salutary curb on the spirit of war."[24]

While president, however, Jefferson made one grand gesture that not only exceeded his constitutional powers but also entailed a good deal of borrowing. Over considerable domestic opposition, he bought the Louisiana Territory at the equivalent of an international foreclosure sale. France needed the money to finance its interminable wars against Great Britain, and Jefferson wanted the property as buffer against the encroachments of the European powers.

Technically, the United States bought Louisiana not from France but from the underwriters of the deal's eight million dollars in bonds, Hope and Company of Amsterdam and Barings and Company in London. Barings, the world's most prominent merchant bankers at the time, did the deal despite the fact that the proceeds would allow Napoleon to continue his war against the country Barings called home. To close the deal, the United States cancelled nearly four million dollars in French debt and paid three million down in gold. In all fairness to Jefferson, a fertile, mineral-rich chunk of real estate three times larger than France made for some fairly substantial collateral.

Five years after the purchase, Jefferson returned to his beloved country home, Monticello. Upon settling in, he could see that frost was playing havoc with his tobacco crop. He promptly informed his business agent that he would not be able to make his regular payments on the eight thousand dollars he had borrowed from a widow named Mrs. Tabb.[25] Then, all too typically, Jefferson threw his energies not into cash crops but into his gardens. The widow woman would have to wait.

Jefferson would spend most of the remaining seventeen years of his life at Monticello or thereabouts, until he died so providentially on the fiftieth anniversary of the signing of the Declaration of Independence—July 4, 1826, the same day on which the Declaration's coauthor John Adams also died. For all his good work on the national scene, at home Jefferson was a chronic deadbeat. He stumbled from debt to debt, from financial crisis to financial crisis. Indeed, in the dictionary of American clichés, his picture should be the illustration next to the phrase "misplaced priorities." Despite a recurrent inability to meet his overhead, he continued to spend his money on books, wine, horses, and especially that colossal money pit of a house.

To make ends meet, in 1817 Jefferson went to his good buddy at the Bank of the United States, its president Wilson Nicholas, and asked to borrow $6,000. Nicholas happily agreed to cosign for the loan, and the bank approved it. Six months later, in April 1818, Nicholas asked Jefferson to cosign on a $20,000 loan to Nicholas himself, at 12 percent annual interest, and Jefferson obliged.[26] Bad move. Nicholas defaulted and Jefferson was stuck with the debt. To get out from under, Jefferson took out another loan and persuaded his grandson and protégé, Jeff Randolph, to cosign. As collateral, Jefferson put up nearly 1,000 acres that would have passed to Randolph and, in so doing, stuck his descendants with the consequences of his own prodigality.

In his public life, at this same time, Jefferson was stepping up his attacks on the nation's debt. In 1813, for instance, he lamented that "the aggregate body of fathers may alienate the labor of all their sons, of their posterity, in the aggregate, and oblige them to pay for all the enterprises, just or unjust, profitable or ruinous, into which our vices, our passions or our personal interests may lead us."[27] It would be too easy to accuse him of hypocrisy. More likely, he was projecting his own personal turmoil. He knew how unsettling debt could be. In 1820, after saddling his grandson with his own debt, he wrote, "It is incumbent on every generation to pay its own debts as it goes. A principle which if acted on would save one-half the wars of the world."[28]

One restless night in January in the last year of his life, the distressed eighty-two-year-old Jefferson was lying awake, desperately trying to plot the family's financial redemption, when an idea descended upon him, in his daughter's words, "like an inspiration from the realm of bliss."[29] The family would sponsor a lottery. For as little as one dollar, an everyday Joe could have the chance to secure a large swath of Jefferson property. Jefferson hoped to raise sixty thousand dollars, enough to pay off the debts and allow him and his daughter to live out their days in something like comfort. Jefferson even harbored the hope that the state of Virginia would purchase the tickets and burn them all, as a way of acknowledging Jefferson's years of public service.

As a younger man, this is exactly the kind of entitlement that would have set his democratic teeth on edge. Unfortunately for Jefferson, the young legislators of Virginia inherited that spirit and rejected the lottery. "I see in the failure of this hope, a deadly blast of all my peace of my mind during my remaining days," he wrote to Jeff Randolph. "For myself I should not regard a prostration of fortune, but I am overwhelmed at the prospect of the situation in which I may leave my family."[30]

It is instructive to compare Jefferson's postpresidency with Harry Truman's. Upon leaving office, Truman drove to Missouri in his own car and settled in the humble Independence home he and his wife had once shared with his mother-in-law. Not wanting to demean the office of president, he turned down all corporate and commercial offers. In this era before presidential golden parachutes, he lived on his army pension and the proceeds from his memoir. "Had it not been for the fact that I was able to sell some property that my brother, sister, and I inherited from our mother," he said in 1957, "I would practically be on relief, but with the sale of that property I am not financially embarrassed."[31] No, economic virtue was not left behind in the nineteenth century.

sixteen

Jackson Days

IF THERE WAS ONE THING ABOVE OTHERS THAT HARD-MONEY ADVOCATES disliked about the Bank of the United States, it was the kind of cluster back scratch described in the previous chapter: Ex-president Thomas Jefferson asks bank president Nicholas to borrow $6,000. Nicholas cosigns, his board approves. Six months later, Nicholas asks Jefferson to cosign a $20,000 loan to Nicholas himself, the board approves. These deals went down in 1817 and 1818 respectively. The Second National Bank of the United States had opened for business in January 1817. The back scratchers did not waste time.

Jefferson had been mugged by his own self-inflicted reality. In 1791, he had opposed the establishment of the First Bank of the United States. As secretary of state, he had attempted to persuade President Washington to veto the bank bill then pending, as it "violated the laws of mortmain, alienage, forfeiture and escheat, distribution and monopoly"[1] and many other laws that Washington likely understood little better than the contemporary reader. More fundamentally, Jefferson distrusted a centralized, monopoly banking operation, even if it were to be 80 percent privately owned.

Secretary of Treasury Alexander Hamilton thought otherwise, and his opinion prevailed. Congress granted the bank a twenty-year charter in 1791. Among its powers was the printing of bank notes to counter a presumed shortage of specie—gold and silver coins—then in circulation.[2] These bank notes could be used to pay taxes on a par with specie, and this endowed them with a status very much like legal tender. At the time, the government collected revenues almost exclusively through excise taxes, basically a sales tax on products produced domestically, and customs duties, a sales tax on products produced abroad.

Even in the very first administration, however, revenues were insufficient to meet the needs of a growing federal government, and the new government took to borrowing from its new bank. This infusion of credit and paper money led inevitably to a spike in inflation and a growing resentment among the proto–Tea Party types of the day. When the bank bill came up for renewal in 1811, the battle lines in America's oldest and most enduring civil war were drawn: the soft-money forces versus the hard. Although the makeup of the respective coalitions would change over time, the intensity rarely flagged. In 1811, the hard-money forces prevailed by a single vote in the House and in the Senate. The Bank of the United States ceased to be.

Although philosopher George Santayana was not talking about central banking when he said, "Those who cannot remember the past are condemned to repeat it," he might as well have been. In this case, he could have safely said ". . . are condemned to repeat it within the next five years." That is how long it would take before the resurrection of the Bank of the United States. As it happened, the state-chartered banks that had begun to emerge even before the demise of the original Bank of the United States were severely tested by America's only war, named for the year it began, 1812.

Wars, of course, demand a great deal of money to finance, and the easiest ways to secure it are first to borrow it and then, if need be, to print it. The government did the former, and the state banks obliged them by doing the latter. The only problem was that the banks, especially those outside of fiscally conservative New England, did not have the specie—gold or silver—to back up their notes. In the years from 1811 to 1815, while the amount of specie in circulation declined slightly, the amount of bank notes nearly doubled. By demanding that their more reckless peers redeem their notes in specie, the New Englanders threatened the very existence of those banks and, by extension, the war effort.[3]

The U.S. government solved the problem by permitting all banks to suspend specie payments. Although contractually obligated to do so, the banks no longer had to redeem outstanding notes in gold or silver. Just twenty-five years earlier, the framers drafted Article I, section 10, of the United States Constitution, the so-called Contract Clause, expressly to prohibit states from granting private relief to favored individuals or institutions. Now, their successors were using the power of the U.S. government to do the very same thing they denied the states.[4]

"You never want a serious crisis to go to waste,"[5] presidential advisor Rahm Emanuel would argue two centuries later. The supporters of a central bank did not need Emanuel to tell them this. They exploited the economic chaos of the war and the postwar period—the specie suspension remained in effect until 1817—to militate for a renewed Bank of the United States. That was one solution. The other solution, the hard-money solution, and a hard political decision as well, would have been to compel all banks to redeem their notes in specie. This would have forced many banks to close. Their unbacked notes would have been liquidated, and the "good money" that had been driven underground would have come back out of hiding.

By chartering a Second Bank of the United States, Congress chose to play for time. For the first eighteen months of its existence, the new central bank, if anything, encouraged the inflation that the war had engendered and failed to rein in the more promiscuous of the state banks. So much money was in play, in fact, that the New York stock-jobbers who had been trading curbside for a century or more decided it was time to come inside. They rented a space at 40 Wall Street for two hundred dollars a month, and on March 8, 1817, grandly renamed their organization "New York Stock & Exchange Board."[6]

By mid-1818, however, officials of the Second Bank and responsible parties in the Monroe administration realized they had little choice but to call the party to a halt. The bonds that had been sold to European investors to finance the Louisiana deal were coming due—four million dollars' worth in gold or silver. As the government's fiscal agent, the bank had to call in its loans to commercial banks and insist that they repay in specie. The ensuing contraction—and it was huge—completed America's first artificial boom-bust cycle. There would be many more.

Wrote hard-money economist William Gouge of the Panic of 1819, "The Bank was saved, and the people were ruined."[7] The panic did, however, spawn a new movement, one that would soon enough find its champion in Andrew Jackson. Jackson would defiantly take up the cause of sound money and go after central bankers the way he had the Seminoles, but the banking tribe would prove a good deal harder to tame.

Andrew Jackson was undeniably a man of many talents, but it is hard to imagine which of them the modern Democratic Party remembers at its annual Jackson Day celebrations. A new off-Broadway musical, *Bloody Bloody Andrew Jackson: The Concert Version*, nicely captures the contemporary liberal take on Old Hickory. As John Lahr observes in his *New Yorker* review, Jackson is played as "gun-toting, Indian hating, land-grabbing Old Stonewall, who 'put the "man" in manifest destiny.'"[8] So fixed is this image that the playwrights feel free to parody it.

Jackson's life story is well enough known. Born fighting in 1767 to Scotch Irish parents, he served as a teenage courier in the Revolutionary War, almost died in captivity, lost both his parents as a result of the war, taught himself law, got himself elected to Congress, was appointed colonel in the Tennessee militia, fought lots of Indians, won the Battle of New Orleans, married a married woman, engaged in some thirteen duels, many of them defending his wife's honor, killed at least one of the duelers, took a few bullets himself, and, oh yes, owned some 150 slaves.

Contemporary Democrats would find little more to celebrate in Jackson's economic program than they have in his slave owning. Jacksonians favored lean, tight governments, the smaller and closer to home the better. They saw the primary role of government as the upholding of property rights. As translated to banking, this philosophy argued for the separation of bank and state, a move from inflationary paper money to pure specie, and 100 percent reserve banking in the place of the fractional reserve alternative.[9] God cannot possibly allow the dead to spy on their living descendants, because if, by some miracle, Jackson got to heaven, watching the TARP rollout in 2008 would have been pure hell.

Beyond ideology, Jackson had political gripes with the Second Bank. He suspected that its autocratic president, Philadelphia blue blood Nicholas Biddle, was using the bank's power and money to defeat his 1828 presidential bid.[10] In 1824, Jackson had won a plurality of both popular and electoral votes but lost to John Quincy Adams when the election was thrown to the House of Representatives. Jackson was more than a little suspicious about how this "corrupt bargain" had come to pass. In 1828, when he contested Adams's bid for reelection, the bank was sufficiently indiscreet in its get-out-the-vote effort that it alarmed even its supporters.

At the time, Biddle had even more power than a Federal Reserve president does today. The federal government appointed just five of his twenty-five directors. Neither the Congress nor the president had any control over the bank's operation, save to withdraw the government's funds or to decline renewal of its charter when it expired. In 1828, Biddle worried about neither of these possibilities. He was the master of his own universe. In the summer of 1832, toward the end of Jackson's first term, Biddle's mastery was confirmed when both houses of Congress voted to recharter the bank.[11]

Shortly before a close vote in the House, Congressman Samuel Carson of North Carolina changed his mind and voted *for* the recharter bill. When he inquired, Attorney General Roger Taney learned that Carson had just received a $20,000 loan from the bank. "Now I do not mean to say that he was directly bribed,"[12] wrote Taney. He blamed instead the proximity of this "mammoth money power" to so many needy public functionaries. The ever-judicious Taney would later be appointed chief justice of the Supreme Court.

In July of that year, Jackson vetoed the recharter bill and did so in thundering terms. "It is to be regretted that the rich and powerful too often bend the acts of government to their selfish purposes," Jackson began, and he kept hammering from there. He argued that distinctions will always exist in society, but when the law adds "artificial distinctions," the humbler members of society "have a right to complain of the injustice of their government."[13] He then delegated to himself—and to Congress as well, if its members chose to exercise it—the power to rule on the constitutionality of an issue. Biddle actually welcomed the speech. He considered it so over the top that in November the voters would surely reject Jackson and his "manifesto of anarchy" and "relieve the country from the dominion of these miserable people."[14] Not for the last time would a central banker misread the mood of the country. Jackson easily beat Henry Clay in the November election and promptly turned his attention to Biddle.

The bank still had four years left on its charter and ample resources to manage a future override of a Jackson veto. Not shy about taking matters into his own hands—during the Seminole wars, he had taken Florida without anyone's permission—Jackson decided to pull the federal deposits from the Bank of the United States and put them in reliable state banks. "My object, sir, is to save the country, and it will be lost if we permit the bank to exist,"[15] Jackson told his dissenting secretary of treasury. He gave the order to withdraw beginning October 1, 1833. When questioned by his own supporters as to motive, especially given that he could veto any future effort to recharter, Jackson contended that the bank would "buy up all Congress" if its survival were threatened. Not wanting to risk that, Jackson intended to take "the means of corruption"[16] out of Biddle's hands.

Biddle struck back. A week after the order went out to remove deposits, Biddle met with his board in Philadelphia. "Nothing but the evidence of suffering abroad will produce any effect in Congress,"[17] Biddle told the directors. By "abroad" he did not mean overseas. He meant abroad as in "abroad in the land." And "suffering" he meant literally. Americans, he believed, had to see the consequences of a credit clampdown if they were to turn against Jackson, and Congress had to feel their pain. The directors heeded Biddle's call to arms, called in loans, and tightened credit.

The battle came to a head in the spring of 1834. The old general knew a thing about strategy. He turned to the *Globe*, a newspaper that preached "the true faith,"[18] meaning whatever Jackson wanted it to print. Using the paper as megaphone, Jackson shared his concerns with the citizens of the then just twenty-four states that Biddle had turned the bank into a "permanent electioneering engine."[19] For this and sundry other good reasons, he told the people, he had decided to withdraw the government's deposits.

A century before FDR's fireside chats, Jackson was the first president to make such a direct appeal to the people. In the process, he so thoroughly outmaneuvered his opponents that they cried foul. John Calhoun, the vice president during Jackson's first term, placed Jackson's appeal "among the alarming signs of the times which portend the overthrow of the Constitution and the approach of despotic power."[20] Not to be out-demagogued, Henry Clay echoed Calhoun's charge of despotism and insisted that if Congress did not act boldly, "The fatal collapse will soon come on, and we shall die—ignobly die—base, mean, and abject slaves."[21]

Calhoun and Clay made these accusations on the floor of the Senate. In this rough-and-tumble era, no one would have accused them of Jackson-bashing. "Bashing" back then meant walking onto the Senate floor, as South Carolina congressman Preston Brooks did in 1856, and beating Massachusetts senator

Charles Sumner very nearly to death with the fat end of a cane, while a gun-wielding fellow congressman held off bystanders.

Calhoun and Clay could afford to attack Jackson because, as senators, they held six-year terms and were not elected directly by the people in any case. Congressmen had no such insulation. On April 4, 1834, an election year, the House voted that the deposits should remain in the state banks and that the Bank of the United States ought not be rechartered. "I have obtained a glorious triumph," Jackson crowed. "That mammoth of corruption and power" had finally been "put to death."[22]

A month after Jackson left office, just as his vice president and now successor Martin Van Buren was easing into power, commercial houses in New York started failing—exchange brokers, stock-jobbers, real estate speculators. It would take five years for America to fully recover from the Panic of 1837.[23] Nearly two hundred years later, history has offered no definitive proof as to why the crash happened, but what was undeniable even then was that the party in power would catch the heat. A pattern had begun to establish itself.

On the plus side, the Panic cleared out an awful lot of financial deadwood—overextended banks, shaky investments, hairy speculations. Van Buren, meanwhile, withdrew the government's money from all the "pet" state banks and stored it in pure specie in government vaults. For the first and only time in American history, the government had established an independent treasury system, free from any entanglement with the nation's banks and with all of its finances grounded in hard money. These halcyon days would extend for twenty years, until the Civil War made printing "greenbacks" once again seem like an attractive way to cover the national debt.

As to the Bank of the United States, it continued on as a wobbly state-chartered bank and contributed its own share to the Panic of 1837. Biddle finally stepped down in 1839, and the bank closed just two years later. Biddle died in 1844 in Philadelphia at age fifty-eight, a year before the seventy-eight-year-old Jackson. But the idea of a central banker did not die with him. No silver bullet, no stake in the heart, no president could keep that idea dead.

seventeen

A Mountain Load of Debt

ALEXIS DE TOCQUEVILLE ARRIVED IN THE UNITED STATES IN MAY 1831, the third year of the Jackson presidency. At the time he was a twenty-five-year-old French dandy, but one with a remarkably keen eye. He left nine months later. Three years after that he produced the enduring classic that we know as *Democracy in America*. Neither before nor since has anyone captured the American psyche with such precision.

Tocqueville conceded that there was nothing unique about American character traits. He had known of people in other countries who were hard-working, restless, ambitious, religious, egalitarian, and individualistic. He had not known, however, nor had the world seen, a whole nation of such people. To understand those people one had to understand the paradox of equality, and this Tocqueville assessed early on.

As Tocqueville observed, in a society where aristocratic privileges have been abolished and where all career paths are open to anyone willing to work hard, the citizen could readily delude himself into thinking "that he is born to no common destinies."[1] Although Tocqueville did not dwell on the question of credit, he understood why Americans would avail themselves of it. "When an immense field for competition is thrown open to all," he continues, "when wealth is amassed or dissipated in the shortest possible space of time amid the turmoil of democracy, visions of sudden and easy fortunes, of great possessions easily won and lost, of chance under all its forms haunt the mind." Under these circumstances, "The present looms large . . . and men seek only to think about tomorrow."[2]

Charles Dickens had a more malign view of America's flirtation with debt. In his sour grapes tour of America ten years after Tocqueville's, Dickens added "the love of 'smart' dealing"[3] to the causes of the nation's periodic insolvency. Although Dickens surely overstates the problem, he did not invent it. Visiting in the wake of the Panic of 1837, he points out the consequences of the various swindles and "defalcations" (his word, meaning a category of bad acts that taint a particular debt such that it cannot be discharged in bankruptcy). "This smartness," he contends, "has done more in a few years to impair the public credit, and to cripple the public resources, than dull honesty, however rash, could have effected in a century."[4]

Dickens talked specifically about "that ill-fated Cairo,"[5] the Illinois town at the confluence of the Ohio and the Mississippi Rivers. The attempt by speculators to make Cairo the rival of St. Louis was undone, Dickens claims, by "gross deceits." When revealed, these deceits eroded confidence in America and discouraged foreign investment. This all, of course, is at least partially true. The fact that Cairo today has three thousand people compared to the nearly three million in metropolitan St. Louis suggests that the scheme to put Cairo on the map was not a roaring success. Still, it was the schemers and dreamers who unbound the West and built most of its cities. Had "dull honesty" been America's defining characteristic, Chicago would still be a swamp and Kansas City a floodplain.

It was not just foreign social critics who were fretting out loud about the easy acceptance of debt by both individuals and governments. Mark Twain told of a speculator overheard boasting, "I wasn't worth a cent two years ago, and now I owe two millions of dollars."[6] Famed orator Edward Everett—he whose two-hour speech at Gettysburg was eclipsed by President Lincoln's two-minute address—blamed the Panic of 1857 on "a mountain load of debt" assumed by citizens, communities, businesses, and governments in unwitting concert. Everywhere Everett looked he saw a "natural proclivity to anticipate income, to buy on credit, to live a little beyond our means."[7]

For better or worse, a variety of businesses emerged in nineteenth-century

America to accommodate those who lived beyond their means. Although pawn-broking had been common in both the Greek and Roman empires, as well as in Europe, the first American pawnshops did not open, at least legally, until the early decades of the 1800s. The late start had as much to do with demographics as with local customs. Pawnbroking is an urban business. The broker needs a critical mass of wage earners to make the business model work. New York City recognized its first legal pawnshop in 1803. By 1897 that number had climbed to 134. Said one crusading journalist toward century's end, "The city can no more dispense with the pawnbroker than it can with the baker or the milkman."[8]

That model was simple enough and remains so. A customer needs cash. She—most nineteenth-century customers were women—brings an item to the pawnshop that she thinks has value. The pawnbroker assesses it with an eye to its potential resale value. Experienced pawnbrokers, as many a disappointed customer can attest, have remarkably good eyes. They have seen and heard everything. The pawnbroker then loans the customer money at an interest rate typically limited by law and holds the item as collateral. If the customer repays the loan on time with interest, she gets the item back. If she extends the loan, all the better for the pawnbroker. If the customer does not finally repay the loan, the pawnbroker resells the item.[9]

The institution took root in American cities because of the advantages to the customer. There was no humiliating interview as there would have been for a charity, no credit checks, no elaborate contracts. The drawback, of course, was the interest rate. Although most American states had adopted usury laws, now defined as excessive interest, there could be no real consensus on what "excessive" meant.

New York City, for instance, allowed 2 percent monthly interest on loans over one hundred dollars, but 3 percent under that amount.[10] Although this did not seem fair to reformers, small loans consumed as much of a pawnbroker's time as large ones but with less return. To get around legal usury limits, pawn-brokers often charged a variety of fees that could run annual interest rates up as high as 300 percent. In the second half of the century, when the reformers started opening their own charity pawnshops, not unlike the *Monte di Pieta* of medieval Italy, even they had to charge as much as 1.5 percent a month to meet their minimal overhead.

In a historical note, the universal pawnshop symbol of three suspended golden balls can be traced back to the Medici coat of arms. To share in the magic of the Medici name, lesser lenders simply ripped off their logo. The unauthorized spread of this symbol represents what is likely the first documented case of trademark infringement. Speaking of infringement, American publishers were ripping off Dickens's work without paying royalties, which helps explain why he was such an ungracious guest.

As convenient as they were, pawnshops had no monopoly on lending to the working classes of nineteenth-century America. In New York City, for instance, an estimated two-thirds of the lending was done by small loan agencies. These shops flirted with legality throughout most of the century, especially in those jurisdictions that enforced an interest ceiling less than 10 percent. To turn a profit on small loans with high default rates, these agencies had to charge 20 percent interest per annum or more. As collateral, they accepted chattel mortgages or attached a worker's wages, the latter being the *modus operandi* of today's payday loan operations.

As one might expect, these small agencies did not enjoy a particularly favorable press. In fact, some time in the late nineteenth century, reformers adapted the slur on real estate speculators, "land shark," to the more memorable "loan shark" applied to small lenders. Despite the mob connotations of the phrase, these lenders rarely, if ever, broke legs. Generally, the worst pain they inflicted on a deadbeat borrower was to sic a "bawlerout" on them. Almost always a female, the bawlerout would try to catch the defaulter in front of friends or coworkers and—you guessed it—bawl her out. Shame was still a viable currency in the nineteenth century.

Borrowers often turned to loan sharks to settle up debts incurred through a seductive new phenomenon known as installment buying. In the early part of the nineteenth century, this phenomenon was reserved for people of means and was offered by retailers as something of a minor honor. Not until the 1880s did the working classes get in on the game. To recruit them, large retailers hired "pullers-in," middlemen who spoke the customer's language, literally, and introduced them to the wonders of buying on the installment plan, American-style.[11]

Late-century American cities were more diverse than they had ever been or have been since. New arrivals, and they came by the shiploads on a daily basis, did not show up wearing Kobe Bryant jerseys with iPods on their belt. They came as strangers to a strange land and appreciated the rope-showing service of the retailers' middlemen. A memoirist of the period recounts how one female middleman—middleperson?—sold the writer's mother a sewing machine, then showed up once a week for the next twenty-five years to collect the twenty-five cent installment owed, in the process becoming a close family friend.[12]

At the time, when people thought of installment credit they thought first of sewing machines. To be clear, Isaac Singer did not invent the sewing machine, never claimed to. He was too busy fathering children in any case—twenty-four with five different women, only two of whom he married. What the Singer Manufacturing Company did invent was the formalized installment plan. The company sold more than 250,000 sewing machines in 1876 alone, roughly half of the machines sold nationwide and most of these "on time."[13] No technology has affected domestic America more.

For most of the nineteenth century, buying one's home on time was thought radical to the point of being taboo. The orthodox approach was for a family to save its money until it could afford to buy a house and then purchase one. The building-and-loan associations changed all that. "I met with several kinds of associations in America of which I confess I had no previous notion," Tocqueville would write, "and I have often admired the extreme skill with which the inhabitants of the United States succeed in proposing a common object for the exertions of a great many men and in inducing them voluntarily to pursue it."[14] By happenstance, Tocqueville visited Philadelphia—"the only city in the world where it has occurred to people to distinguish the streets by numbers and not by names"[15]—in the same year that America's first savings-and-loan association was founded there, 1831. By 1893, there were nearly six thousand such associations.[16]

In the beginning, they were just that—associations. Indeed, many had no offices or salaried officials, let alone Learjets parked in company hangars. Would-be homebuyers would buy shares in the association in the amount equal to the money they hoped to borrow. The homebuyers were allowed to pay the association the cost of the shares over time, and they also paid 6 percent interest on the money borrowed.[17] Without intending to, the associations had pioneered the amortization of home loans.

Amortization derives from the Middle English *amortisen*, meaning "to kill"— a meaning that might resonate with people burned in the recent subprime crisis. More generally, amortization has come to mean the payment of interest and principal together in fixed monthly installments. Although moralists were troubled by the voluntary assumption of debt, rigorous installment plans for essential items had the effect of making families more, not less, conscientious in the budgeting of their income. If they wanted to stay in their homes, they had to put money aside each month. To work, this system of payment needed honorable mortgage lenders and a morally responsible customer base.

In 1890, the U.S. census estimated the private debt of the nation's households to be eleven billion dollars. The superintendent of the census was sufficiently unnerved by the proof of America's "debt-creating mania" that he pleaded with his fellow citizens to come "to their sober senses" and launch a new era of "retrenchment and debt-paying."[18] Although this plea may sound judgmental by contemporary standards, Tocqueville thought such moralizing the proper role of the public official. Government had the obligation, he reasoned, to "teach that wealth, fame, and power are the rewards of labor, that great success stands at the utmost range of long desires, and that there is nothing lasting but what is obtained by toil."[19]

Although Tocqueville acknowledged the role of the church in inspiring "a love of the future" and conceded that Americans "wish to be as well off as they can in this world without forgoing their chance of another,"[20] he underestimated the power of the pulpit and the public opinion it generated. Christianity exercised a useful restraining influence throughout the nineteenth century. "Debt is an inexhaustible fountain of dishonesty," warned popular late-nineteenth-century evangelist Henry Ward Beecher in righteous indignation. "It has opened in the heart every fountain of iniquity; it has besoiled the conscience, it has tarnished the honor, it has made the man a deliberate student of knavery, a systematic practitioner of fraud."[21] This famed abolitionist had no more use for loan sharks than he did for slave traders, and he was one out of thousands preaching the same message.

For all the inducements to indulge, most Americans managed to strike a balance between success in this world and access to the next. Artemus Ward, Abraham Lincoln's favorite stand-up comic, wryly summed up the forces at war within the American soul. "Let us all be happy, and live within our means," he joked, "even if we have to borrer money to do it with."[22]

eighteen

Cross of Gold

THE ELECTION OF 1896 REPRESENTS THE MOST DRAMATIC PARTY REALIGNMENT in the history of American politics. The party of Jefferson, Jackson, and Grover Cleveland—hard-money men all—went soft. The transition was not an easy one. Said the party's eventual nominee of the struggle, evoking the language of the Civil War, "Brother has been arrayed against brother, and father against son. The warmest ties of love and acquaintance and association have been disregarded."[1]

The struggle centered not on war and peace or prohibition or segregation, all potentially hot topics, but on a single issue that could be summarized in a single word: gold. The insurgent soft-money forces, America's debtor class, were rising up in righteous indignation against their creditors, the "few financial magnates who in a backroom corner the money of the world."[2] Standing in the way of the insurgents were the so-called Bourbon Democrats, who were alleged to do their financial masters' bidding. What the insurgents demanded was nothing less than an abandonment of the gold standard. Said their thirty-six-year-old leader in the speech that would net him the party's nomination, "You shall not press down upon the brow of labor this crown of thorns. You shall not crucify mankind upon a cross of gold."[3]

By this time the Republicans had already nominated William McKinley as their candidate for the presidency. But William Jennings Bryan, the "boy orator of the plains," was savvy enough to know that he was facing a more formidable opponent than McKinley—a more formidable opponent, for that matter, than the power broker behind McKinley, Mark Hanna. No, to win, Bryan would have to best the man whose power Hanna brokered, America's most formidable banker ever and arguably the most powerful man in the world circa 1896, John Pierpont Morgan.

The ascent of the house of Morgan gives a reassuring ecumenical coloring to the history of investment banking: they were the Protestants to the Medicis' Catholics to the Rothschilds' Jews. The Morgans, a term used here to include partners as well as family members, would also oversee, quite literally, the shift of the world's financial power from London to New York. As with the Medicis and the Rothschilds, their story begins with a hardworking patriarch and reaches its ascendancy with a son.

In 1837, the year of the Panic, the year coincidentally that Pierpont was born, Baltimore merchant George Peabody (pronounced *PEE-buh-dee*) moved to London. Already respected in international circles, Peabody opened a merchant house and began to do business. He traded in dry goods—a catchall phrase for textiles, clothing, and the equally elusive "sundries"—and financed other trades as well. Businesses like his were known as merchant banks, the progenitors of today's investment banks.[4] Merchant bankers dealt exclusively with institutions and what we have come to call—isn't there a better phrase?—"high net-worth individuals." They issued stocks and bonds, financed overseas trade, and brokered commodities among other services. Theirs was a world without teller windows or Christmas clubs or velvet rope lines in the lobby.

Not content to blend into London's oaken woodwork, Peabody positioned himself as an American banker. This was risky. At the time Peabody was establishing himself, Dickens was writing home about America's "gross deceits" and, yes, "defalcations," and his was an opinion shared by many, if not most, London bankers. Defaults by various states on British loans were further tainting the British perspective on the American national government. When the Americans attempted to borrow from Britain in 1842, James de Rothschild sent its agents packing: "Tell them you have seen the man who is at the head of the finances of Europe, and he has told you that they cannot borrow a dollar, not a dollar."[5]

Merchant bankers developed their reputations by delivering on the securities they sponsored. When officials in Peabody's native Maryland defaulted on their obligation, they took Peabody's credibility down with them. Friends shunned him. The best clubs blackballed him. "You and I will, I trust, see that happy day," he wrote a fellow citizen, "when as formerly, we can own ourselves Americans in Europe, without a blush for the character of our country."[6]

Given the consequences for them—personally as well as for the body politic—if debts went unpaid, bankers have had a history of doing what they had to in order to set things straight. What Peabody and his partners at Barings did was to sponsor an image campaign back in Maryland on behalf of debt resumption. They were not above bribing influential citizens, Senator Daniel Webster foremost among them, to endorse their campaign. "Your payment to Mr. Webster would not appear very well if it should get out,"[7] wrote a senior Barings official to his American bagman in something of an understatement. Happily, the strategy worked. Interest payments were resumed, and the depreciated bonds Peabody had himself bought regained their value. He made a small fortune in the process and restored his reputation.

A bachelor with a predilection for prostitutes, Peabody had no legitimate heirs. As he grew older and less well, he began to cast about for a partner to carry on his business. Junius Spencer Morgan, a forty-year-old banker from Boston, came highly recommended. When he moved to England in 1854, Morgan took along his wife and his sickly adolescent son, John Pierpont. Peabody was a pain to work with, but the down-the-road payoff was sufficiently promising that Junius kept his gripes to himself. The Crimean War had driven up wheat prices, and the railroads that shipped the wheat were sharing in the good times. For the Brits who wanted to invest in America—at least a billion dollars had been pumped into railroads already—Peabody and Morgan were the go-to guys.[8]

All good things come to an end, including, of course, the Crimean War. Wheat prices collapsed as surely as they had swelled. This set off a general panic in 1857. Gold payments out of New York banks were suspended, and Peabody found himself desperately overexposed. Only an emergency credit line of 800,000 pounds from the Bank of England saved the firm from tanking. This brush with disaster rattled Junius and his twenty-year-old son Pierpont, then working as an intern on Wall Street. "Let what you now witness make an impression not to be eradicated," wrote the father to the son, one of many such missives, "slow & sure should be the motto of every young man."[9]

For the next twelve years, the now healthy, strapping, confident Pierpont represented his father's interests on Wall Street. Peabody had retired in 1864, and the firm now bore the name of J. S. Morgan & Co. In 1869, Pierpont made a move that set him apart from his peers and insinuated him into the American power structure in a way that no banker had been before. The prize at stake was of itself small potatoes, the 143-mile Albany & Susquehanna Railroad.[10] For hardball financier Jay Gould, however, the railroad represented a link in a chain that he was trying to hammer together. When the railroad's founder, Joseph Ramsey, resisted his overture to buy it, Gould, himself just a year older than Pierpont, attempted a hostile takeover.

In 1869, hostile did not mean "your lawyers yell at our lawyers" as it does today. Hostile meant recruiting an armed posse of 800 thugs off the streets of New York and shipping them upstate to do battle with Ramsey's army of 450 hardened country boys. The battle climaxed with a literal head-on collision between the trains of the respective forces and a pitched battle in which at least ten people were shot, the Ramsey forces prevailing.

Pierpont did not play this way. He came in after the bones were set and the dead buried, bought six hundred shares of the railroad for his New York firm, got Ramsey his job back as president, and, as reward, asked only for a seat on the board of directors. At the time, this was a novel move. Bankers did not sit on boards. But as Pierpont realized, when you sit on the board, no one is going to take your business away.

While his father remained in England, Pierpont continued to build the American end of the business. A devout Episcopalian and dogged moralist, he eschewed idleness, extravagance, and gambling. "Among robber barons," writes Morgan biographer Ron Chernow, "he was unique in suffering an excess of morality."[11] His moral restraint served him well in 1873. Financier Jay Cooke, who had made his fortune with one hand in the government's pocket, overreached on a railroad deal and precipitated the Panic of 1873. Drexel, Morgan—the name of Pierpont's group—was secure enough to take advantage of the failures that followed. "I don't think there is another concern in the country [that] can begin to show such a result,"[12] wrote Pierpont to his father about the more than one million dollars in profit the firm pocketed in that panicky year.

Over the next twenty years, with Cooke out of the way, Pierpont made the name J. P. Morgan synonymous with wealth and power. Fond as he was of moral order, he proceeded to "morganize" one business after another, particularly the railroads. When a mismanaged railway fell into receivership, he would step in on behalf of its investors, often British, streamline the business, reorganize it, and transfer control to himself. "In reorganizing railways," observes Chernow, "[Morgan] ascended to a new plateau of power, beyond what any other private businessman had yet achieved."[13]

When panic struck again in 1893, the resulting failures opened up a host of new power opportunities, including the rescue of a floundering new high-tech outfit called General Electric. The panic would also offer Morgan a different kind of opportunity, the grandest one of his career. In the way of background, the United States had resumed the gold standard in 1879. Despite widespread fears of a liquidity crisis, the 1880s proved to be arguably the most productive decade in American history.[14] While prices fell, wages soared. This resulted in an increase in savings and capital formation, which in turn fed the nation's hunger to industrialize. Hard-money advocates may have resented the National Banking Acts (passed during the Civil War and left in place), but otherwise the 1880s were as close as America ever got to a *laissez-faire* economy.[15] The Democrats who accused George W. Bush of running a *laissez-faire* shop would have amused the critics of a real free-market champion like Democrat Grover Cleveland.

In 1890, during the gap in Cleveland's split presidency, the nation's soft-money party, the Republicans, decided to muck with success—three times. First, they passed the Sherman Silver Purchase Act, whose effect was to put America back on a bimetallic standard, a sure way to make "Gresham" a household word once again. Second, they passed the McKinley Tariff Act of 1890, which hiked the price of imports and reawakened inflation. And third, the New York subtreasury began to settle accounts with bank notes instead of gold. The cheapening of America's money alarmed America's creditors abroad. Still smarting from the anti-Americanism he had experienced as a teen in England, and wanting to preserve the nation's honor, Morgan applied enough pressure to get the Silver Act repealed in 1893.

The indebted farmers of the West and South had no use for the tariff, but they welcomed the inflation that came with a cheapened currency. This they saw as the best way to balance their books with the big-city bankers, about as welcome in their world as boll weevils. So deep was the hostility that several Western states outlawed bankers, and Texas banned them altogether. The contempt for Wall Street only heightened with the Panic of 1893, as it has after every panic, and the farmers began to militate for a fresh supply of cheap currency. The *Atlanta Constitution* preached, "The people of this country, outside the hotbeds of goldbuggery and Shylockism, don't care how soon gold payments are suspended."[16]

As the *Constitution* implied, though admittedly without much tact, Jews had made their presence felt on Wall Street. Many of them had begun, like Nathan Rothschild, as dry-goods merchants. Among them were the German-Jewish founding fathers like the Lehmans in Alabama, Lazard in New Orleans, Kuhn and Loeb in Cincinnati, and Goldman in Pennsylvania.[17] By the turn of the century, Wall Street had become culturally bipolar, with Kuhn Loeb and the Jews occupying one pole and J. P. Morgan and the WASPs the other. Despite his own distaste for certain Jewish banking houses, Morgan may have defused a good deal of the populist anti-Semitism by emerging as the public face of the gold standard.

In 1895, the United States found itself, in Morgan's words, "on the brink of the abyss of financial chaos."[18] For a variety of reasons, the United States Treasury was hemorrhaging gold. The government was weeks away from being unable to honor its debts. The one man in the world who could save the gold standard took a train down to Washington and, without invitation, demanded to see the president, Grover Cleveland. When Cleveland obliged him, Morgan laid out an ambitious scheme in which the Morgan and Rothschild houses would collaborate to secure 3.5 million ounces of gold, half or more from Europe, and exchange it for roughly sixty-five million dollars' worth of thirty-year gold bonds.

When the deal went down, the financial markets responded enthusiastically. The hinterlands, however, were manifestly less pleased. The populists did not know why America needed a gold standard in the first place. To them Cleveland was little more than a tool "of Jewish bankers and British gold."[19] Even the New York *World*, obviously indifferent to New York's changing demographics, picked up on the anti-Semitism, calling Morgan's syndicate a pack of "bloodsucking Jews and aliens."[20] Not above a little race-baiting himself, albeit with a literary tone, William Jennings Bryan asked the clerk of the House to read aloud Shylock's bond from *The Merchant of Venice*.[21] In Bryan's cross of gold analogy, it was Morgan who played the role of Pontius Pilate. His unspoken sin was to have reminded his fellow citizens that America was still a debtor nation.

A Republican, Morgan used his considerable influence to steer the Republicans to the gold standard. At the Republican convention in June 1896, Morgan's man at the convention, Senator Henry Cabot Lodge of Massachusetts, laid out the game plan for Hanna and McKinley: stick to gold, stop talking about greenbacks and silver, and the Morgan forces will work for you; abandon gold, and the Morgans will work against you.[22] Morgan, they knew, had backed Cleveland. They would not secure his support simply by appealing to his Republicanism. With the Democrats headed in the opposite direction, Hanna and McKinley saw the political value in hewing to the Morgan line.

On the other side of the aisle, the Panic of 1893 had made Cleveland's bid for renomination unlikely, and his blessing of the Rothschild-Morgan deal had made it unthinkable. Economic downturns, no matter their cause, have always stirred the American people to righteous wrath, and in this case the populists were quick to exploit it. Bryan, however, brought something else to the party—his Midwest pietism. For the last generation, the Democrats had been the *laissez-faire* party, both socially and culturally. In Cleveland's first campaign, 1884, the Republicans had notoriously identified his party with "rum, Romanism, and rebellion." In 1896, under Bryan, the Democrats pulled a political one-eighty. They shifted, in today's terminology, from the economic right to the left and from the cultural left to the right. To say the least, this confused the base.

The electoral map dramatically changed coloration from 1892 to 1896. In 1892 Cleveland had won most of the big industrial states with heavy Catholic populations, including New York, New Jersey, Connecticut, and Illinois. He also swept the South—Southerners would vote for a "yaller dog" before they would vote for a Republican—and beat Benjamin Harrison, the incumbent Republican. In 1896, Bryan held the South but McKinley carried New York, New Jersey, Connecticut, and Illinois, as well as every contiguous state in an arc from North Dakota to Maine, and won the election.[23] In subsequent elections, both parties moved to a mushy progressive center, and the difference between them blurred. This may account for the falloff in voter turnout as well. Too much echo, not enough choice.

In the seventy-five years between the fall of the Second Bank of the United States and the rise of the Federal Reserve, J. P. Morgan was the closest thing America had to a central banker. Unlike official central bankers, however, Morgan had his own chips on the table, and in 1907, he got to play his last big hand before the Feds nationalized the game.[24] In October of that year, while attending the Episcopal convention in Virginia, the market started wobbling. Seventy years old and semiretired, Morgan boarded his private railroad car and headed back to the Street.

As in every such occasion, there are a thousand reasons offered as to why the markets crashed and rarely ever a consensus. Some laid the blame on President Theodore Roosevelt. Teddy had, in fact, kept the financiers off balance, Morgan included, with his frequent criticism of them as "great malefactors of wealth" and his threats to check their power. More honest than most pols, he would later concede that his "assaults and exposures" may have helped precipitate the panic.

The trust companies deserved their share of the blame as well. These companies managed the trust accounts—wills, estates, and the like—that banks at that time could not. Though usually conservative, the more adventurous had found the law's loopholes and begun to speculate. As happens, especially with amateurs, the speculators failed to anticipate certain risks—in this case, for instance, a collapse in copper shares—and the tightly coupled Wall Street institutions began to derail.

Enter J. Pierpont Morgan stage right. What he did over the next few weeks has become the stuff of legend. He literally strode Wall Street like a colossus, "the embodiment of power and purpose," said his awestruck son-in-law, Herbert Saterlee. "The thing that made his progress different from that of all the other people was that he did not dodge or walk in or out, or halt or slacken his pace. He simply barged along, as if he had been the only man going down Nassau Street hill past the subtreasury." Morgan summoned bankers, trust presidents, industrialists, government officials, and when he called, they came. When he demanded money to stem the bleeding in the markets, they provided it. "Within two weeks," writes Chernow, "he saved several trust companies and a leading brokerage house, bailed out New York City, and rescued the Stock Exchange."[25]

Even the progressives of the era—Woodrow Wilson and Theodore Roosevelt among them—were awed by the job that Morgan had done. His efforts, however, got them to wondering how much better a central bank could do the same. With a properly constituted "Federal Reserve," they reckoned, the nation might never experience a market crash again.

nineteen

Wizard of Finance

IF THERE WAS ANY ONE EVENT THAT TRIGGERED THE PANIC OF 1907, it was an attempt to corner the stock of United Copper, an attempt that failed rather spectacularly. Among the investors in that would-be corner was one Charles W. Morse. A classic Wall Street wheeler-dealer, Morse had succeeded in cornering the New York ice market a decade earlier—with a little help from Tammany Hall—and earned himself the sobriquet "the Ice King."[1]

On the heels of the panic, the political class, as it typically does, went looking for scoundrels to prosecute. Morse fit the bill as well as anyone. He was promptly convicted of bank fraud and sentenced to fifteen years in a federal penitentiary in Atlanta. He arrived in January 1910. Soon after checking in, he met another new arrival, a charming and ambitious wisp of an Italian immigrant. With impeccable old-world manners and only the slightest accent, the tiny Italian captivated Morse and was in turn captivated by him. Within ten years of their prison rendezvous, Morse's advice and support would inspire his Italian friend to earn his own millions as well as the title "the wizard of finance."

The reader who guesses that the wizard in question was Amadeo Giannini guesses wrong. In 1910, Giannini was in San Francisco happily growing the Bank of Italy according to the rules. He had founded the bank six years earlier in a building whose previous tenant had been a saloon. Immediately after the earthquake in 1906, Giannini had cleverly hauled the bank's vault to his home in then rural San Mateo. When a subsequent fire consumed most of San Francisco's major banks, he was uniquely positioned to meet the city's immediate liquidity needs—other than water—and earned a solid reputation in the process. In 1928, Giannini merged his expanding business with a Los Angeles bank and kept its rather grandiose name, Bank of America.

Giannini is the kind of financier that cities name schools after. San Francisco's Giannini Middle School is testament to the same. No one, however, has named a school after Morse's Atlanta friend, but his name endures nonetheless. One hears it much more than Giannini. In fact, one has heard the wizard's name more in the last year or two than in the decade or two prior. That name, of course, is Ponzi.

In 1910, twenty-eight-year-old Charles Ponzi had boarded a southbound train from Montreal with five undocumented Italian immigrants. Just seventeen days earlier, Ponzi had been released from a Montreal prison, where he had served two years for forging a check. Fortune still was not smiling on Ponzi. He and his homeboys, his *goombahs*—an American corruption of *compa* or *compare*—got busted together crossing into the U.S. The Italians testified against Ponzi, the alleged "coyote," and were set free. Ponzi was sent to Atlanta for his fateful meeting with Morse.[2]

Not inclined to physical work, Ponzi had grown up in an affluent Italian household, spoke several languages, and headed off to America only after squandering all his money at the gaming tables while at college in Rome. In America, he would redeem himself, or so he convinced his indulgent mother.[3] In 1912, however, when released from the federal pen in Atlanta, redemption did not seem near at hand.

While bouncing around the South, looking for some quick way to make a fortune, Ponzi heard of a young woman desperately in need of skin grafts. A sentimentalist, he volunteered seventy-two square inches of his own skin to help patch her up. The account of his sacrifice made the local paper, and Ponzi sent a clipping of it to the warden back in Atlanta.[4] Though emotionally rewarding, his selfless act was not nearly redemptive enough, at least not on the terms that this lapsed Catholic hoped to be redeemed.

In 1917, after thirteen unproductive years in North America, Ponzi made his way back to his port of entry, Boston. A potential job as a clerk at an import-export firm attracted him. What held him in Boston was a woman he met soon after arriving. Ponzi married his American rose, Rose Maria Gnecco, within a year of their first meeting.[5] Without trying, she turned this capricious dreamer into a committed schemer, one determined to support her in the style he thought she deserved.

Ponzi found his inspiration in, of all places, his stamp collection. In 1906, the U.S. and some sixty-two other countries had gathered in Rome to find a hassle-free way to send mail across international borders. The solution they hit upon was built upon a standard note that could be redeemed for stamps in any participating country. Ponzi thought its very name—the International Reply Coupon—had marketing gravitas.

Before the Great War, exchanging the coupon for stamps was equitable and straightforward. After the war, however, currency devaluation meant that a dollar could buy three times as many coupons in Italy as it could in the United States. With all of the other unsettled business after the war, no one had yet recalibrated the coupons. There was, of course, one minor drawback to Ponzi's scheme: although he could convert coupons to stamps, he could see no feasible way to convert either stamps or coupons to cash. That problem he put off thinking about. He was always stronger on dreams than details in any case.

In early December 1919, Ponzi stopped in to see pawnbroker Max Rosenberg at Uncle Ned's Loan Shop. There he swapped some of Rose's rings for cash to start his business. He tried to entice Rosenberg into investing, but Rosenberg had grown too used to holding collateral in hand.[6] He was not about to swap gold for paper.

In the middle of December, Ponzi paid the state the fifty cents necessary to register the name of his new enterprise, and that same day the Securities Exchange Company opened for business in a musty upstairs office above School Street in downtown Boston. Before the new year was through, this cash-strapped son of Italy would make and lose millions.

It all started slowly. In the first month, Ponzi had persuaded only eighteen people to invest, and they gave him all of $1,770 in cash. As he told them, he would invest their money in International Reply Coupons, make his profit by exploiting exchange rates, all perfectly legal, and then return their investment plus 50 percent within ninety days, forty-five if things went well.[7] Although the diminutive financier had no clue as of yet how to convert coupons to cash, he convinced himself that it could be done and brought that confidence to the table. The word seeped out, at first among Italian-Americans, and slowly, surely outward from there.

In March 1920, Ponzi attracted 110 investors who put down $25,000. Ponzi was able to redeem the rings from Rosenberg that he had pawned to start this business just a few months earlier. In April, when his initial investors realized that Ponzi was actually willing to pay 50 percent interest as promised, the news spread like the Spanish flu. That month 471 customers invested $140,000. Although a few of the early customers cashed in, most took another throw of the dice. In May, more than 1,500 investors ponied up $440,000. This was turning into real money.

On May 5 of that same year, two other Boston Italians made their first mark on American culture when they were arrested for the murder of Alessandro Berardelli, a security guard killed in a South Braintree payroll robbery three weeks earlier. What Nicola Sacco and Bartolomeo Vanzetti had in common with Ponzi—beyond their good looks and shared ethnicity—was that they, too, were as guilty as sin.[8] Unlike his countrymen, however, Ponzi would not claim ethnic victimization. Even after his arrest, Ponzi reminded the press that he was a "hearty endorser of the established government."[9] Besides, when Ponzi looked at his heritage, he did not see the oppressed masses. He saw the Medici. He reminded one critic who questioned his background that "banking had its origin in Italy and that the bill of exchange was devised by Italians."[10]

In the summer of 1920, Ponzi was too busy counting money to worry about arrest. In June, 7,800 people invested $2.5 million with the Securities Exchange Company. In July, 20,000 investors plunked down $6.5 million. That $6.5 million had a value comparable to $69 million today. "Hope and greed could be read in everybody's countenance [or] guessed from the wads of money nervously clutched and waved by thousands of outstretched fists!" Ponzi would later remember the experience. "Madness, money madness, the worst kind of madness."[11]

Although one newspaper would note that "foreigners predominate"[12] among the crowds, Ponzi's appeal had long since transcended its ethnic base. At least five Boston police inspectors had bought in, as well as hundreds of ordinary cops. The average size of each investment suggests that the people buying in were not all bootblacks and paperboys. Ponzi had become a multi-cultural, multiclass phenomenon.

The nation's social critics are likely to conclude, as Ponzi himself had, that "Nobody gave a rap for ethics" or that "we are all gamblers. We all crave easy money."[13] But even in 1920, the year that the Black Sox scandal broke, neither generalization was close to true. There were any number of people who were bothered by what Ponzi was doing and a greater number still savvy enough to stay away from School Street.

The *Boston Post* sniffed a fraud early on. So did a posse of state and federal officials, most notably the state's incorruptible bank examiner, Joseph Allen. Bostonian Clarence Walker Barron, the father of American financial journalism, was particularly critical. Even before he knew Ponzi was running a scheme, he considered the underlying currency manipulation immoral. Evoking images of medieval divines, he intoned, "When a man gets money from the government without performing a service, it is just the same as when a man takes money from an individual without performing service for that money."[14] The *Boston Globe* added a Darwinian twist to the same sentiment. "In those parts of the planet which nourish high-grade human stock," the *Globe* opined, "there is no such thing as living without working."[15]

The various investigations were, however, slow getting untracked. For one, Ponzi's explanation of how he generated his revenue sounded credible. For another, he was not violating the state's usury laws. If anything, he was the victim of the usurious demands of his clients, who expected 50 percent interest every ninety days.

Soon enough, though, several newspapers and investigative agencies were hot on his case. By the end of July, under enormous pressure on all sides, Ponzi submitted his business for a public audit and agreed to stop taking investments. This was something of a relief to Ponzi, as the more investments he took, the deeper was the hole he dug for himself. He had long since given up hope of trading coupons for cash.[16] His investors, however, wanted to keep on believing. Depending on the rumor of the day, they would either storm his office hoping to get their original investment back or storm his office trying to invest some more. The air was slipping out of this bubble surprisingly slowly.

A series of damning newspaper articles, including revelation of Ponzi's early arrests, finally punctured it. The run on Ponzi's operation ended up taking out a couple of Boston banks—and almost the whole Boston banking complex—so deeply was he invested in several of them. And truth be told, in the era of fractional reserve banking, the banks' positions were nearly as exposed as Ponzi's were.

The denouement revealed a Ponzi as gracious and dapper as ever, and an America far more tolerant than historians credit it to be. In August 1920, Ponzi was arrested. The following month, in an incident that would crudely prefigure the attacks of September 11, 2001, Italian anarchists pulled a wagon filled with dynamite in front of J. P. Morgan's headquarters at 23 Wall Street and let her rip. The ensuing blast killed more than thirty people, wounded hundreds more, and wrecked the interior of the Morgan building. This blast capped a year of terror bombings by the followers of anarchist Luigi Galleani.

In the same years that Ponzi was being tried first by the federal government and then by the state, so were Sacco and Vanzetti. As the Soviet propaganda arm projected the latter case, Sacco and Vanzetti were powerless immigrants persecuted for their unpopular political belief and ethnic origins. The Massachusetts legal establishment was the evil instrument of the pair's "judicial murder."[17] And the twelve members of the jury who convicted the pair were bigots all, easily inflamed by the state's disinformation campaign.

The treatment of Ponzi helps put a lie to this nonsense. Even after he was arrested and convicted, even after he had defrauded half the citizens of Boston, the crowds continued to cheer him on. In December 1920, a few days after his guilty plea in the federal case, the *New York Times* conceded, "There was something picturesque about him, something suggestive of the gallant about him." The press and the people of Boston had gone easy on Ponzi, the *Times* claimed, due to "a lack of sympathy for those whom he robbed . . . [The victims] showed only greed—the eagerness to get much for nothing—and they had not one of Ponzi's redeeming graces."[18]

As the Melonie Griffiths-Evans case in the opening chapter suggests, the people of Boston have changed less than their media have.

twenty

Jekyll Island

THE MEETING OF THE TWO CHARLESES IN THE ATLANTA PEN WAS NOT THE
most memorable financial confab of that year, 1910—not by a long shot. That
honor fell to a gathering of faux duck hunters on a small private island off the
coast of Georgia. There were only six men in the group. The task of recruiting
the hunters was given to Henry Pomeroy Davison, the handsome young senior
partner *chez* Morgan and a veritable rock star on Wall Street. That he invited
some guests to go duck hunting attracted little attention. A born sportsman,
Davison had graduated from deer and rabbits around his humble Pennsylvania
boyhood home to moose in Maine and rhino on the White Nile.[1]

For at least four of the six, the trip to Georgia was draped in mystery. Each
guest was instructed to show up at Hoboken Station on November 22 and there
board the private railroad car, blinds drawn, of Senator Nelson Aldrich. Aldrich,
they knew, was John D. Rockefeller's man in the U.S. Senate and the father-
in-law of Rockefeller's son. He and Davison would accompany them on the
journey to a destination that had been secured by J. Pierpont Morgan himself.

Each guest arrived individually at the station as requested and kept his
distance from the others during the journey to Brunswick, Georgia. There,
the six men boarded a boat headed for Jekyll Island, a hunting retreat for the
elite described by one magazine as "the richest, the most exclusive and most

inaccessible club in the world."[2] The names among its fifty or so members, in addition to Morgan, included Rockefeller, Pulitzer, Astor, Vanderbilt, Gould, and others of the turn-of-the-century household variety.

For the next ten days, the six men and a small skeleton staff had the island to themselves. They emerged at retreat's end with a document that, with a few modifications, would soon enough reshape the world of finance. For the record, the duck hunters owed their invitation to the Panic of 1907 and the man who calmed it. That crisis had found Morgan at the peak of his powers. As early biographer Frederick Lewis Allen noted, "Where there had been many principalities, there was now one kingdom, and it was Morgan's."[3] Morgan had succeeded too well. Now more than seventy years old, he caused Wall Street and Washington to wonder what would happen in a future emergency if there were no Morgan among them. "Something has got to be done," Senator Aldrich worried out loud. "We may not always have Pierpont Morgan with us to meet a crisis."[4]

Neither Pierpont nor Wall Street had confidence that Pierpont's forty-year-old son, Jack, had the banking chops to pick up where the old man left off. Although not incompetent, Jack Morgan was not his father. Besides, few Americans of any stripe were keen on a ruling Morgan dynasty.

Even before the panic, academia had been quietly militating for a solution to future crises that did not involve Morgan or any other independent agent. Leading the charge was a professor of economics at Columbia University, E. R. A.—as in Edwin Robert Anderson—Seligman. The American-born Seligman had studied in Europe and picked up a little Marx along the way. He would not be the last academic economist so influenced. Over the winter of 1907–1908, he presided at three conferences, each of which called for the creation of that ultimate fix-all, a central bank. Seligman disdained "the horde of small competitors"[5] that made American commerce, banking in particular, so difficult to manage by experts like himself.

Also speaking at the Columbia conference of 1907 was one Frank Vanderlip, a banker and former assistant secretary of treasury. He, too, argued that a competitive, decentralized banking system caused the panic, "one of the great calamities in history." Vanderlip saw central control along scientific principles as a solution to a free and competitive market. His outspokenness on this issue earned him a round trip to Jekyll Island.

Following Vanderlip at Columbia was Paul Warburg. Born into a Jewish banking family in Hamburg, Germany, Warburg married into the American Loeb family and moved to the United States in 1902 as a thirty-four-year-old partner in the investment banking house of his in-laws, Kuhn, Loeb & Company. No one in America knew central banking better than Warburg did. "Small banks constitute a danger,"[6] he told those gathered at Columbia in arguing for the benefits of European-style banking. Warburg, in fact, had a problem with the whole idea of a free, self-regulating market. He hoped to replace Adam Smith's "invisible hand" with the "best judgment of experts," himself high among them. In 1910, Warburg, too, took up duck hunting on Jekyll Island.

Aldrich kept the reform ball rolling in the Senate. He managed to get a minor banking bill, the Aldrich-Vreeland Act, passed in 1908. The reformers took note of a seemingly minor amendment to the bill that Aldrich's fellow senators paid little heed to: the creation of a National Monetary Commission (NMC) to study proposals for restructuring the banking system. Wrote one reformer in the *Wall Street Journal*, "In no other way can such education be effected more thoroughly and rapidly than by means of a commission . . . [that] would make an international study of the subject and present an exhaustive report, which could be made the basis for an intelligent agitation."[7]

Aldrich set up the NMC promptly in June 1908 and started agitating. Although various senators and representatives filled the seats in the conference room, the Aldrich-appointed staff did the real work. It was agreed from the beginning that the NMC would be run as a discreet, ecumenical alliance among Rockefeller, Morgan, and Kuhn, Loeb. On Morgan's advice, Aldrich named Henry Davison chief advisor. "My idea is, of course, that everything should be done in the utmost quiet manner possible," Aldrich told a colleague, "and without any public announcement."[8]

The NMC, its agents, and its allies spent the next two years hammering out proposals and winning support. To woo the reluctant bankers in the Midwest, the planners insisted that any new national bank would be decentralized through regional complexes. For those worried about private control, planners assured that the government would oversee the operation through an appointed governing board. To drive the message home, the *Wall Street Journal* launched a fourteen-part front-page series on the need for a central bank.[9]

Feeling the need to goose the project along, Davison called the meeting at Jekyll Island. In addition to Aldrich, Warburg, and Vanderlip, A. Piatt Andrew and Benjamin Strong donned their hunter togs. Andrew was just finishing his tenure as assistant secretary of treasury and had served before that as a director of the United States mint. Indiana born, he had been educated at Princeton and in Europe and had taught economics at Harvard.

Of the six men in attendance, none would prove more influential than Strong. Then the president of Banker's Trust Company, the thirty-nine-year-old Strong owed his career to Davison, who had hired him six years prior, and to Davison's boss, Morgan. Strong and Davison were the two Morgan men in attendance. Aldrich and Vanderlip were Rockefeller men. Warburg represented Kuhn, Loeb; and Andrew, an economist, was friendly to all camps.

The only duck or wild turkey the men saw during the ten-day retreat was on their dinner plates. They ate well, their sole reprieve during sixteen-hour workdays. They even celebrated Thanksgiving together. Vanderlip would much later describe their shared time as "the highest pitch of intellectual experience that I have ever experienced,"[10] but he kept this experience to himself. Before leaving, he and the others took a pledge of secrecy. It would be four years before anyone got wind of the meeting and twenty years before any of the men admitted being there. Given the secrecy and the seriousness of the enterprise, the swamps of Jekyll Island would serve as the primordial stew for a thousand conspiracy theories, some of which are close to accurate.

Strong and Vanderlip drafted the "Aldrich Plan," the document mentioned above that summarized the strategy agreed upon at the retreat. The plan called for the creation of a "national reserve association," a sort of banker's cooperative that replicated the function of a central bank without calling it such.[11] The association would have the authority to issue currency and lend to commercial banks. Although government appointees would sit on the association's board, the bankers themselves would control it.

Aldrich had recommended a straightforward central bank on the European model, but the nonpoliticians knew better than he that a central bank could be more readily sold to the public if packaged as a decentralized bank.[12] That sell was complicated by the fact that the Democrats had taken Congress in 1910 and would take the White House in 1912.

The marketing campaign for the Aldrich Plan kicked off at a National

Board of Trade meeting in January 1911. After a rousing speech in its favor by Andrew, delegates voted to back the plan. The group's chairman then appointed a seven-person committee to market the plan, headed by none other than Warburg. The delegates, of course, had no knowledge that Andrew and Warburg had helped draft the document they were about to promote.

To give the illusion of a grass-roots effort, the committee of seven launched a National Citizens League for the Creation of a Sound Banking System and headquartered it in Chicago, rather than New York.[13] While the Citizens League drummed up enthusiasm on Main Street, a parallel campaign was launched to win over Wall Street.

Congress would prove more difficult. A three-time presidential loser by 1910, William Jennings Bryan still held sway over much of Congress. His soft-money supporters saw the hard-money hand of Morgan behind a central bank and resisted. To win over Congress, supporters of the plan would have to lose the Aldrich name and find a Democratic sponsor. Happily for them, Carter Glass, the head of the Banking Committee in the House, stepped up to champion the cause in the House.

The House Democrats and now President Wilson insisted on changes. They demanded not only the appearance of decentralization, but also at least a smidgen of reality. There would be twelve private regional reserve banks in the system, and these would be placed under central political control. A Washington board, which included the treasury secretary and presidential appointees, would oversee the whole system.

On March 31, 1913, J. P. Morgan died. On December 23, 1913, President Wilson smiled and signed into law the hybrid concoction that was to replace Morgan, the Federal Reserve. The Jekyll Island men smiled too, and they knew what they were smiling about. In analyzing the beast, they had figured out that the control of it could very well reside with the presidency of the Federal Reserve Bank of New York if that first president were shrewd and resourceful. They had just the man in mind. From 1914 until his death in 1928, their own Benjamin Strong would preside over the New York Federal Reserve and set the monetary policy for the nation. The Federal Reserve Act had not reduced the power of the duck hunters and their backers. It had merely reduced their responsibility.

twenty-one

Birth of the Consumer

On June 19, 1877, the *New York Times* ran an all-cap headline, "A SENSATION AT SARATOGA."[1] As the subhead went on to explain, the sensation was this: the Grand Union hotel in Saratoga Springs, New York, had changed its rules to exclude Jews and turned away the prominent Wall Street banker, Joseph Seligman.

The incident had to have been upsetting for Seligman. Forty years prior, he had immigrated to America from Germany as an eighteen-year-old and promptly gone to work as an itinerant peddler working the farmer beat in rural Pennsylvania. Seligman sold enough implements and sundries that he was able to send for his two brothers, William and James. In time, the brothers upgraded their enterprise from peddling merchandise to merchant banking and by the time of the Civil War, they had built one of the most formidable such houses in America. So deeply did Seligman identify with his adopted country that when his son was born eleven days after the fall of Fort Sumter, he named him after the Union general who defended the fort, Edward Robert Anderson.[2] Thus began the career of E. R. A. Seligman.

The younger Seligman was encouraged to believe in the American dream. Indeed, Horatio Alger Jr. tutored him as a child, and the dream does not get much purer than that. Although E. R. A. chose not to pursue his father's career,

151

he never strayed too far from Wall Street. As previously noted, he played a significant role in the birth of the Federal Reserve from his perch at Columbia University. Perhaps the leading public intellectual of his era, Seligman was eager to show the relevance of the economist in the everyday life of the republic. In 1925, when he got his chance, he would make the most of it. Before he was through, he would almost single-handedly legitimize personal credit and sire the consumer revolution.

If the sewing machine had introduced the working classes to installment buying, it had failed to make buying on credit respectable among the middle classes. In *The Century Dictionary* of 1889, for instance, the listing for "installment plan" reads like a warning label. According to the entry, "the seller retains the ownership until payment, and stipulates for the right to retake the article, without return of some or any part of what has already been paid, if the buyer makes default in any instalment."[3]

In his 1886 novel *The Minister's Charge*, popular author William Dean Howells has his protagonist learn that he can buy the suit he longs for "on the installment plan" if, that is, he does not mind shopping "on a degenerate street, in a neighborhood of Chinese laundries."[4] In his 1906 novel *The Jungle*, Upton Sinclair dedicates almost as much anxious attention to his character's installment purchases as he does to his packinghouse miseries.

Arguably the leading voice in the anticredit movement was then-popular novelist Irving Bacheller. In his 1912 best seller *Charge It*, Bacheller lays out a philosophy that would have found favor with Martin Luther. His aptly named character Socrates Potter speaks for the author when he pontificates that "credit is the latest ally of the devil," and that "the two words 'charge it' have done more harm than any other in the language."[5]

In his more ambitious 1910 novel *Keeping Up with Lizzie*, Bacheller boldly links corruption in the microeconomic order to a breakdown in the macroeconomic one. This linkage deserves exploration, even if Bacheller's plot wanders all over the lot. As told, each of the town's two leading grocers has indulged his child. These two young adults, Lizzie and Dan respectively, have learned to savor the high life at their fashionable colleges. When they return home, they try to keep up with each other. Their competition eventually sucks in the whole town. The grocers have to hike their prices to fund their children's needs, and inflation follows. Just about everyone descends into debt.

The townspeople mortgage their homes and file for bankruptcy. A young cashier at the bank embezzles eighteen thousand dollars to keep up and then blows his brains out in self-disgust.

Happily, Socrates Potter has been saving his money. He lectures the hapless prodigals before bailing them out and helping them restart their lives. Dan marries Lizzie. They return to the farm, and the town returns to normal. Memories of inflation, bankruptcies, and moral breakdown embed themselves in the town's chastised collective consciousness.

As sincere as he was, Bacheller was no Aristotle, no Aquinas, no Adam Smith. Despite widespread anxiety about the "morphine of credit," neither he nor anyone in turn-of-the-century America spoke with universal authority. The nation's moral thunder was strained through a thousand filters. All the nation's social workers, newspaper editors, pastors, academics, and home economists together did not carry the weight of one run-of-the-mill medieval pope.[6] America's pluralism was dissipating the message of the largely Protestant advocates of the social gospel.

Still, the crusaders against debt might have prevailed were it not for the introduction of one new technology, the same technology, by the by, that helped undo America's sexual morality—the automobile. In 1906, when Woodrow Wilson, then president of Princeton University, first sensed its potential, he feared for the nation's future. Everyone would want a car, he reasoned. Few could afford them. The frustration would lead to socialism.[7]

Henry Ford helped head off the feared revolution. In 1903, he and a half dozen investors launched the Ford Motor Company.[8] In 1908, they rolled out the Model T Ford for $825, and overnight a new car seemed within reach of just about every wage-earning guy across the fruited plains. Many Americans, however, especially those disinclined to save their money, stood like Tantalus in their own self-imposed Hades, forever reaching for those keys only to see circumstances snatch them away. Banks offered little help. A car violated just about every traditional standard of sound commercial banking.

In an extended 1916 study, an independent consultant to Ford, Edward Rumely, offered a way around bank recalcitrance. "Because of certain facts of human nature," he fairly observed, "there are always more people who will buy when they can pay for a thing gradually in the course of the next six months, than there are people with cash in their pockets to buy outright."[9]

Rumely recommended that Ford stay out of the lending business for a variety of good reasons, but suggested instead that the Ford Motor Company set up a subsidiary banking company.

Henry Ford would have none of it. He believed in cash. His distaste for installment buying, bankers, banking, borrowing, lending—the whole financial enchilada—was becoming the stuff of legends. Accordingly, Ford sold all of its cars for cash to dealers. The dealers, however, were increasingly working with local finance companies to move their autos off the lot. This whole end of the business did not much concern Henry. In 1920, every other car in the world was a Model T. He had reason to believe that his cash-centric sales strategy was working.

Alfred P. Sloan was not feeling nearly as complacent. The rising executive at upstart General Motors understood that a credit-financing arm would help GM increase sales and stabilize production. It would also enable GM to cut into Ford's market dominance among low-end buyers. And so in March 1919, the company took the plunge and launched the General Motors Acceptance Corporation.[10]

After a sharp postwar recession in 1920, which the still humble Federal Reserve let work itself out, the economy took off, and everyone wanted a car. By 1923, 46 percent of GM buyers were taking advantage of GMAC's installment plans.[11] This not only put marginal buyers in the low-end market, but it also allowed middle-class drivers to "buy up." By this time, young males had come to understand that a sharp-looking car could make them smarter, taller, and better-looking. And if it made them poorer in the process, it made them at least *look* wealthier. The status they were buying may have only been symbolic, but it worked.

The anticredit forces were not about to be run over. Henry Ford led an unlikely coalition in resisting what one old-school merchant called "the Slimy Coils of Installment Evil."[12] For obvious reasons, savings banks still discouraged installment buying. In fact, they used the nation's two thousand school-banking programs to educate these future depositors on the virtues of putting their money in banks. Union leaders worried about collecting their dues and fretted that strikes would be harder to call if their members had installment payments to meet. Clergy of all stripe railed against debt as they had been doing since Moses. And now, even America's emerging socialist wannabes were joining the chorus.

Not wanting to appear insensitive to a culture war it had helped launch, GM commissioned a study to explore the effects of installment selling on society.[13] If the results came back positive, GM could take credit for pioneering these credit innovations. If they came back negative, GM could profit by tightening its credit while simultaneously posing as guardian of the nation's morals. And who more credible to undertake this study than the nation's most prominent economist, E. R. A. Seligman?

Contemporary universities would be hard-pressed to find people on their faculties who think as Seligman did. Although no friend of *laissez-faire* economics, he believed in progress and wasn't afraid to say so. He understood that social progress was tied to economic performance. This worldview predisposed him to rule favorably on the credit issue, and this he did in his highly influential 1927 report, *The Economics of Instalment* [sic] *Selling*. Too confident to equivocate, Seligman argued that credit was helping drive the "business revolution" and constituted "a significant and valuable contribution to the modern economy."[14]

Seligman went well beyond charts and graphs in making his case. He editorialized that the whole language of credit should be changed, not only to make the discussion more rational, but also to make credit more acceptable. At the time, economists tended to divide credit into two categories: "productive credit" that was advanced for income-producing products and "consumptive credit" for purchases that were bought largely for convenience or pleasure.

Seligman had real problems with the word *consumptive*. For one, it sounded like a disease. At the time, tuberculosis—the AIDS of its day, much feared and perversely fashionable—was routinely called consumption. For another, *consumptive* gave the impression that the product was consumed, as in used up and wasted. Seligman insisted that a much more useful word would be *consumer*, as in "consumer's credit." The word stuck, and in no time America transformed itself from a nation of citizens to a nation of consumers. GM's Sloan gave Seligman full credit for eroding the resistance of the nation's bankers and businessmen to the credit revolution.[15]

Others took up the crusade where Seligman had left off. Notable among them was department store honcho Julian Goldman. When Goldman opened his first high-end store in 1916, he could see how middle-class reluctance to buy on time was limiting sales. Seligman's book inspired him to devise an ad strategy that would overcome that reluctance. In one memorable 1928 ad, headlined "A factory or a fur coat," Goldman followed Seligman's lead in breaking down the moral distinction between productive and consumptive buying. The ad flattered the female purchaser into seeing herself as a "good business woman," one who financed her "business" in the "only practical modern way."[16] Not only that, but her purchase of the fur coat would help stimulate the economy, put more money in circulation, and keep people employed. In 1930, Goldman published a book called *Prosperity and Consumer Credit* that was grounded openly in Seligman's theories.

Implicit in the history of credit and debit is a cultural reality that historians choose to avoid: from the nineteenth century forward, major innovators in the management of credit and debit were disproportionately Jewish, very much so. As the twentieth century progressed, this trend would continue. A parallel trend had developed as well: those who resisted credit innovation, both on Wall Street and off it, were disproportionately Protestant. Catholics played little role in this ongoing dialectic. Although Catholic doctrine did not discourage enterprise, Catholic culture in America subtly did. Beyond the brigand Joe Kennedy and the banker Amadeo Giannini, it would be hard to name a single Catholic of real consequence in the financial field, especially in the first half of the twentieth century.

What was impressive about America, especially given the state of the world circa 1930, was how well its citizens, its financiers especially, kept this culture war civil. If the tension between Jews and Protestants—shorthand for the latter: WASP or "white shoe"—was a constant, resentments were rarely given voice by either side. In his recent best seller *The Israel Test*, George Gilder attributes this to the fact that anti-Semitism "tends to wane under a growing and expanding capitalist system."[17] For those who disdained capitalism, Karl Marx most notably, this was merely a sign that Jewish values had corrupted an entire culture. Those who championed free enterprise, on the other hand, had to appreciate how well Jews played the game, even if it occasionally came at their expense. Says Gilder, "Americans should not conceal the triumphs of Jews on our shores but celebrate them as evidence of the superior freedoms of the U.S. economy and culture."[18]

On Main Street, open hostility seldom moved beyond the fringe. When it did, as in the Seligman hotel incident, it made headlines. Although denied certain club memberships and subjected to a variety of comparable slights, Jews felt secure enough in the rule of law to continue to innovate. Like the Rothschilds in the nineteenth century, however, the founding fathers of German-Jewish Wall Street—what author Stephen Birmingham famously described as "our crowd"—tended to be circumspect. As successful as they had been, as closely as they mimicked the dress, speech, manners, and public altruism of their WASP counterparts, they could not quite take their success for granted. Still, it does Jewish-American culture an injustice to portray its businesspeople as victims. By the beginning of the twentieth century, they were warriors in an occasionally rough but usually civil war, fully capable of giving and taking.

As he did on any number of fronts, Henry Ford broke the civility mold. From 1919 to 1927, Ford published the *Dearborn Independent* and expressed his views indirectly through its editors. The *Independent* charged, among other things, that the national debt was a Jewish creation, which was slowly enslaving America. Ford saw the Federal Reserve as part of this larger plot and laid the blame on the one Jewish duck hunter, Paul Warburg. As to Jews, he thought of them as an "international nation" of people, whose internal cohesion gave them an unfair advantage in competition with the more individualistic Christians.[19]

In 1920, the *Independent* published the notorious *Protocols of the Learned Elders of Zion*. At the time, this tract was widely believed to be the working document of a Jewish cabal plotting world domination. In reality, the Paris branch of the Russian secret police had taken an original document drafted to discredit the Jesuits and redrafted it to throw suspicion on the Jews and their allies in the anti-czarist ranks. Of the twenty-four protocols, one is titled "The Tyranny of Usury." This protocol matter-of-factly describes how a state borrows money before purporting to explain how the dynamics of money lending have changed, seemingly as planned:

> So long as loans were internal the GOYIM only shuffled their money from the pockets of the poor to those of the rich, but when we bought up the necessary persons in order to transfer loans into the external sphere, all the wealth of States flowed into our cash-boxes and all the GOYIM began to pay us the tribute of subjects.[20]

If this sounds extreme today, in 1920—after a century of Rothschild dominance in European money markets—it did not. Had J. P. Morgan also been
Jewish, the paranoia that raged through Europe might have infected America
as well. But Morgan saved the day once more. The debate over whether consumers should indebt themselves remained secular and civil and was largely
settled by the end of the 1920s.

The June 1928 issue of *Century Magazine* relates a history of installment
credit that was both amusing and accurate. It tells the tale of the "Bad Boy"
of the business world known as "Instalment Buying," who was "despised
by his affluent brother Cash Down, and his more respectable cousin Charge
Account." After years of abuse, the tables turned.

> The Bad Boy grew up to be a fine member of society, and today leads the mer-
> chandising parade by many millions of dollars. He has changed his name and
> now appears in the best circles as the Acceptance or Finance Plan. . . . Scholarly
> economists laud his works; books are written about him, philosophies evolved,
> and he is gradually taking his place as a power in the land.[21]

By 1928, the spirit of borrowing to buy stuff had spilled over into Wall Street.
It was about to suffer a setback.

twenty-two

Expelling the Money Changers

IF THERE IS ANY ONE IMAGE THAT EVOKES THE OCCASIONAL WHIMSY OF the New Deal, it is this one: President Franklin Delano Roosevelt sitting in his bedroom with Secretary of the Treasury Henry Morgenthau Jr., deciding what the daily price of gold would be. Imagine an antsy Gene Wilder as Morgenthau and a capricious Zero Mostel as Roosevelt. The scene that follows is reportedly true:

> **FDR**: Now, Henry, how much should we hike gold today?
>
> **MORGENTHAU**: Uhhh, ten cents?
>
> **FDR**: Oh, Henry!
>
> **MORGENTHAU**: Fifteen cents?
>
> **FDR**: Let's go . . . twenty-one cents!
>
> **MORGENTHAU** (alarmed): Twenty-one cents?
>
> **FDR** (jauntily waving cigarette holder): Three times seven—it's a lucky number!

Said fallen away New Dealer Raymond Moley, in a wee bit of an understatement, "Roosevelt gravely marred his image as a responsible statesman, by the early-morning bedside guesses with Morgenthau about what the price of gold was to be that day."'[1]

Just five or so years earlier, America had sat astride the economic world, the repository of most of its gold and even more of its hope. The president at that time, Republican Calvin Coolidge, could not have differed more from FDR. In her breakthrough reassessment of the Depression, *The Forgotten Man*, Amity Shlaes nicely summarizes Silent Cal's humility and restraint: "Coolidge had long ago determined that the world would do better if he involved himself less."[2]

Presidential discretion, Coolidge believed, led to economic stability.[3] Businesses, he believed, welcomed an administration whose approach to its business clientele mirrored what consumers would later see in a 1970s-era Holiday Inn ad campaign: no surprises. Businesses could plan more confidently if they could trust their government. This strategy seemed to be working. As vice president under Harding, Coolidge had seen how the administration's hands-off approach to the downturn of 1920 had allowed businesses to cut their losses, trim their payrolls, and get back to work quickly. The years since had, by all accounts, been years of sustained and substantial growth, inspired in no small part by the explosive growth in the auto and radio industries.

As to the precipitating event that led to the crash of 1929, fingers point in a thousand directions, but a surprisingly high number of them point to still another private conclave among financial wizards, this one on the north shore of Long Island in August 1927.[4] In attendance were the chief central bankers from Germany, France, Britain, and the United States. Representing America was Benjamin Strong, president of the New York Federal Reserve and one of the Jekyll Island Six. Over the years, Strong had developed a deep personal relationship with Montagu Norman, the head of the Bank of England.

Not too long before the meeting, Britain had returned to the gold standard after a wild inflationary run during the Great War. Unwilling to accept a diminished pound, a symbol of its own humbled standing in the world, Britain had pegged its currency artificially high, but the world wasn't buying. Gold continued to flow into the United States. Norman leaned on his American friend to help prop up the British pound by lowering interest rates on U.S. Treasury bonds, thus making foreign investment here less attractive.

Strong knew the risks of obliging. The stock market was running hot as it was. Typically, lower interest rates stimulate borrowing for production and consumption and make stocks relatively more attractive than bonds. As Strong confided to the French representative, a rate cut would give the market "un petit coup de whiskey." But hey, what are friends for? A few days after the Long Island meeting, Strong overrode bitter resistance among his fellow Fed presidents and forced the rate down from 4.0 to 3.5 percent.

Morgan partner Russell Leffingwell was among those who had a squirrelly feeling about the meeting. "Monty and Ben sowed the wind," he said in March 1929, seven months before the crash. "I expect we shall have to reap the whirlwind. . . . I think we are going to have a world credit crisis."[5] In fact, stocks had begun the irrationally exuberant phase of their rally immediately after the rate cut in August 1927. This was not likely a coincidence. The Fed had helped turn a rally into a bubble.

This year, of course, also happened to be the year that E. R. A. Seligman had given his blessing to buying on time. In 1928, *Century Magazine* had proclaimed "credit" the cat's pajamas. When ordinary citizens discovered they could put as little as 10 percent down on a stock purchase and borrow the rest "on margin" in the anticipation that the rise in stock prices would pay the interest, they bulled through the financial china shops in unprecedented numbers. The story is told that financier Joe Kennedy grew wary of the market when he was offered a hot stock tip by a shoeshine boy.[6] With shoeshine boys buying in, Kennedy bailed out just in time.

This new consumer class, bootblacks and barbers and beekeepers, did not need much encouragement. As Charles Dickens had pointed out a century earlier, everyday Americans had a fondness for speculation and "smart dealing." By 1929, women had joined the ranks of investors. Although history has been oddly silent about their role in goosing the market, some one-third of the new speculators were female.[7] Brokers had taken to opening offices in New York's more fashionable shopping districts to attract their business. In August 1929, the *Ladies' Home Journal* published a feature on investing that might have served as a manifesto if its message—Everyone Ought To Be Rich—had not proved so unfashionable just three months later.

Of course, not everyone was keen on speculation. In February 1929, Alabama senator Tom Heflin introduced a resolution asking the Federal Reserve to tame the market. "Wall Street has become the most notorious gambling center in the universe,"[8] he thundered. But the hip new investor class did not exactly share this yokel's view that the stock market was a "monstrous evil." Meanwhile, the Fed—with its power divided between the regional presidents and the Washington governing board—dithered. The death of Benjamin Strong the year earlier had left a power vacuum that his successor, George Harrison, was never quite able to fill.

As early as 1925, Coolidge's activist commerce secretary Herbert Hoover had been warning against the dangers of speculation, but his concern had been premature. The market was not yet overheated. As Coolidge would say of "Boy Wonder" Hoover, "That man has offered me unsolicited advice for six years, all of it bad."[9]

Hoover's remarkable success had made him a know-it-all. Orphaned as a boy in Iowa and shipped out to his California relatives, Hoover had majored in geology and engineering at Stanford and within a few years of his graduation had virtually reinvented gold mining. His mastery of this art had become as hot a commodity as the gold he knew how to find. At the age of thirty, he was reportedly the highest-paid man of his generation. During and after World War I, Hoover single-handedly, or so it seemed, managed the massive food relief efforts throughout Europe. Author Sherwood Anderson would describe his face as that of a man who "had never known failure."[10] This was about to change.

The "standard history" of the Depression, as Shlaes notes, is that "Hoover made matters worse through his obdurate refusal to take control, his risible commitment to what he called rugged individualism. Roosevelt, however, made things better by taking charge. His New Deal inspired and tided the country over."[11] Only in the last few years has the grip of this history on our national consciousness begun to ease, and with good reason: the narrative is more false than true in every detail. Beyond that, it ignores the critical role of the Federal Reserve. As the events of 1987 proved, a market crash does not necessarily lead to depression, even recession. That it did in 1929 and thereafter owes more than a little to the misadventures of the still-learning Federal Reserve.

Sworn in as president eight months before the crash, Hoover contributed his own fair share to the unraveling, but not by being passive. Passivity was not his style. "Words are not of any great importance in times of economic disturbance," he announced. "It is action that counts."[12] Unfortunately, just about every action Hoover took proved to be the wrong one. He raised taxes, browbeat businesses into sustaining wages and employment, bullied the stock market, and signed into law the flamingly disastrous Smoot-Hawley Tariff Act of 1930, which triggered a fury of retaliatory measures around the world and sharply cut American exports as well as imports.

By and large, economists are as hard on the Federal Reserve as they are on Hoover.[13] They argue that the Fed was tightening the money supply when it should have been loosening it. The hard-money economists who make up the so-called Austrian school—Van Mises, Hayek, and their allies—dispute this interpretation. The Austrians argue that Hoover and the Fed tried their best to inflate, but that their efforts were "foiled by the good sense, and by the increasing distrust of the banking system, of the American people."[14] What seems beyond dispute is that, for whatever reason, the actual supply of money in the United States dropped by 4 percent between the end of 1928 and the end of 1930.[15]

In the place of a Morgan striding down Wall Street, solving problems as he strode, America got a Mexican standoff. The New York Fed, the regional banks, and their Washington overseers were all looking at each other and saying, "Now what?" The paralysis was obvious before the crash in the Fed's inconsistent response to an overheated market and even more obvious afterward.[16] Under Hoover and the Fed, the government had assumed for the first time the responsibility for the nation's prosperity. Profit, however, has a cool logic of its own that politicians have never quite understood.

The patrician Roosevelt did not even care to learn. In his March 1933 inaugural address, Roosevelt may have eased the fears of the ordinary citizens, but he intensified the fears of those he most needed to assuage, the investor class. "The rulers of the exchange of mankind's goods," he insisted, "have failed through their own stubbornness and their own incompetence."[17] From that day forward, no businessperson could anticipate FDR's market logic *du jour* any better than he could his gold price.

Although Roosevelt had several trusted Jewish advisors, Morgenthau among them, he seemed to have been dangling a little fresh Semitic meat in front of the inaugural crowd when he railed about "the unscrupulous money changers" who had brought America to its knees. According to Roosevelt, these "self-seekers" could only propose "the lending of more money" as solution to theirs and the nation's problems. To drive the point home about the evils of such wanton usury, he continued with an analogy that America's biblically literate population surely understood, "The money changers have fled their high seats in the temple of our civilization. We may now restore that temple to the ancient truths."[18]

Whether intentionally or not, Roosevelt was rephrasing the themes that Karl Marx had laid out in his treatise "On the Jewish Question." Marx, it should be recalled, saw salvation for Jews and for society at large only after society had "succeeded in abolishing the empirical essence of Judaism—huckstering and its preconditions."[19] Roosevelt was sophisticated enough to know that WASPs had as much financial clout as Jews. If not as explicitly as Marx, however, Roosevelt implied that there was something inherently Jewish about the source of that clout, "the mad chase of evanescent profits," and something inherently Christian about the "ancient truths." These Roosevelt described as "social values more noble than mere monetary profit."[20]

After describing a variety of actions to get people back to work, Roosevelt turned his inaugural sights once again on "the evils of the old order." That this order had made America so prosperous that its dispossessed Okies could drive their own cars to California was lost on Roosevelt and his allies. "There must be a strict supervision of all banking and credits and investments," he railed, fully ignoring the role of government in creating the mess he had inherited, "there must be an end to speculation with other people's money, and there must be provision for an adequate but sound currency."[21]

Roosevelt proved to have unusual ideas as to what exactly constituted a "sound currency," especially when it came to gold. Two days after the inauguration, he used the legal cover of the wartime Trading with the Enemy Act to declare war on those who were "hoarding" gold.[22] Three days later, he signed into law the Emergency Banking Act. This bill, which evoked unfond memories of John Law's tyrannical endgame in eighteenth-century France, gave FDR the authority to demand the surrender of all gold by American citizens in exchange for paper money. A month later, he set May 1, 1933, as the deadline for the surrender. As the conspiracy-minded noted, this just happened to be International Workers' Day in the socialist world. Those who failed to surrender their gold could face as many as ten years in prison.

The motive for the seizure of gold was simple enough. Roosevelt wanted to inflate the currency to appease the indebted, especially the farmers. If citizens had the right to redeem currency in gold, as they did under the gold standard, they would turn in their cheapened paper dollars for gold and withdraw the gold from circulation: Gresham's Law. So the Roosevelt administration criminalized the very possession of gold. In July 1933, Roosevelt denounced the gold standard as one of the "old fetishes" that needed to be replaced. In August 1933, FDR issued an executive order demanding that all U.S. gold producers sell their output to the secretary of treasury at a price that he (with his predilection for lucky numbers) and the secretary would determine.

"It may be that an unprecedented demand and need for undelayed action may call for temporary departure from that normal balance of public procedure,"[23] Roosevelt had promised in his inaugural. He was as good as his word. The civic strip mining of America's gold was executed without benefit of a single Congressional hearing. Needless to say, this process did not inspire a lot of confidence within the business community.

Roosevelt was just as adventurous on the banking front. Immediately upon taking office he ordered all banks that were closed to remain closed, even though he had no authority under the Constitution to do this. The Emergency Banking Act, which he had Congress pass immediately thereafter, gave him the power not only to close banks but also to print money wartime-style as he saw fit.

From day one, Roosevelt had done his best to dethrone the "privileged princes of these new economic dynasties,"[24] FDR-code for influential bankers. He joyfully imputed a feudal hauteur to their resistance. "These economic royalists complain that we seek to overthrow the institutions of America," he argued at the 1936 Democratic National Convention. "What they really complain of is that we seek to take away their power."[25]

Ironically, however, it was bankers like the Morgans who were diversified enough to weather the Depression and protect their depositors.[26] It was not economic royalism that led to the great majority of bank failures, but myopic legislation designed to protect local monopolies. Some 90 percent of failures occurred in states whose "unit" banking laws forbade banks from branching out beyond their base. Canada, which had no such laws, had no such problems. Those one-office banks that hung on clamored for federal deposit insurance to protect them against the self-defeating regulation that was making survival difficult.

In June 1933, Roosevelt signed into law the Glass-Steagall Act. In the apt words of author Michael Lewis, the act "cleaved mankind in two."[27] Banks now had to choose between investment and deposit banking. They could not do both. A classic in political scapegoating, the act rewarded those banks that had done the worst and punished the banks that had done the best. It provided deposit insurance for the struggling banks and forced the successful ones to divest their investment banking operations. As Morgan biographer Ron Chernow observes, "The Glass-Steagall Act took dead aim at the House of Morgan."[28]

The intellectual force behind much of this new legislation was Louis Brandeis. As a public advocate twenty years earlier, he had taken on the Morgan & Co. in its plan to expand the New Haven Railroad. Anticipating FDR, he argued that the company symbolized "a monopolistic and predatory control over the financial and industrial resources of the country"[29] and prevailed. Brandeis had counseled Woodrow Wilson in his 1912 run for the presidency and was rewarded with a seat on the Supreme Court, the first Jew so appointed.

Not overly squeamish about the separation of powers, Brandeis continued to advise presidents, Roosevelt included, using his daughter as a liaison to the president. The Morgans blamed Brandeis for Glass-Steagall. "I have little doubt that he inspired it, or even drafted it. The Jews do not forget. They are relentless," lamented Russell Leffingwell to his fellow Morgan partner Thomas Lamont in still another chapter of Wall Street's ongoing culture wars. "The reason why I make so much of this is that I think you underestimate the forces we are antagonizing."[30]

In 1934, a year after Glass-Steagall, the Morgans lobbied just as hard against the impending Securities Exchange Act, a sweeping piece of legislation that placed the sale of stocks and bonds under federal control. The Morgans argued that the proposed regulations would turn Wall Street into a "deserted village,"[31] but they did not deter Congress or the White House. To aggravate the Morgans all the more, Roosevelt named their old nemesis, Joe Kennedy, to be the first chairman of the Securities and Exchange Commission.

In 1935, forced to choose between deposit banking and investment banking, the house of Morgan shocked Wall Street by abandoning the side of the business that had made them rich and famous. Leffingwell explained his decision in a letter to Roosevelt, asking him to repeal Glass-Steagall: "Nobody can afford to be in the business unless he has a good bread and butter business to live on. A house exclusively in the underwriting business is under too much pressure to pay overhead and living issues to pick and choose the issues it will underwrite."[32]

A blue chip off the old block, thirty-four-year-old grandson Henry Morgan, along with partner Harold Stanley and a few others, split from the mother ship and in 1935 launched the investment banking house of Morgan Stanley. Within a year, the new firm had achieved nearly 25 percent market share in public offerings. Over the next seventy-five years, no investment bankers would do consistently better than Morgan Stanley. Not to worry: J. P. Morgan & Co. would be heard from again as well.

For all of the sound and fury of FDR's reign, and for all the soothing charm of his style, the New Deal did not deliver. And no one knew that better than an eventually disappointed Morgenthau. "We are spending more money than we have ever spent before and it does not work," he told a Congressional hearing in 1939. "I want to see this country prosperous. I want to see people get jobs. We have never made good on our promises. I say after eight years of this administration we have just as much unemployment as when we started and an enormous debt to boot."[33] In 1939, seventeen—as in a 17 percent unemployment rate—was no one's idea of a lucky number.

twenty-three

Holy Land

IN POST–CIVIL WAR AMERICA, THE ONLY DECADE MORE ANOMALOUS than the 1930s was the 1940s. For much of that decade, history skidded sideways, particularly the history of credit and debit. Ford was selling tanks and planes—more than four hundred B-24s in a single month—not Model As and Model Ts. There was only one buyer and no installment plans. Consumers were investing not in stocks and bonds but in War Bonds. Homes were not being built, let alone sold.

Most anomalous of all was the behavior of individual consumers: they were saving money in unprecedented amounts. The numbers astonish: personal savings rose from $3.8 billion in 1940 to $37.3 billion in 1944, a nearly tenfold increase.[1] Businesses were setting aside money as well. When the extreme fiscal and monetary policies of the wartime government righted themselves after the war, the cumulative savings of both individuals and business stimulated both investment and consumption. The Depression was not coming back.

The signs of regeneration were nowhere more obvious than in Southern California. In 1950, just south of Los Angeles and east of Long Beach, developers got to work on ten square miles of scrubland and lima bean fields. There they built an instant city and called it, for no apparent reason, Lakewood.

In the first ten months of Lakewood's existence, the developers sold 7,400 single-family homes. As Lakewood city administrator D. J. Waldie notes in his wonderful memoir, *Holy Land*, "Buyers needed only a steady job, and the promise they would keep up the payments."[2] The city of Lakewood was incorporated in 1954. By 1960, it would house 67,000 people, virtually every one of them in his or her own home.

The average age of the wives in that early 1950s wave of Lakewood home-buyers was twenty-six, the husbands thirty-two. Most of the men had served in World War II, Korea, or both. Many were the first members of their extended families to own their own homes. They had title to these houses due in no small part to the efforts of the federal government to put people in their own homes. Lakewood residents were not unique in this regard. Orange County, immediately to the south of Los Angeles County, would see its population swell from 200,000 people in 1950 to 2 million by 1980, and the majority of these people in their own homes as well.

In fact, the federal government had been in the home credit business since at least 1862, when President Lincoln signed the Homestead Act, a subtle anti-slavery bill that gave settlers free title to fifty acres of public land with the only condition being they live there and develop it. Although well intentioned, the act was exploited by a fair share of sharp dealers who hoped to cash in on government largesse. The act also put an awful lot of people into properties that they could not sustain. Do we see a pattern developing here? The homeowners most vulnerable were those on the Western plains, beyond dependable rainfall. The Depression-era Dust Bowl would send many of these families packing, and many of their children would find themselves homesteading with government help in places like Lakewood and Orange County.

The first president to make a serious effort at finding homes for the nation's nonfarm citizens was can-do Herbert Hoover. In fact, Hoover started his home-owning campaign while still secretary of commerce. "Nothing is worse than increased tenancy and landlordism,"[3] he preached. Living in a Hooverville, even without a landlord, might strike the residents thereof as a tad worse, but such independent living was still a few years away.

In 1922, Hoover launched the "Own Your Own Home" campaign, arguing that the homeowner tends to be happier and more productive than the renter.[4] For all his genius, Hoover failed to ask a question that has escaped lesser political lights as well: does home owning make people more happy and productive or are happy and productive people more likely to own homes?

Hoover's campaign, aided by new rules that allowed nationally chartered banks more latitude with home loans, resulted in a surge of home building. From mid-1927 to mid-1929, the mortgage lending of the national banks grew 45 percent. At the time, most home loans were relatively short-term. The borrower presumed that, if need be, he could refinance as the note came due. After the crash of 1929, however, the marginal borrowers that Hoover had prodded into home buying often lacked the wherewithal to refinance the homes he had prodded them to buy.

As the market froze, Hoover used his bully pulpit to try to warm it up, but this seemed no more effective than his earlier efforts to cool down an overheated Wall Street. In the process, he proved that presidential bluster was no match for market momentum. After a series of false starts, Hoover signed the Federal Home Loan Bank Act in 1932. Launched with a dozen banks and $125 million in capital, the FHLBank System was designed to provide funds to "building and loan" institutions so that they, in turn, could make mortgages available to consumers.[5] Sluggish even by federal standards, the program granted a total of three loans in its first two years. By 1933, despite Hoover's efforts or perhaps because of them, banks were foreclosing on some one thousand homes every day.

Upon taking office, Roosevelt found it more politic to assail the banks than to assess the role government had played in the housing crisis. More aggressive than Hoover, he and his administration launched the Home Owners' Loan Corporation (HOLC) in 1933 to make low-interest loans to families in danger of foreclosure, and followed that up with the more permanent Federal Housing Administration (FHA) in 1934.[6] Unlike the HOLC, the FHA did not make direct loans but instead guaranteed the loans that private commercial banks would make. Amidst the rash of New Deal programs, the FHA is among the few that actually seemed to work as planned.

In 1938, to assure that lending institutions had ample money to lend, the New Dealers launched the Federal National Mortgage Association (FNMA), affectionately known as Fannie Mae. Although it seems hard to believe today, for nearly the first seventy years of its existence Fannie Mae was, in fact, looked upon favorably. Fannie Mae's mission was to help keep lenders liquid by buying their loans and, for a small fee, assuming the risk of default. This service created what has come to be known as a secondary mortgage market.

In 1944, Congress enacted the Servicemen's Readjustment Act, which in turn begat the VA home loan, a program that in one mutation or another has helped put some eighteen million families in homes of their own. As with FHA loans, the government did not lend the money but rather guaranteed loans made by private mortgage lenders against loss of principal, were the veterans to default. No doubt many, if not most, of the first flush of Lakewood residents came wrapped in a government guarantee. In California, home ownership rates increased from 43 percent in 1940 to 58 percent in 1960, a figure just slightly below the national average of 61 percent.

The federal urge to put people in homes inevitably put pressure on housing prices. To continue to meet their political commitments, the VA and FHA began to loosen their lending standards. Loosening, of course, led to increased foreclosures. In 1960, FHA-insured loans were failing at five times the rate they were in 1950, and VA loans were failing at twice the rate.[7] The economy was not a factor: failures in conventional mortgages remained flat throughout the decade. Traditional lenders had stuck to their underwriting standards.

The civil rights movement put more pressure still on lenders. Beginning in the 1960s, they would be asked to factor in the would-be borrowers' cultural variables, not just their creditworthiness. Washington presumed that lenders, if not watched closely, would ignore their own best interests and discriminate willy-nilly against certain minorities. Private lenders, as well as the FHA and VA, were routinely accused of "red-lining," that is, consciously denying loans to those who lived in predominantly black neighborhoods.

The statistics, however, tell a more interesting story. Between 1940 and 1960, for instance, the period when red-lining was allegedly epidemic, home-ownership increased substantially across the board—by 24.2 percentage points among whites and by 18.6 among blacks. As is obvious, white ownership rates did increase faster during this period, but as a Vanderbilt University study notes, "Controlling for factors other than race eliminated nearly all of the increase in the gap between 1940 and 1960."[8]

The primary reason for the increased gap was obvious to anyone who wanted to see: the vast migration of blacks from the South, where home-ownership rates were high, to the central cities of the North, where home-ownership rates were low among all races. Between 1960 and 1980, home-ownership rates increased among blacks more quickly than among whites and almost as quickly as charges of red-lining. The perception that banks routinely discriminated against blacks, even in the face of numbers to the contrary, would shape lending practices in the years to come with less-than-optimal results.

To narrow the home-ownership gap, the Lyndon Johnson administration took its War on Poverty into the housing market. In 1968 new legislation enabled poor families to receive FHA-insured loans with down payments as low as $250.[9] With the lure of FHA-backed loans, and occasionally with the help of well-greased FHA inspectors, smart-dealing real estate agents were then able to finesse low-income minorities into homes they could not afford to keep up.

Many of the new homeowners were not nearly ready to own a home. Single mothers, for instance, received some 20 percent of these mortgages in already vulnerable cities like Philadelphia and Detroit. Since roughly 1960, the federal government had been on an unwitting campaign to drive fathers from the home. That was the year that the Aid to Dependent Children Program became the Aid *to Families* with Dependent Children, or, more realistically, Aid to *Moms* with Dependent Children. A working dad at home did not fit the state definition of family. In 1964 the Feds sweetened the pot for forsaken moms with food stamps and in 1965 with Medicaid.

Foreclosures followed in record numbers—Philadelphia had more in three years of this program than it had in the previous thirty-three with FHA loans. When foreclosures reached critical mass, neighborhoods turned into ghettos. When aspiring arsonists learned just how much fun it was to watch abandoned buildings burn, ghettos turned into kindling.

"The program could not work," Harvard historian Louis Hyman recently commented, "because it tried to solve a problem of wealth creation through debt creation."[10] This much should have been obvious at the time, but when a road to a particular hell is paved with good intentions, there is no turning back the hell-bound.

Single motherhood was not unique to the poor and/or black. As it often did, California was paving a new road, if not to hell, at least to purgatory. In 1953, when *Harper's Magazine* asked the young homemakers of Lakewood what they missed most in moving there, they usually replied, "My mother."[11] So many of these young families were so removed from their roots that they did not have a close friend or relative in the same time zone. When familial tension built, there was often no one there to mediate it.

Divorce was spreading like Continental dollars. In 1969, rather than stabilize the currency, the state abandoned the band-of-gold standard and introduced no-fault divorce. Bad marriages promptly drove out the good. In 1970, the first full year of the no-fault law, the state registered a record 112,942 divorces—a 38 percent increase from just the year before.[12] In 1960, there had been only 105,352 *marriages* in California. Population growth—27 percent for the decade—accounts for some of the discrepancy, but the marriage/divorce ratio, no matter what the qualifiers, signaled a massive disruption in family life.

By 1980, California had registered a new record: 138,361 divorces. In other words, more than 276,000 Californians got divorced in 1980 alone. That was more than twice as many as in 1966, and in 1966, the California divorce rate was already 50 percent higher than the national norm. The nation, however, was eager to catch up. By 1985, just about every state in the union had adopted no-fault divorce in one form or another, with predictable results. By 1980, the nation's divorce rate was higher than California's was in 1969. Embarrassed by its own numbers, California stopped tracking divorces after 1980. By the year 2000, only 57 percent of the homes in the still functional Lakewood had a married couple dwelling within, and by California standards, that was high.

The results of these trends were not immediately obvious. The effect of divorce and single motherhood on home owning was something the chattering classes chose not to chatter about. Like an unpaid debt, these were worries that would be passed down to the next generation.

twenty-four

The Market's Fools

ON OCTOBER 6, 1979, PAUL VOLCKER, THE NEWLY APPOINTED CHAIRMAN
of the Federal Reserve—and at six foot seven the only one who could dunk
a basketball—made a short speech that rocked the economic world. Volcker
announced that after several years of economic malaise and high inflation,
the money supply would no longer fluctuate with the business cycle: the Fed
would fix the money supply and allow interest rates to float.[1] This move, which
increased the allowable range in the federal fund rate from 11.5 percent to 15.5
percent, had some totally unexpected consequences.

On Main Street, where many savings-and-loan associations were actually
located, the news hit hard. Protected by the federal government more vigilantly
than bald eagles or Chinook salmon, S&Ls, often called *thrifts*, stumbled into the
mid-1970s with some 53 percent of the nation's home mortgage market.[2] The
reason for their success was simple enough: the Federal Reserve, in an effort to
pump more money still into the swelling mortgage market, allowed them to pay
higher interest than commercial banks. Congress also provided deposit insurance
for the thrifts and carved out various tax loopholes. Home ownership was, after
all, an American birthright. On the downside, for no reason anyone could remember, thrifts were not allowed to offer checking accounts or invest in anything but
home mortgages. The government giveth. The government taketh away.

As a consequence, until the mid-1970s at least, running an S&L had been no more challenging than chairing the local Rotary, which many thrift presidents actually did. Within the industry, these gents were said to belong to the 3-6-3 club: borrow money at 3 percent, lend at 6 percent, tee off by 3 p.m.[3] Double-digit interest rates threw this whole understanding out of whack. When the 3-6-3 clubbers found themselves in a 12-10-whenever world, they stopped making home loans. It made no sense to lend at 10 percent if they had to borrow at 12. In the three years after the Volcker speech nearly 25 percent of the nation's four thousand thrifts collapsed.

On Wall Street, however, bond traders had not heard news this good since V-J Day. By allowing the interest rates to swing within a broad range, the Fed assured that bond prices would swing as well—inversely in lockstep to rates of interest. Suddenly, investors looked at bonds with fresh eyes, seeing them not just as repositories of wealth, but as generators of the same.[4] In a veritable eyeblink, Volcker had turned the bond market from a sleepy backwater into the Bellagio Las Vegas. Better still, by getting the money supply under control and reining in inflation, the Fed helped turn credit into the world's greatest growth industry. Between 1977 and 1985, the combined indebtedness of American governments, corporations, and consumers increased by an incredible factor of twenty.[5] Most of that money was filtered through Wall Street.

Not all Wall Street was celebrating, however. The Volcker move brought only gloom to the Medici quarter at Salomon Brothers. That Salomon's Italians would be relegated to a ghetto within the historically Jewish firm shows just how entertaining a country America can be. The larger story begins in 1910, when the original Salomon brothers—Arthur, Herbert, and Percy—split from their dad, lured away his clerk, and opened a small office on Broadway near Wall Street.[6] They soon recruited a Baltimore department-store tycoon as partner, largely for his seat on the Stock Exchange.

By this time, Jewish bankers of German origin—Abraham Kuhn, Solomon Loeb, Joseph Seligman, the Lehman Brothers, Marcus Goldman and his son-in-law Samuel Sachs—had very nearly reached white shoe status on Wall Street. Their heirs thought of the humble Salomon brothers and their successors as tradesmen and treated them accordingly. Though resentful of the treatment, Salomon execs took pride in their scrappy, black-shoe backgrounds. The image the firm projected, writes Salomon bond-salesman-turned-author Michael

Lewis was "of clannish Jews, social nonentities, shrewd but honest, sinking its nose more deeply into the bond markets than any other firm cared to."[7]

In the late 1970s, Robert Dall, one of those Salomon partners nostril-deep in bonds, sniffed out a mother lode of possibility. Although Wall Street had historically brought borrowers and lenders together, its wise men had somehow overlooked the single greatest stash of capital in America: home loans. The stash had grown from $55 billion in 1950 to $700 billion in 1976 without anyone mining its riches.[8] By the time of Volcker's speech in 1979, the home mortgage industry had passed the trillion-dollar mark and surpassed the New York Stock Exchange as the largest capital market in the world.[9]

Finding gold was one thing. Extracting it was another. The Government National Mortgage Association—Ginnie Mae—had discovered the truth of this some years earlier. Spun out of Fannie Mae's side in 1968, Ginnie Mae bundled the home mortgages of the least affluent homeowners and sought to sell them as bonds, the only mortgage-backed securities guaranteed by the federal government.[10]

In 1970, Salomon partner (and later treasury secretary) William Simon, had a dustup with Ginnie Mae. This fully federal entity would not correct what Simon saw as the security's fatal flaw: the ability of the homeowner to prepay his mortgage. A purchaser of a long-term bond wanted the assurance that the bond would pay a given return throughout its specified life. If, however, homeowners could pay off their mortgages when interest rates dipped and refinance at a lower rate, the bondholder could be left with cash in a low-interest environment. Institutional buyers, in particular, had little interest in bonds of unknown maturity.

While Simon ignored the Ginnie Maes, Dall, who worked under Simon, started dabbling. He quickly saw the untapped potential in home loans, and in 1977 he and a colleague persuaded Bank of America to package its home loans in the form of a bond, the first private issue of mortgage securities. They then persuaded investors that these bonds had a high enough yield and a low enough risk to offset the prepay liability. They attracted enough attention within the firm that Salomon Brothers established a separate mortgage department in 1978, the first on Wall Street.

In 1970, the government had launched the semiprivate Federal Home Loan Mortgage Company, or Freddie Mac, to compete with the semiprivate Fannie

Mae and create a more competitive secondary mortgage market. Now, with Salomon Brothers in the game, there was a fully private player in the secondary market to complement these government-sponsored enterprises, or GSEs. And unlike the GSEs, Salomon Brothers could deal in what are called nonconforming loans—loans either too large or too risky to conform to GSE standards.

Dall knew he would need a hard-nosed trader to make the operation work, and he got his first pick, thirty-year-old Lewie Ranieri. The Brooklyn-born Ranieri stepped into the mortgage department straight out of central casting. A college dropout, he had begun just ten years earlier as a seventy-dollar-a-week night shift clerk in Salomon's mailroom.[11] He did his job well, got promoted, seized opportunities, and soon enough found himself on Salomon's trading floor—sloppy, loud, fat, effective, and unabashedly Italian.

When Dall took ill, Ranieri took over the department and started hiring loyalists from the back office—John D'Antona, Peter Marro, Bill Esposito, Ron Dipasquale, Michael Mortara. No fool, Ranieri hired the occasional whiz kid, often Jewish, out of Wharton or wherever, not to appease his bosses, but to do the math. In the streets of Brooklyn, Jews and Italians had often collaborated in the loan business—Italians typically on the collection side of the industry. On Wall Street, at least, their collaboration was legal. Oddly enough, at Salomon it would be left to Ranieri and family to uphold the firm's streetwise Jewish heritage.

For the first year or two, few begrudged the Italians their fiefdom because no one was getting rich or close to it. Home loans, no matter how pretty the package, were a tough sell. When Volcker allowed interest rates to range upward in October 1979, the selling got much tougher at every level of the mortgage market. New home starts tanked and so did Ranieri's business. So sluggish was his operation that Salomon management started making noise about shutting it down. Meanwhile, the mortgage departments of would-be competitors—Merrill Lynch, First Boston, Goldman Sachs—died aborning. More stubborn than prescient, Ranieri hung on and ended with the kind of autonomy granted only to the ignored and irrelevant.

On September 30, 1981, the government gaveth once more. To rescue the floundering thrifts, Congress passed a generous and complicated tax break. As exploited, it allowed the thrifts huge tax write-offs, but only if they sold off their old loans. Sunbelt thrifts had little money and lots of demand. Rust

Belt thrifts had lots of money and little demand. It made sense for the Rust Belters to supply needed cash to the Sunbelters by buying their mortgages.[12] Everyone wanted to trade, and the hottest exchange in town was *chez* Lewie.

Amazingly, Ranieri and his crew were unaware of the legislation until after it had passed.[13] For them, it was like Christmas morning, and they had found a pony under the tree—it was that serendipitous. With only half an idea of what he was doing, some congressional staffer had just created the greatest market in the history of Wall Street and, oh yes, planted the seed for the eventual destruction of the American economy. But in 1981, who knew?

The 3-6-3 guys were to Ranieri's crew what H. G. Wells's soft-boiled Eloi were to the omnivorous Morelocks—lunch, or what Wall Street calls the market's fools. On more than one occasion, Ranieri had to scold a trader for making too good a deal at the expense of some utterly clueless thrift exec.[14] Not all the execs were clueless, of course, but even the savvy ones had to play to keep their doors open. If they sensed they were just pushing their problems down an unknown road, they felt they had little choice but to do so.

By decade's end, of course, the whole system would implode at great expense to the taxpayer. Said the head of the Resolution Trust Corporation, the entity created to clean up the S&L mess, "[The government] provided them with such perverse incentives that if I were to defend the S&L gang in court, I'd use the defense of entrapment."[15]

The same year that Congressional manna descended on Salomon Brothers, 1981, the firm morphed from partnership to corporation. This was something of a trend on Wall Street, and it had its critics. Wall Street legend—and Salomon veteran—Henry Kaufman was not alone in regretting the change of culture. "The trust and intimacy that once typified relations between investment banks and their clients," he observed, "has been supplanted by a transaction-driven ethic that favors profit maximization at every turn."[16]

Michael Lewis, who worked for Salomon in the mid-'80s, came to a similar conclusion, phrased a bit more succinctly: "Short-term greed," he reckoned, was driving out "long-term greed."[17] In his best-selling satire of 1980s New York, *Bonfire of the Vanities*, Tom Wolfe heard the mantra of the traders at the barely fictionalized Salomon Brothers as "Make it now!"[18]

The shift to corporate management had as a side effect the shift of knowledge and power from the vested top to the ambitious middle. This shift was enhanced—or aggravated, depending on one's perspective—by the advent of personal computing in the early 1980s.[19] The young guys coming out of grad school—and in the mortgage department at Salomon they were all guys until 1986—began to invent unholy new ways to subdivide the mortgage pie.

The inventors schemed to lessen the effect of loan prepayment, the possibility of which made mortgages unreliable income generators. In 1983, First Boston beat Salomon to the punch and created perhaps the most important financial innovation of the 1980s—the collateralized mortgage obligation (CMO). To put a CMO together, an investment house would gather multi-millions of dollars of ordinary mortgage bonds—Ginnie Maes, Freddie Macs, Fannie Maes—and place them in a trust. The investment bankers would then sell interest-earning shares in the trust in certificate form. These were the CMOs. This part is all straightforward enough.

Where the CMO got tricky and interesting was when the pool was subdivided into what are called tranches (rhymes with launches). Although there are any number of ways to structure a CMO—or, more generically, a CDO, "collateralized debt obligation"—a common one was to divide a mortgage pool into three tranches based on risk exposure: senior, mezzanine, and equity. All tranches would receive interest payments from the assembled loans, but the investors in the senior tranche would receive all of the principal paid in by all the mortgage holders in the pool until their principal was repaid. Only then would the principal be repaid to those in the mezzanine tranche and, after them, those in the equity tranche.[20] The lower tranches offered higher reward for added risk.

Investors in a senior tranche faced minimal risk and consequently received minimal reward, usually just slightly more yield than a U.S. Treasury bond. Importantly, this process also shortened the life of the senior tranche in a fairly predictable way, all but negating the nagging unpredictability of the prepaid mortgage. This restructuring had astonishing effects. The certainty and security of the CMO unleashed the market potential of the home loan in ways that few anticipated.

As an aside, the reader who finds this explanation hard to follow ought not feel abashed. Wall Street veterans like Henry Kaufman were warning early on that these products were "too complex to be understood by those who trade them."[21] Confirms Michael Lewis, "Across Wall Street, CEOs have made this little leap of faith about the manner in which their traders are making money, because they don't fully understand what their traders are doing."[22]

Roger Lowenstein of the *New York Times* made a good effort at illuminating the process by tracking one particular bundle of 2,393 loans with a total face value of $430 million. Lowenstein followed the loans from their origination at an unnamed "nonbank lender" to a New York investment bank, which packaged them, to the analyst's desk at Moody's, the rating service where they were evaluated.[23]

Moody's had access to aggregate data on the loans and the borrowers but not to the loan files. Using historical performance criteria, its analysts assessed which percent of the loans were subprime, where the loans originated, what kind of loans were involved, and other relevant data before rating *not the loans themselves*, but the bonds issued by the "special purpose vehicle" that the investment bank had created to house the loans.

To get an investment grade rating for at least some of its bonds, the investment bank sliced this bundle into twelve classes. The upper classes, the ones that were to get repaid first, Moody's rated triple-A, even though this particular bundle of loans was all subprime (and more on that phenomenon later).

The asset-backed securities described above derive their value from real assets, namely, the mortgages of actual homeowners. A CMO is one step further removed from reality. Investors do not buy mortgages. They buy bonds that are based on mortgages, these sliced into tranches and evaluated tranche by tranche by the rating agencies.

Although the assembly of a CMO is somewhat less complicated than that of an atom bomb, the CMO has potentially greater fallout, having value only to the degree that investors value it. Typically, investors purchased senior tranche CMOs because they promised a higher return than Treasury bonds with only slightly more risk. If, say, 2 percent of the loans in that mortgage pool default, the CMO has not necessarily lost 2 percent of its value. It may have lost 20 percent of its value or more. A sudden uptick in defaults would make the market jittery and the security suddenly toxic. No one may want to purchase a low-yield asset with high-risk exposure.

Ironically, investment houses like Salomon put CMOs together with the avowed intention of minimizing investor risk. To further reduce risk, they offered insurance policies against loss to buyers of a senior tranche. Known as credit default swaps (CDS), these policies proved highly popular in the home loan gold rush.[24] As secure as the home mortgage business had historically been, the issuers of CDSs thought they had found a perfectly legal way to print money. There were no messy fires or car crashes or suicides to adjudicate. The insured paid in and the insurers cashed out. Although complex, insurers had confidence in their own smarts, and of course, no insurer was smarter than AIG.

Complicating matters is that the primary purchasers of CMOs, CDOs, and credit default swaps have been the hedge funds. These largely unregulated investment groups owe their name to their historic strategy of hedging a "long" position by buying comparable stocks short. Although hedge funds have continued to employ long-short strategies, they have helped pioneer countless new ways to slice and dice debt. A loss in a hedge fund investment can ripple through the financial system because most such purchases are highly leveraged.[25] In other words, a hedge fund partnership often increases its investment by a factor of five or ten by borrowing the additional money from a bank. In short, when a hedge fund tanks, a lot of people get nervous.

Meanwhile back at Salomon, its heady traders made a killing in the CMO revolution, at least for a while. The problem was that the CMO had standardized the packaging of home loans and turned it into just another bond that could be priced and traded on the open market.[26] Ranieri and his dropout colleagues were losing market share. All that accrued backslapping knowledge of buyers and sellers was depreciating in value. Ascendant now were the Ivy League PhDs who were packaging home loans in a thousand different ways and turning old-school horse-trading into something like a science. To end run regulation and attract new business, investment houses, Salomon included, were hiring these rocket scientists and paying them in a good year what they had paid their fathers in a lifetime.

In the rush to modernity, the new corporate Salomon was also purging its streetwise Jewish heritage, the last defenders of which were, of all people, the Ranieri crew. In July 1987, Salomon fired Ranieri, the firm's best earner in the previous decade. The family followed in quick order—Mortara, D'Antona, Dipasquale, Marro, Gonella. The lone member of the crew left on the mortgage trading desk, Paul Longenotti, showed up at work one day after the purge wearing a button that said, "Fire me, I'm Italian."[27] Only in America.

twenty-five

Membership Has Its Privileges

IN 1946 OR 1947, THE DATE IS IN SOME DISPUTE, A FELLOW NAMED JOHN Biggins, about whom little is known, introduced an item that would pump fresh new blood into American finance. Biggins worked for the Flatbush National Bank of Brooklyn. There he got it into his head that if customers were given a bank card, and that card allowed them to charge items at various stores, the bank would build loyalty among the customers and merchants both. Biggins called the card Charg-It, and, without fanfare, introduced the first universal credit card.[1] True, the universe extended only to stores within a two-block radius of the bank, but it was a start.

Within a few years, banks across the country were experimenting with credit cards. The first bank to explore its potential in a big way was Amadeo Giannini's Bank of America, which launched the awkwardly named BankAmericard in 1958.[2] The card's acceptance throughout California led the bank to embark on a regional strategy. Among its licensees was Seafirst Bank in Seattle. When a free spirit named Dee Hock came to work for Seafirst in 1968, he discovered that Seafirst was actually losing money on the card. The technology was primitive. The accounting was messy. And fraud was rampant among customers, merchants, and criminals alike.

At a BankAmericard convention in Ohio, Hock rallied his fellow licensees, all as frustrated as he was, to form a cooperative. Over the next ten years, he led the charge for technological and accounting upgrades. He also made a branding recommendation that stuck: replacing the ungainly BankAmericard with the sleek and sophisticated Visa, the card that puts you "everywhere you want to be."

Although Hock understood that profit was what kept a bank's doors open, profit was not what drove him. A true visionary, he was intrigued by the idea of electronic money. He saw it as a way to liberate the ordinary Joe from the physical restraints that cash imposed: the need to extract it from suspicious bankers, to have it handy at all times, to carry large sums when away from home in case of emergency. Hock and his fellow pioneers, like Citibank's Walter Wriston, were about to change all that.

What Hock could not anticipate was the role that credit cards would come to play in a still inchoate anti-debt revival. In the absence of universal Christian sanctions, Catholic or Protestant, this revival would be wholly secular, but its leaders would be no less zealous than Luther, Calvin, or Savonarola. Before the advent of the universal credit card, twentieth-century America had, of course, seen sporadic attacks on the peddlers of debt, but the credit card gave focus to those attacks. In the financial morality play of postindustrial America, if the user were Everyman, the credit card dispenser would embody greed, the only one of the seven deadly sins that social puritans cannot abide.

These secular moralists go about their business with the charm and detachment of New England divines preaching infant damnation. Yet for all their grim preachiness, social puritans have been remarkably successful in spreading their message and enforcing their themes. Virtually every media news story on credit cards adheres to their template: consumer starts innocently; card company lures consumer; consumer dabbles; consumer has crisis; consumer turns to credit cards; consumer gets hooked; card company harasses consumer; consumer goes bankrupt; consumer accepts minimal blame; reporter exonerates consumer; reporter condemns card company. If this paradigm sounds familiar, recall the century-old advice of anti-usurer Dr. George Bush, who compared debt to a serpent's bite "often so small as to be scarcely perceptible at first, yet the venom soon spreads and diffuses itself till it reaches the vitals."[3]

Such profiles may concede some responsibility to the consumers in their card usage, but almost never do they question the lifestyle choices that left them vulnerable. Social puritans can be remarkably singular in their zeal. Many recognize no other sin, admonish no other behavior, crusade against no other evil than the promiscuous dispensing of credit.

Among the high priests in the unorganized and unrecognized social puritan movement is one Robert Manning, the author of the influential 2000 best seller *Credit Card Nation* and the custodian of the Web site of that same name. Playing to a crowd that styles itself nonjudgmental on any other subject, on the subject of credit cards he and his audience can be as self-righteous as a boatload of Venetian monks. Words like *insidious, usurious, punitive,* and *credit-gouging* pepper the book.

The stories that Manning tells flip the Tolstoy maxim that "happy families are all alike; every unhappy family is unhappy in its own way." In the Manning retelling it is the unhappy, bankrupt families that are all oddly alike. Take the case of Catherine, a fiftyish policy grunt in the New York City mayor's office. Catherine has grown up in a household where personal debt is seen as a moral failing, "a kind of Jewish Calvinist guilt thing."[4]

After graduating from college debt-free and working in publishing, Catherine returns to graduate school "as a means for personal advancement that would enable her to avoid debt."[5] She has a stipend, but then the seemingly unexpected happens: the tuition increases and her scholarship is reduced. She turns to her credit cards. At a friend's suggestion, she wraps her credit card debt into a student loan and reduces her interest from 18 percent to 3 percent. At the time, Catherine "thought she had made the right decision."[6] That the taxpayer was now subsidizing her credit card debt troubles neither her nor Manning.

After grad school, Catherine goes to work for a nonprofit, presumably in development. This job demands "champagne taste with a draft-beer pocket-book."[7] She honors that demand with credit cards. When the inflation of the late 1970s sets in (1975–79 annual average: 8.06 percent), she concludes that spending is the only way to beat the system. "Those macroeconomic circumstances profoundly influenced her decision to abandon the cognitive connect between earnings and consumption,"[8] writes Manning, as though inflation had reached the disorienting levels of Weimar Germany, where it took a wheelbarrow full of cash to buy a loaf of bread. As addicted to hyperbole as Catherine was to credit, Manning claims that this short-lived "age of inflation" spelled an end to the "Puritan work ethic" in general.

In any case, Catherine loses her job, moves in with her parents, and then marries a Middle Easterner. "After a year," Manning writes blithely, "irreconcilable cultural differences led to divorce."[9] Now it is back to grad school for another master's, more student loans, more credit card debt; then a career shift, more graduate school, more loans, more debt, a recession that stymies her job search; then in the early 1990s, a job with a salary that cannot "keep up with inflation" (1992–95 annual average: 2.85 percent), more credit card debt. In 1996, a year when employers were scrambling to find workers, "the nonprofit sector was implementing serious budget cuts."[10] Catherine loses her job, and the credit card companies turn on her.

Finally (reluctantly, of course), Catherine decides on bankruptcy. She reasons, with Manning's tacit approval, "Why should I feel so bad after all the S&Ls that went broke and the corporations that filed for bankruptcy?" The one catch is those seemingly benign student loans. The bankruptcy court won't discharge them. Still, she finds a decent job and a rent-controlled apartment. Were it not for that apartment, says Catherine, who has obviously become accustomed to living on other people's money, "I would be leading the workers' revolution. . . . There is no way a single woman can survive on my salary and pay a market-rate rent in New York City."[11]

Catherine was one of literally millions in the late 1990s who contributed to an unprecedented phenomenon: a dramatic spike in bankruptcies during a period that even Manning concedes was one of "economic prosperity and low unemployment."[12] He offers no explanation for this rise other than the "lax lending policies of the banking industry that offered easy consumer credit to increasingly higher-risk, lower-income workers."[13]

The role of divorce, delayed marriages, single motherhood, and a media that elevates prodigals to victims does not seem to factor in. From Manning's perspective, that single women were "the fastest-growing subgroup"[14] among the bankrupt is merely further proof of their exploitation by the banking industry. Nowhere does he acknowledge the hell that banks would pay if they were more selective and that selectivity led to "disparate outcomes" along race and gender lines, as it inevitably would.

Protected by the media, social puritans do not feel obliged to think through their positions. On the one hand, Manning chastises banks for making credit too accessible. On the other, he laments the fact that "low-income minorities, new immigrants, and the struggling lower middle class" are finding access to banks "increasingly difficult."[15]

Those denied credit are condemned to a world of payday loans, pawnshops, rent-to-own stores, and loan sharks, a world in which even Manning admits the 19.9 percent APR of a Citibank Visa begins to look attractive. He argues that the cost of credit to these people represents a "new feature of social inequality," unaware, obviously, that reformers have been making this same argument for the last three millennia. Like most such reformers, he ignores the risk factors that drive up credit costs to the poor. But then again, he pretty much ignores the poor. They net one page in a four-hundred-page book, credit cards being a sexier subject altogether.

The credit card epidemic, Manning assures the reader, is so virulent that not even the "spiritually guided" are immune.[16] To prove his point he cites the case of one Reverend Robert Trache. Appointed the Episcopal bishop of Atlanta in the year 2000, Trache had to withdraw when his superiors learned he had recently been "overwhelmed with the worldly affairs of personal finance"[17] and forced to file for bankruptcy. This case, Manning tells us, belies the stereotype of the irresponsible, spiritually adrift credit card abuser.

Trache, however, tells a different story. In a recent interview, he claims that he "had to withdraw because my marriage was in trouble," adding, "I'm on my second marriage now."[18] Not exactly old school, he says that the two historical people he would most like to meet are Henry VIII and Mary Magdalene—"I believe Jesus learned a lot from her"—and the purpose of religion is to "discover the interconnectedness between people and the universe."[19] Trache may belie some stereotypes, but that of spiritually grounded Christian is not one of them.

Manning concedes there are consumers "on the Puritan side of the moral divide."[20] These people adhere to a traditional ethic, reject the seductions of the banks, and pay their credit card bills at the end of each month. Manning has mixed feelings about this lot. After a grudging bit of left-handed praise, he scolds them for "tak[ing] advantage of the punitive social underpinnings of the moral divide as convenience users."[21] To reinforce his point, he adds that bankers "disdainfully" refer to such people as "deadbeats." In the real world, a more accurate adverb would be *ironically*.

In researching his book and documentary of the same name—*Maxed*

Out—James Scurlock made a pilgrimage to Manning's office at the Rochester Institute of Technology. Although Scurlock has a redeeming sense of humor and a bit more detachment, he largely accepts Manning's contention that the financial industry is to blame for the indebtedness of so many Americans and the death of the Puritan ethic.

In the same paragraph that Scurlock chides Citibank's Walter Wriston for his "disregard of history," he celebrates those "stodgy old bankers whose fathers and grandfathers had warned them about the need for regulation—the ones who were quite comfortable operating the small banks in the small towns and granting credit to individuals only with great caution."[22]

In truth, bankers have always resented regulation except, as is only natural, when it benefits them. It was the small-town bankers, after all, who pushed for unit-banking legislation to protect their local monopolies. Unfortunately, the legislation left them without diversified resources when the Depression hit, and they failed in great numbers. In truth, too, customers have always resented bankers who would deny them their dreams. Has there been a bank lobby scene in any movie in which the naysaying banker is portrayed as something other than a judgmental prig?

Like Manning, Scurlock celebrates a history that did not exist. Like Manning, too, he singles out financial freedom as the one freedom that should be denied Americans, especially American youth. Bizarrely, the same people who insist that adolescents should be able to drive, drink, cohabit, vote, and get an abortion without their parent's consent are horrified when a bank sends these kids a credit card application.

Among the stories that Scurlock tells, all of which hold to the social puritans template, is that of Elizabeth Warren, a professor at Harvard Law and a crusader for bankruptcy rights. In the late 1990s she had been tasked with discovering why so many Americans were going bankrupt during a time of seeming prosperity. She had presumed the answer would be too many people spending irresponsibly for too many unnecessary goods.

What she found was "shocking," at least to Scurlock. "The most reliable predictor of whether someone would declare bankruptcy," he continues, "wasn't the number of credit cards or the pairs of shoes in the closet, it was whether or not they were females. And then whether or not that woman had a child."[23]

A traditionalist would be inclined to address the underlying problem:

women, often with children, making their way through life without husbands and the financial protection they provide. For the social puritans, the phenomenon of single women with children is not inherently a problem. The problem is that greedy bankers seduce these women with easy credit, and then mean-spirited public officials deny them easy bankruptcy. In pitch-perfect social puritan patois, Scurlock lays the problem off on a capitalism that "worked for a long time but that has been released from its tethers and has mutated into a relentlessly efficient and voracious machine."[24]

A traditionalist like Michael Novak would counter that democratic capitalism works best when all of its agents assume responsibility. "How can a people govern a whole society," he asks, "that cannot, each of them, govern themselves?"[25]

twenty-six

The Greed Decade

THE SO-CALLED GREED DECADE FULFILLED ITS CINEMATIC POTENTIAL on the evening of September 15, 1986. The setting was the bar mitzvah of the thirteen-year-old son of real estate developer Gerald Guterman.[1] The lad was named Jason, as was every other thirteen-year-old in America in 1986. Guterman was also celebrating, however belatedly, the bat mitzvahs of his two daughters by a previous marriage—and in 1986 who did not have at least one previous marriage?

This was not your grandfather's bar mitzvah. As befitted a decade of excess, Guterman had rented the QE2 and its thousand-person crew at a price approaching one million dollars for an overnight, forty-six–mile "cruise to nowhere." This price did not include the hiring of the Peter Duchin orchestra or the services of Stu Feinstein, one of America's premier party planners. Feinstein, in fact, still ranks this event number one among the top ten events he has ever planned.

"The Guterman's [sic] had simply instructed me to create unique surprises and total fun," he notes on his Web site. "I armed myself with a 40+ member ensemble from Le Clique, 200 costumes and props and total artistic freedom. Our goal was to help convert this excursion into a fantasy voyage of epic proportions. We had a ball!"[2] To pull this off, Feinstein had to corner New York's entire mime market for the weekend, a break for the city at large.

At the actual ceremony, the hired rabbi sang the praises of Jason's parents. "In a home that has everything," he said, "Linda and Gerry also stress to their children that which gives us purpose."[3] Given the circumstances, the guests had to wonder what the "that" could possibly have been. They were not likely to learn from the evening's most special guest. Having intentionally missed the launch, he descended onto the ship in a twin-engine helicopter and stepped out in black tie and tails to a swell of laughter and applause. Ace arbitrageur Ivan Boesky had arrived.

"Don't ever use my helicopter again for a stunt like this," a friend scolded Boesky after the fact. "Revolutions are made of this. People get put in gas ovens."[4] The friend would have been even more disturbed had he known that the day after the ship docked, Boesky would surrender to federal authorities for his role in a massive insider-trading scheme.

What speaks well of late-century America is that Boesky, Jewish as he was, paranoid as he was, never had to fear an anti-Semitic backlash, let alone gas ovens. Neither did his coconspirators, especially the prominent ones like Martin Siegel, Dennis Levine, and Michael Milken. Although all of the major players, as well as many of the minor ones, were of Jewish descent, in the Gentile imagination the greed decade had no particular ethnic connotation. At the time, Jewish religious leaders worried that it might. Prominent rabbi David Gordis feared that Boesky and pals would evoke ancient stereotypes of Jews as "exploiters of the economy, parasites, profiteers."[5]

At a panel on ethics in April 1987, Gordis insisted that lessons be learned from the scandals. "As a people," he implored, "we must look more deeply into the recesses of our tradition, our experience, and our values. The prophets and sages of Jewish history preached and taught a doctrine of justice, honesty, and social responsibility."[6] Influential socialist Michael Harrington sat on that same 1987 panel. To no one's great surprise, he attributed the scandals to "a larger ethos of egotism and greed promoted under the Reagan presidency."[7] A lazy and partisan media preferred Harrington's spin to Gordis's introspection.

A quick Google search for "greed Reagan" produces nearly eight million hits, many of them seething. The first listing on this particular day reads, "Purveyor of greed, Reagan: his body should have been left in the street for the dogs." The second one is less charitable still: "I would have to agree with the characterization of the 1980's being a decade of 'greed' because Reagan was president, a g****, f*** ing conservative who . . ." The postings do not get much kinder.

Given the rage about greed, stoked anew in the last few years, the nation has done well to avoid an ethnic identification. Our sensitivities, however, have precluded us from any kind of meaningful cultural analysis, either of greed in general or the eighties in particular. Those who have looked cursorily at the decade, and have transcended the Reagan fixation, might be tempted to think that Wall Street had gotten too Jewish. Those who look deeper might conclude, as Gordis did, that Wall Street was no longer Jewish enough.

"I want to be a latter day Rothschild,"[8] Boesky had boasted in 1985, a year before his downfall. He had gone so far as to buy into a savings-and-loan to establish a base for his rise as merchant banker in the Rothschild mold. What Boesky failed to understand is that even if they'd had helicopters in the nineteenth century, the Rothschilds would never have made a flashy landing at a seagoing bar mitzvah. Their enduring success hinged on discretion, restraint, tradition, family, faith. Boesky had none of this. He was only as interested in Judaism as his investors were.[9]

Born in 1937, Boesky had grown up comfortably in suburban Detroit, but he was definitely not part of Our Crowd. His father, a Russian immigrant, owned a chain of topless bars. When discussing his past, Boesky would refer to them as "delicatessens."[10] He starred at wrestling in high school but little else. After some false starts, he finally graduated from inner-city Mumford High, the school made famous by Eddie Murphy in *Beverly Hills Cop*. He attended the less-than-prestigious Wayne State, but did not graduate. He did, however, get a law degree from the Detroit College of Law, an institution so fly-by-night it did not require a college diploma for admission. Boesky's breakthrough came when he married up. Seema Silberstein was the daughter of a wealthy real estate developer. That marriage and Boesky's scrappy chip-on-your-shoulder ambition would make all the difference.

Culturally, the conspirators had much in common: a grounding in a modest family business, an outsider's insecurity, and an indifference to the faith and tradition that channeled their ancestors' ambitions. Authors Ehrlich and Rehfeld would class them among the New Crowd, the brash, energetic, ambitious—sometimes too ambitious—generation of Jewish entrepreneurs on Wall Street who had pushed Our Crowd aside and elbowed their way past their established WASP competitors.[11]

Martin Siegel grew up in a Boston suburb with little paternal contact. His father and uncle worked seven days a week struggling to keep their retail shoe business afloat. The eventual collapse of the business would haunt Siegel. A good student, he was the first member of his family to attend college, Rensselaer Polytechnical Institute. After college, he enrolled at Harvard Business School in 1969 and got caught up in the antiwar movement sweeping American campuses.[12]

Once hired at Kidder, Peabody out of grad school, Siegel quickly shucked his pacifism for the trench warfare of mergers and acquisitions. Since no one else at this white shoe firm had much interest, Siegel focused on hostile takeovers, despite their unsavory taint. Writes James Stewart in his authoritative account of the scandals, *Den of Thieves*, "Many of the WASP investment banks and law firms preferred to leave such work to the other firms, many of them Jewish."[13]

A marriage to a Kidder, Peabody WASP, Jane Day Stuart, the second for both, was thought a bit scandalous, even though Siegel was nonreligious. Still, it helped smooth out Siegel's "obvious ambitions and sometimes rough edges."[14] With his Harvard degree and Hollywood good looks, Siegel was off and running. Unfortunately, he ran into Ivan Boesky along the way. At the end of the day, Siegel was convinced that Boesky planned to kill him for cooperating with the authorities. That cooperation kept his prison time down to two months and probation to five years. Boesky, who was also cooperating, would serve more than three years.

Dennis Levine, born in the modest Queens neighborhood of Bayside in 1952, had little going for him but an almost pathological ambition. His father was a "tin man," a dealer in aluminum and vinyl siding, who kept his cash and his business records under the bed. During his senior year at a city college, Levine applied to every investment house on Wall Street and got cold-shouldered by them all.[15] The lack of a white shoe pedigree doomed him, he was convinced, and he remained bitter the rest of his career.

Levine used his bitterness as a wedge to recruit others into his schemes. After getting a job at Citicorp, he met a cultured and complacent Harvard grad named Bob Wilkis at a company reception. "You know, we're just nice Jewish boys in a hostile, WASP environment," he told Wilkis. "Screw the system!

Screw the boss!"[16] Insistent and ingratiating, he leaned on a reluctant Wilkis to swap inside information. As reward, Wilkis earned a year in prison, five years probation, and the loss of just about everything he owned. Levine got two years in prison on top of an eleven-million-dollar fine.

Easily the most interesting and genuinely innovative of the conspirators was Michael Milken. Milken had grown up as far from Wall Street, emotionally and physically, as a person could—Encino, in Los Angeles' much-maligned San Fernando Valley. The son of an accountant, Milken was wired into business from boyhood on. While others at Berkeley were busily burning down the campus in the late 1960s, Milken was managing portfolios for family friends and majoring in business administration.[17] After graduation and marriage, he headed off to Philadelphia and the Wharton School. While at Wharton he took a summer job at the old-line Philadelphia firm then known as Drexel Harriman Ripley. After graduation, lacking the kind of polish and connections that opened doors on Wall Street, Milken stuck with Drexel and went to work in its Wall Street office.

It did not much matter where Milken worked or what his title was. He was not to be denied. At Berkeley, he had come across an antique but still relevant study. Its author had reached a startling conclusion: a large and well-diversified portfolio of low-grade bonds would produce higher yields over time than a comparable investment in high-grade bonds.[18] Since Berkeley, Milken had been testing this idea and honing it. He would leave investment-grade bonds, the kind that major companies issued, to the Morgan Stanleys. They held about as much excitement for him as U.S. Treasury bonds. Instead, he would deal in the bonds issued by shakier outfits—"fallen angels," start-ups, and highly leveraged acquisitions. Given their lower credit rating, these companies had to pay a higher rate to attract investors. That higher rate translated into high-yield bonds.

At Drexel, Milken began assembling and trading and making money. His colleagues were not impressed. Said one, "The high-grade bond guys considered him a leper."[19] Not surprisingly, their complacency was dragging Drexel down. Despite an infusion of cash from Firestone Tire and Rubber (and a subsequent new name, Drexel Firestone), Drexel was starting to wobble. A Wall Street hustler named Tubby Burnham saw an opportunity. As the head of a small, prosperous, and "submajor" brokerage house, he figured he could achieve "major" bracket status—this mattered on Wall Street—by buying the faltering Drexel. In deference to Wall Street protocol, Drexel had to come first on the nameplate, and so was born Drexel Burnham.

The culture wars were about to begin. Drexel had been the quintessential WASP firm. Burnham was something else. Robert Linton, *né* Robert Lictenstein, Drexel Burnham's chairman in the early 1980s, denied that Burnham had been, strictly speaking, a Jewish firm. He explained, "None of the top people practiced their religion. I mean, we weren't lighting candles."[20] This much would become obvious as the decade wore on.

Only after the purchase did Tubby Burnham learn about Drexel Firestone's primary asset. It was not its name, bracket, or client lineup. The firm's chief asset was an odd, intense, bewigged twenty-five-year-old working in his own little magical kingdom of schlock bonds. Drexel Firestone's president advised Burnham that Milken, one of the old Drexel's handful of Jewish employees, would need special care and feeding if Burnham expected to keep him. When Burnham saw the numbers Milken was producing, he knew this was a leper he could learn to love.

Levine set his sights on Drexel Burnham as soon as he caught wind of its new go-go corporate culture. Once hired on, he set about recruiting likely conspirators, among them a young attorney named Ilan Reich. As a boy in Brooklyn, Reich had attended a *yeshiva* where he spent half the day studying religion. At Columbia University, Stewart explains, "He became increasingly estranged from his family, discarding their orthodox Jewish values without any clear sense of what would replace them."[21] While people like Reich drifted and Levine brooded, Milken filled the void in his religious life with a newfound faith. In what was surely the most unfortunate branding in modern history, this faith came to market under the name *junk bonds*.

"He only cared about bringing the truth," reminisced one Drexel employee of Milken. "If Mike hadn't gone into the securities business, he could have been a preacher."[22] This was a recurrent theme among those who knew him. "He was like a messiah, preaching the gospel," recalled one junk bond buyer. "He had this total singlemindedness of purpose."[23] Biographer Connie Bruck describes his life in terms equally well suited to a medieval monk: "a sublimation of all things personal and an utter consecration to his mission."[24]

Milken almost never stopped working—seven days a week, twelve, sixteen, twenty hours a day. "I come in in the morning sometime between four-thirty and five," he would write in an SEC deposition describing his workday. "Sometime around ten forty-five to eleven-fifteen they put some food on my desk which I eat in anywhere from one to five minutes."[25] After moving the entire junk bond operation back to Los Angeles, the now supremely wealthy Milken bought a home not in Beverly Hills or in Bel Air but in Encino. He put eighty thousand miles on a battered yellow Mercedes before he sold it. An egalitarian at work, he had no office of his own and no taste for luxury. Milken's was not textbook greed.

To a certain point, Milken's mission had real value. He quickly discovered that Drexel could underwrite public high-yield issues on behalf of a poorly rated company and market them directly to the public. Junk bonds were not just for trading. In his hands, they were highly useful for raising capital. That capital could breathe new life into aging companies and energize start-ups. Milken also hit upon the idea of offering small investors a diversified portfolio of high-yield bonds—in other words, junk bond mutual funds.

Through high-powered salesmanship—he occasionally crossed paths with mortgage trader Lewie Ranieri in the hunt for investors—the Encino Man was making himself the most powerful manipulator and marketer of debt on the planet. When Milken and his investors bought a company's bonds, he transformed the traditionally passive role of the bondholder. "You're working for me," he told one CEO. "You own a lot of the equity in your companies, but I own your debt. And your equity is not worth the paper it's printed on unless your bonds are valuable."[26]

As his power grew, his ego grew with it. A perfectionist, he demanded of his staff what he demanded of himself and paid them so outrageously well they put up with his screaming and abuse. "It's a slave ship out there," said one Drexel investment banker, "high priced slavery."[27] But it was more than just the pay. The staff was awed by Milken, "a charismatic and messianic leader," says Bruck, "whom many of his figures came to see as larger than life."[28] Milken's L.A. group, the tail that was wagging the Drexel dog, turned into junk bond apostles. "We owe it all to one man," said a member of that group, "and we are all extraneous. Michael has denuded us of ego."[29] Chalk it up to his California origins: Milken was the first financier to turn an investment bank into a cult.

As the 1980s progressed, Milken began to use junk bonds to finance hostile takeovers and leveraged buyouts. This, he saw, was where the real power and money were. So keen was he on this use of junk bonds to finance takeovers, and so indifferent had he grown to public opinion, that he began to call his annual high yield conference the Predators' Ball—the second worst branding call in the history of finance.

Even at this point, there was nothing inevitable about Milken's downfall. What undid him was his hunger for information. He may have been a god to his employees, but he was not omniscient. In the takeover business, information was everything. An arbitrageur like Boesky—that is, someone who specialized in anticipating takeovers—was tempted to secure information any way possible. Think *Wall Street* and Michael Douglas's character Gordon Gekko, who was reportedly modeled on Boesky. The line between what an arbitrageur should know and what he should not was easily crossed. Boesky crossed it often—with Milken, with Levine, with Siegel. "This is a highly technical business," Boesky once explained to a colleague, "and there are grey areas."[30]

Rudy Giuliani did not see it that way. Then the U.S. attorney for the Southern District of New York, he had, writes Stewart, "a Catholic, even Jesuitical view of the world, one marked by clear divisions between right and wrong, friend and enemy."[31] The chief of the fraud unit, Charles Carberry, like Giuliani a product of Catholic schooling, shared his worldview, as did their collaborators at the SEC. They were also a good deal more competent than Boesky and Milken ever suspected. When Levine was arrested, writes Stewart, "it suggested a level of securities enforcement that neither had previously believed existed."[32] These Reagan appointees also belied the notion that his administration had turned a blind eye to securities fraud.

None of the conspirators was a hard guy. "Wall Street types weren't strong in a criminal sense," Carberry concluded. "They cared too much about respectability."[33] As George Gilder might have phrased it, in an increasingly secular environment, the Jewish "need for achievement" had persisted while the culture's "rigorous moral framework" had been set aside.[34] Still, the conspirators were all just one generation removed from leading lawful, respectful, traditional lives. When finally brought to justice, Milken "emitted bloodcurdling screams."[35] Reich "began sobbing";[36] Siegel "put his head in his hands and began to weep."[37] This was the way the greed decade ended: not with a bang, but a whimper.

Though a decade lasts for only ten years, greed is both forever and universal. "The avarice of mankind is insatiable,"[38] Aristotle observed some 2,300 years ago, and little has happened in the years since to disprove him. The notion that the 1980s was distinctively greedy can be seen in retrospect for what it was: mischievous anti-Reagan agitprop.

For Bernie Madoff, now serving 150 or so years in prison for defrauding thousands of investors out of billions of dollars, the 1980s was merely the third decade out of five in which he spun his impressively sticky web. In fact, he was arguably less greedy in the 1980s than he was in the 1990s and in the 2000s, when his Ponzi scheme was cranking full throttle. And unlike Milken, whose genius revolutionized Wall Street, Madoff did nothing more constructive than steal other people's money and spend it.

Madoff's biography reads much like Boesky's. The grandson of immigrants from Eastern Europe, the son of a struggling plumber turned broker named Ralph, Madoff went to public high school in Queens, bounced around before graduating from *déclassé* Hofstra University on Long Island, dropped out of Brooklyn College Law School, and saved enough money from installing sprinkler systems to start up a humble brokerage firm immodestly called Bernard L. Madoff Investment Securities. Like Boesky, Madoff married up. His well-connected father-in-law may have helped with start-up costs, and he certainly helped his son-in-law recruit investors.[39]

Although not religious by inclination—he described himself as "a lox and bagel Jew"[40]—Madoff played on tribal loyalties to snare customers. He proved particularly skillful in exploiting his fellow Jews' pride in their historical business savvy. "This isn't about a bunch of widows and orphans that got taken in by some huckster selling vacuum cleaners door-to-door," one insider told Mark Seal, the *Vanity Fair* writer who has done some of the best reporting on Madoff. "He hit smart people. The ones who are really rich have big egos, and they don't want to look stupid."[41]

Among his customers, for instance, was old buddy and New York Mets owner Fred Wilpon, who would invest hundreds of millions with Madoff. For years, Wilpon boasted about the Madoff connection. "He must feel like a total fool," one Wall Street observer said of Wilpon after Madoff's arrest. "Here's a nice enough guy, decent and honorable, but he tended to brag that he had deals that were better than other people's."[42]

If Madoff's business model was pure Ponzi, his style was more Goldman Sachs. He moved in the best circles, donated to the right causes, and paid out only 10 to 12 percent annual interest, not the outrageous returns that Ponzi had. But Madoff paid that percentage year in and year out, good years and bad. This consistent high yield attracted investors. So, too, did the snob appeal. Getting in with the imperious Bernie was like getting a table at Le Cirque on a Saturday night. He did not take everyone.

Ground zero in Madoff's world was Palm Beach, specifically the Palm Beach Country Club. The predominantly Jewish club accepted members not on how much money they had—a $350,000 initiation screened out the chiropractors in any case—but on how much money they gave away. There was no self-reporting allowed here, as there was on home loans. Charitable histories were reviewed and assessed. In the age of securitization, club leaders had proved that even good deeds could be bundled and commoditized.

Prominent philanthropist Carl Shapiro, something of a surrogate father to Madoff, opened Palm Beach's golden gates to Madoff. Shapiro's son-in-law, Robert Jaffe, served as gatekeeper. As many as one-third of the club's three hundred members would come calling. Up until the day of Madoff's arrest, Shapiro and Jaffe had no idea of the nightmare they had enabled. Said the ninetysomething Shapiro upon learning of Madoff's deceit, "It was like a knife to the heart."[43]

When Madoff was arrested in December 2008, an emotional tsunami ripped through Palm Beach and sent shock waves around the world. Thousands of people had invested some fifty billion dollars with Madoff—many of them unknowingly, through feeder funds—and, as they learned to their horror, it was all gone. Gone with the money was the confidence, the pride, the sense of personal and communal superiority. "What Hitler didn't finish, he did!"[44] an overly dramatic doyenne of Palm Beach Jewish society told Seal.

Unlike the scandals of the 1980s, the Madoff revelations had a distinctly Jewish face, and Jews everywhere, especially in Palm Beach, were turning red. "The anti-Semites are ecstatic,"[45] lamented one Palm Beach resident. She was speaking not of skinheads in Paducah but the WASPs in Palm Beach. A more accurate word to describe the response is *schadenfreude*, a guilty delight in the suffering of others. One did not have to be an anti-Semite to enjoy it. Nearly a century earlier, after Ponzi's arrest, the *New York Times* readily acknowledged the community's "lack of sympathy for those whom he robbed." These victims, the *Times* editorialized, "showed only greed—the eagerness to get much for nothing."[46]

If the media treated Madoff's victims more sympathetically, they let it be known that investors had every reason to be suspicious. The returns were too consistently good. As early as May 2001, *Barron's* reporter Erin Arvedlund had shared this news with Wall Street. "Even adoring investors can't explain his steady gains,"[47] she wrote in an article titled "Don't Ask, Don't Tell: Bernie Madoff Is So Secretive, He Even Asks Investors to Keep Mum." Arvedlund noted that in a then-recent report, a dozen hedge fund professionals had questioned why no one had been able to duplicate Madoff's numbers. She quoted one investment manager who pulled out of a Madoff fund because "he couldn't explain how they were up or down in a given month."[48]

When Laura Goldman, a broker and analyst, sent this article and others to the members of the Palm Beach Country Club in 2001, the response she got was shockingly cold. "Oh, they were nasty! *Nasty!*" Goldman told Seal. "They said all these publications were jealous of Bernie. They were being anti-Semitic. People called me an anti-Semite. I'm not only a Jew, I live in Israel!"[49]

Madoff's most serious critic, private fraud investigator Harry Markopolos, had no more success than Goldman in warning the public. Markopolos had alerted the SEC as early as 2000, and in 2005 sent regulators a nineteen-page memo entitled "The World's Largest Hedge Fund Is a Fraud."[50] The SEC had neither the patience nor the competence to deal with Markopolos, and, as Goldman can attest, Madoff's investors just did not want to know.

When they found out the truth about Madoff, many of the investors responded with the outraged innocence of a subprime borrower whose adjustable rate mortgage had just adjusted up. "I want to be treated like GM and A.I.G. and Bank of America!" one raged to Mark Seal. "I can't wait years!" Said another, "I need people to know that the SEC failed miserably for at least 10 years, if not more, that they were warned, and that they didn't stop this devil from doing his deed."[51]

Los Angeles rabbi Mark Borovitz, himself a reformed con artist, understood just how Jewish pride had fed into Madoff's ambitions. "Whether it's Latino or black or Jewish or Christian, everybody wants to trust their own. Bernie Madoff took our trust and raped it," said Borovitz. "He took advantage of every vulnerability, because he knew our vulnerable spots."[52]

twenty-seven

Age of Innocence

On January 31, 2006, Alan Greenspan pushed through the final interest rate hike of his eighteen-year career as chairman of the Federal Reserve. This was the fourteenth consecutive increase in a tightening cycle that had begun in June 2004, when the federal funds rate stood at an improbably low 1 percent. The world, however, paid less attention to the hike than it did to the heroics of the man behind it. The headline of the *London Independent* summed up the international take on his career: "Greenspan steps down as Fed chief with his reputation at its zenith."[1]

A continent away in Calabasas, California, the news of still another rate hike had to drain a little color from Angelo Mozilo's eternal tan. A federal funds rate now at 4.5 percent meant a prime of 7.5 percent and a further constriction of the customer pipeline. Still, with shares in his company selling at more than forty dollars and a market share nearing 20 percent, the highest of any mortgage company in the nation, the chairman and CEO of Countrywide Financial enjoyed an esteem, if not at Greenspan's level, not too far below.

Mozilo and Greenspan had grown up within a few miles of each other, Greenspan in the northern reaches of Manhattan, Mozilo in the Bronx. When Greenspan was about three, his parents divorced. He went on to live with his mother, who worked sales in a furniture store.[2] From the age of ten, Mozilo worked in his father's butcher shop.[3] Greenspan graduated from George Washington High School three years behind Henry Kissinger and left for college—on a daily basis—via the A train down to NYU. Mozilo kept to his borough for college as well, graduating from Fordham University, not far from his Bronx home.

Greenspan was Jewish. Mozilo was of Italian descent. His butcher father, in fact, had been an immigrant. That the two New Yorkers would play so crucial a role in stimulating America's economy seems somehow fitting. Jews and Italians had been responsible for much, if not most, of the world's credit innovations. The Medici conceived international investment banking. The Rothschilds perfected it. Salomon Brothers first securitized mortgages. Ranieri godfathered the phenomenon for Salomon and branded it. Ponzi put his name on the pyramid scheme. Madoff put his signature on the Ponzi scheme. Moses, with a little help from above, originated the ban on usury. The Italian popes enforced it.

Greenspan and Mozilo may not have been aware of credit's cultural history, but in the fifty or so years since interest rates had last seen 1 percent, they had watched that history unfold. However gradually, the culture had changed around them. Although it would not have been obvious from following the media, that shift had less to do with the behavior of "usurers" in any of their manifestations—from community banker to bond salesman to loan sharks—than it did with the behavior of consumers, especially the prodigals among them.

Wall Street culture had changed—in some ways for the better. The whiteness of one's shoes still counted, but not as much as it used to. Ethnicity mattered less and merit more than it had just a few decades back. "Quants"—people who could do the math—emerged as real powers. Savvy traders had more value than ever. And up-from-the-mailroom hustlers were still finding their way to the trading floor. In *Bonfire of the Vanities*—the title an allusion to Savonarola's scorching of the Medici—Tom Wolfe captured the essence of contemporary Wall Street through the eyes of ace bond salesman Sherman McCoy:

> He considered himself part of the new era and the new breed, a Wall Street egalitarian, a Master of the Universe who respected only performance. No longer did Wall Street mean Protestant Good Family. There were plenty of

prominent Jewish investment bankers. Lopwitz himself was Jewish. There were plenty of Irishmen, Greeks, and Slavs. The fact that not one of the eighty members of the bond department was black or female didn't bother him. Why should it? It didn't bother Lopwitz, who took the position that the bond trading room at Pierce & Pierce was no place for symbolic gestures.[4]

On the potential downside, the major investment houses had largely shifted from partnerships to corporations, and if this democratized Wall Street, it also diminished long-term loyalty and distanced executives from the consequences of failure. As to ethics, internal controls had eroded a bit in the last century, but enhanced external controls had largely compensated for the erosion.

Wall Street's new corporate culture, however, aggravated a problem with the quants. Unless given lots of room and money, these "young professors" felt free to take their highly profitable show someplace else. The typical CEO, who often had little idea what these guys were doing, hesitated to look too closely. He was, as Michael Lewis put it, the "hostage of his cleverest employee."[5]

Any organized religious opposition to credit that might have existed when Mozilo and Greenspan were boys, and there was little even then, had largely exhausted itself. In its place there surfaced a vaguely socialist animus against the dispensers of credit that had all the moral coherence of a grudge. Ordinary Americans meanwhile retained as sneaky an affection for the "successful scoundrel" as they had in Dickens's time—how many cheerful movies has Hollywood made about con men?—but as Madoff and Boesky could surely attest, the public could turn on those sharp dealers in a heartbeat if its own interests were threatened.

As to consumers, they had, in fact, become more dependent on credit. Between 1980 and 2000, for instance, outstanding consumer debt rose from $355 million to $1,560 million. But raw numbers here mislead. More than 80 percent of consumer debt was tied up in home mortgages. As home prices escalated, mortgages grew, and so did debt. The attitude toward debt, however, had changed little. From the Mayflower on, Americans have struggled with it. If individuals yielded to its seductions as Thomas Jefferson had, most Americans continued to resist, as Benjamin Franklin had implored them to, even in the face of Madison Avenue's siren song. For all the blather about the seductive wiles of the credit industry, at least 40 percent of American credit card users spurned its advances and paid their bills in full on a monthly basis.

If there was a major cultural shift among relevant cohorts over the past fifty years, it had been among prodigals. Their impulse—"to take because they wish to spend"—had not changed since Aristotle's days. What had changed, however, was society's willingness to oblige them when they tried "to take recklessly and from any source." One reason for this was that prodigals had reached a certain critical mass—had, in fact, become something like a voting bloc.

In the 1950 census, families made up 89 percent of all American households. By 2000, that figure had dropped to 68 percent. But even this does not tell the whole story. "Family" figures include single-parent households, and this had proved the fastest growing of family cohorts, from 10 percent of all households in 1970 to 16 percent in 2000. In that same period, the "traditional" family took the biggest hit. By century's end, married couples with their own children made up only 24 percent of all households, down from 40 percent just thirty years earlier.[6]

Accelerating the transition has been the major media's celebration of the new family dynamic. One faux-objective feature after another has sneakily endorsed "the steady, profound change in Americans' concept of family."[7] Unfortunately, all the *People* magazine stories about Madonna or Jodie Foster do not help ordinary single mothers make their mortgage payments. This is not to suggest that alternative families are intrinsically prodigal, but pressure from the media and government to put them in homes of their own was making them so in great numbers.

Despite increasing prosperity, despite the growth in the condominium market, these cultural trends conspired to keep a lid on the home-ownership rate. When Bill Clinton was inaugurated in 1993, the rate was lower than it had been when Richard Nixon was inaugurated in 1969. Yet across the political spectrum, everyone agreed that Americans had a veritable manifest destiny to own their own homes. Indeed, presidents since Herbert Hoover had been doing their damnedest to boost the numbers.

The numbers, however, were frozen. The decline in two-parent families was negating the increase in prosperity. How could it not? In 1993, the average income for households headed by divorced women was 40 percent that of married couples; for unmarried women it was only 20 percent. As the numbers suggest, many of these women could not manage homes of their own. Home-ownership rates for female-headed households struggled to stay above 50 percent. For married couples, they hovered consistently in the 80 percentile range. With blacks overrepresented among single families—by 1993, 57 percent of black children were growing up in a single-parent household, as compared to 21 percent of white children—white home-ownership rates inevitably outstripped those for black home ownership. In the early 1990s, that gap was at least 25 percentage points, around 70 percent for whites and in the low 40s for blacks.[8]

The chattering classes, however, refused to acknowledge family breakdown as a problem, let alone as an explanation for the disparity in home-ownership rates. Their preferred explanation for just about everything unpleasant was the inevitable racism. This they could and would freely impute to less enlightened Americans, especially the business classes. Ignoring all contrary evidence, they found what they were looking for in a 1991 study by the Federal Reserve. According to the study, 61 percent of blacks had been approved in their quest for government-backed home loans as compared to 77 percent for whites.[9] Bingo!

The study conceded a lack of information about "the creditworthiness of applicants" as well as "the adequacy of the collateral offered,"[10] but for the media these limitations were mere quibble. They wanted to believe that lenders in late-century America would willingly sacrifice their own profits to keep the black man down, and they were not about to let facts stand in the way.

"Getting turned down for a mortgage may have more to do with how you look than how much you make,"[11] led a USA Today editorial. A front-page story in the Wall Street Journal began, "When it comes to buying a home, not all Americans are created equal."[12] Focusing only on the negative and using the word twice generously, both the Journal and the New York Times pitched their stories from the perspective that blacks were "twice as likely" to have their home loans denied as whites. This made for a much more sensational hook than "Most black applicants get home loans" or "Higher percentage of whites denied home loans than Asian-Americans."

To make the racism story line work, the media had to ignore another significant set of data, namely, default rates. In 2004, the Department of Housing and Urban Development did a comprehensive study of FHA loans that originated in 1992. The sample size was substantial, nearly 250,000 loans. Given that the

FHA insures only modest loans for low- and moderate-income people, the cross-racial comparisons were for comparable properties. What the study revealed, among other results, was that after the seven prosperous years from 1992 to 1999, blacks were defaulting on their loans more than twice as frequently as whites, and Hispanics were defaulting three times more frequently—the latter in a worrisome 13 percent range. If minorities had been held to a higher standard, their default rates should have been lower than whites, not higher.[13]

Another in-depth study on the years 1991 to 1996 concluded that divorced women were "significantly more likely to default than divorced men and married households."[14] By the end of that period, the default rates among divorced women had more than doubled from 1991. This breakdown fed the surge in bankruptcies. The housing officials of either party had to know this. They simply chose not to share this information, and the media chose not to request it.

At the Fed, meanwhile, Greenspan, a friend and acolyte of überlibertarian Ayn Rand, had accommodated himself to his ironic role as chief regulator of an economy that Rand believed was better left unregulated. He had, however, taken his lumps along the way. In October 1987, just three months into the job, Greenspan got the jolt of a regulator's lifetime when the Dow plunged 508 points. By sheer numbers or by percentage, this had been the greatest one-day descent in the market's history.

In large part, Black Monday owed its scary existence to a series of new products from Wall Street's whiz kids that might generically be described as "portfolio insurance." The insurance could take a variety of forms, but most of them involved derivatives and computer-dependent portfolio math.[15] Theoretically at least, big institutional buyers like pension funds and mutual funds could offset potential losses through a computer-based hedging strategy. The strategy was typically structured in such a way that when the portfolio prices started to drop, the computer program triggered more futures sales to offset the decline.

This system made perfect sense as long as only a few traders were on to it, but when everyone yielded their decisions to roughly the same programs, the computers took over the trading room floor. After a few anxious days at the end of the previous week, and a nervous weekend, the computers kicked off Monday morning, October 19, in a selling frenzy that did not cease until the market had lost 23 percent of its value.

At 8:40 the next morning, Greenspan responded to the crash with just one sentence: "The Federal Reserve, consistent with its responsibilities as the nation's central bank, affirmed today its readiness to support the economic and financial system."[16] This brevity represented not the soul of wit but the soul of uncertainty. Greenspan did not know what else to do, and the market may have sensed it as it continued to crash. Then around 1:00 p.m., some unknown investors commenced to buy the stocks back, and the market began its largest rally in history. "Several people or firms might have operated in concert to manipulate the market," Robert Woodward notes in his Greenspan biography, *Maestro*. "That was technically a scheme and possibly illegal."[17] If so, no one wanted to know. In the spirit of J. P. Morgan, this cabal had quite likely rescued the economy.

As they say, "success has a thousand fathers," and with order restored in the capital markets, Greenspan emerged as patriarch-in-chief. Still, Black Monday had left him feeling as adrift as Dave had upon realizing that Hal was the one running the spaceship in the film *2001: A Space Odyssey*. "I know I've made some very poor decisions recently, but I can give you my complete assurance that my work will be back to normal," Hal told Dave after killing his copilot. "I've still got the greatest enthusiasm and confidence in the mission. And I want to help you."[18] When the quants said much the same to Wall Street after October 19, their bosses had little choice but to listen.

Although nominally Republican, Greenspan sloughed off administration pressure and pushed through a series of rate hikes that triggered a shallow recession and cost George H. W. Bush reelection in 1992. Upon taking office in 1993, Bill Clinton was warned about Greenspan. "Look what he did to Bush," his advisors told him. "He's going to do it to you."[19] Chief economic advisor and former cochair of Goldman Sachs Robert Rubin knew better. He counseled Clinton that if he were serious about the economy, controlling long-term interest rates was essential. "You mean to tell me that the success of the program and my reelection hinges on the Federal Reserve and a bunch of f–ing bond traders?"[20] Clinton asked. The answer was yes. Greenspan was running the show, and by decade's end the media was treating him like a rock star.

Bond traders, however, only get one vote each, and to get reelected after a rocky start, Clinton knew he would have to win over his liberal base. As early as 1993, HUD began to bring legal action against those mortgage bankers who declined a higher percentage of minorities than whites. In 1995, the Clinton administration put teeth in Jimmy Carter's 1977 Community Reinvestment Act (CRA), which had merely "encouraged" financial institutions to "help meet the credit needs of local communities."[21] Under Clinton, regulators moved from encouraging to strong-arming.

The regulators were backed by the street-level bullyboy tactics of ACORN, shorthand for Association of Community Organizations for Reform Now. Founded in 1970 as an offshoot of the welfare rights movement, this mischievous left-wing syndicate turned its attention to housing in the 1990s and proved remarkably effective in a dysfunctional kind of way.

Even before Clinton was elected, ACORN had begun to lobby for a strengthening of the CRA. In 1991, its operatives set the stage for their new focus with a two-day takeover of the House Banking Committee hearing room. Historically, banks had been reluctant to offer home loans to people who might not pay them back, and so ACORN set out to embarrass bankers into overcoming that reluctance. "If there was no community pressure and the law, few banks would do something,"[22] ACORN's housing director Michael Shea told the *New York Times* in 1992.

A sympathetic media romanticized ACORN and turned what might have been a nuisance for the banks into a public relations nightmare. As the *Times* reported approvingly, "The nation's largest banks have come to the negotiating table just to silence objections that could derail or create costly delays to a merger."[23] The *Times* cited a federal regulator who seemed equally at ease with ACORN's soft-core extortion: "Acorn is street-tough and they bedevil the bankers. But they've gotten banks to commit millions they otherwise would not have lent."[24] When the CRA grew fangs, ACORN bit harder. Its enforcers harassed lenders and contested their plans to expand into new branches or new states unless they could show that they were "CRA-compliant." ACORN also lobbied a reluctant Fannie Mae to buy the loans that it had pressured the banks into making.

To make ACORN's task easier, the Clinton administration demanded that banks quantify the progress they were making in giving loans to LMIs—people of low and moderate income. The administration encouraged banks to use "innovative or flexible" lending practices to reach their LMI numbers. Meanwhile HUD, which Congress had made the regulator of Fannie Mae and Freddie Mac in 1992, began to pressure these agencies to set numerical goals for affordable housing, even if that meant buying subprime mortgages. Angelo Mozilo's Countrywide Financial was happy to help. In July 1999, the company announced a strategic agreement with Fannie Mae, promising to allocate "a substantial portion of Countrywide's agency-eligible production to Fannie Mae."[25]

A September 1999 *New York Times* article offers a useful window on the pressures that were being brought to bear on the lending industry. The article blithely cheers on the work of Fannie Mae, then in the process of prodding banks to provide mortgages to those whose credit was "not good enough to qualify for conventional loans."[26] The article leaves the oddball impression that the lenders begged to be prodded. Banks, the *Times* tells us, were "pressing Fannie Mae to help them make more loans to so-called subprime borrowers."[27] The banks, in fact, were responding to the pressure from Washington.

With a gun to their head, the lenders turned to Fannie Mae and Freddie Mac to relieve them of the imprudent loans they were now being forced to make. Before the 1990s, Fannie and Freddie had sufficiently tough lending standards that default was not much of an issue. That would change. In 1999, the newly appointed CEO, Franklin Delano Raines, was boasting of the changes Fannie Mae had already made and the changes to come. As he told the *Times*, Fannie Mae had lowered the down payment requirements for a home and now planned to extend credit to borrowers a "notch below"[28] its traditional standards. That notch was spelled *subprime*.

Few words in recent media history have been bandied about with less comprehension than *subprime*. Typically, reporters use subprime as an adjective to describe a kind of loan when it would be more accurately used to describe a kind of borrower. In the way of background, engineer Bill Fair and mathematician Earl Isaac started a business in 1956 called the Fair Isaac Corporation, whose mission was to measure credit risk. They came up with a model they called FICO, which is now the most widely used credit-scoring system in the world.[29] The system is based on the sensible premise that the best way to judge a would-be borrower's ability to handle credit is to assess how he or she handled it in the past. Lenders consider a borrower with a FICO score in the 650 to 850 a prime credit prospect. Those who score beneath 650 are considered subprime. Historically at least, lenders solicited prime prospects. Subprime prospects solicited lenders. As supplicants, subprime borrowers have had a limited ability to shop for better rates.

Given the greater risk, and their inability to shop, subprime prospects typically have had to pay more interest to secure a loan. Adam Michelson makes the
salient point in his critical look at Countrywide's unraveling, *The Foreclosure of
America*, that higher rates do not bespeak an "evil conspiracy." Says Michelson,
a former Countrywide executive, "If corporations were not additionally compensated for the additional risk they were assuming by underwriting these
Subprime loans, the marketplace would cease lending to those with less than
perfect credit."[30] Wanting it both ways, ACORN and its fellow travelers would
denounce the higher rates for subprime borrowers as "predatory lending."

For investors, high interest translated into high yield. In October 1997, almost
ten years to the day after Black Monday, the investment banks Bear Stearns and
First Union Capital Markets underwrote the first securitization of subprime
loans for a total of $385 million. The triple-A rating of Freddie Mac–approved
loans seemed, at least, to guarantee the payments on these securities. The back-
patting press release announcing the launch hit all the bubble-era hot buttons:
these "affordable" and "flexible" mortgages offered the possibility of credit for
"low and moderate income families" in "traditionally underserved markets."[31]

These securities proved enormously popular. They promised a 7.5 percent
yield in a low-interest environment and, if that were not enough, a chance
to cleanse one's venal Wall Street soul by doing what appeared to be a social
good. "At the time I bought the subprime portfolio," writes Michael Lewis,
here in the satiric guise of a busted hedge fund manager, "I thought: This is
sort of like my way of giving something back."[32]

Bear Stearns would live to regret its involvement in the subprime business,
but then again, the company had built its reputation on risk taking and innovation. Founded in 1923, the firm first got serious about bonds in general in
1933, when partner Teddy Low (born Theodore Lowenstein) recommended
that the firm hire a hulking twenty-four-year-old former pro-football player
named Salim "Cy" Lewis.[33] The son of Jewish immigrants from eastern
Europe, Lewis was charged with investing the firm's own capital in corporate
bonds. Lewis's main chance came with Roosevelt's seizure of the railroads
during World War II.

Although railroad bonds remained in play during the war, no one wanted
to buy them. The reason was simple: they paid no interest. When Lewis saw
that the bonds were selling for as little as 5 cents on the dollar, he bet on the

home team to win the war and started snatching them up. At war's end, these bonds rose to par, and Bear Stearns pocketed the difference. No longer content to make money as mere agent on investor transactions, Bear Stearns now looked for ways to make money with its own money. The private equity era on Wall Street was about to kick into gear.

In 1949, Lewis hired the man who would become his successor, another tough, athletic Jew named Theodore "Ace" Greenberg.[34] As befit the firm's image, Greenberg slighted MBAs in favor of candidates with a PSD degree— poor, smart, and with a deep desire to become rich. To jumpstart its humble "mortgage related securities department"[35] in 1983, Bear Stearns hired PSD Tommy Marano, who in turn hired a controversial but highly effective Lewie Ranieri alum from Salomon Brothers named Howie Rubin. By 1989, Bear Stearns had blown by Salomon Brothers and emerged as the market leader in mortgage securities. The firm surprised no one on Wall Street when it pioneered the subprime market in 1997. The timing seemed good. The year before, 1996, home ownership had crossed the 65 percent mark for the first time since 1981.

A second Greenberg comes into play here: Maurice "Hank" Greenberg, a cousin of Ace.[36] A World War II vet who had participated in the liberation of Dachau, Greenberg was handed the reins of the flailing American International Group (AIG) in 1968 and built it into the world's largest and most prosperous insurance company. It was in 1998 that AIG's Financial Product unit (AIGFP) entered the market for credit default swaps, which had been created by the bankers at J. P. Morgan. The bankers had been looking for an AAA-rated nonbank to insure the debt of public corporations and AIG took the bait. Hugely profitable, credit default swaps helped make AIGFP the most productive of all the insurance giant's divisions.

In his valedictory address at the Democratic National Convention in August 2000, President Clinton celebrated "the highest home ownership rate in our history." At the time, the figure had moved beyond 67 percent and was still rising. Not shy about his presumed accomplishments, the president thanked the conventioneers for supporting his agenda, one that "has taken our country to new heights of prosperity, progress, and peace."

To rally the base a week before the 2000 election, the Clinton administration announced historic new regulations that would put a further squeeze on Fannie Mae and Freddie Mac. "These new regulations will greatly enhance access to affordable housing for minorities, urban residents, new immigrants and others left behind, giving millions of families the opportunity to buy homes," said HUD secretary Andrew Cuomo. "We acknowledge and appreciate that Fannie Mae and Freddie Mac have accepted this challenge."[37]

The regs upped Fannie and Freddie's "affordable housing" quota from 42 to 50 percent. If the political hacks running these allegedly private enterprises protested this new challenge, it did not make the news. In fact, they seemed proud to pioneer this brave new frontier. "We have not been a major presence in the subprime market," said Fannie CEO Raines, "but you can bet that under these goals, we will be." Fannie's CFO, Timothy Howard, added that "making loans to people with less-than-perfect credit" is "something we should do."[38]

By the year 2000, all systems were go for the launch of a massive bubble. All that was missing was an expansionary monetary policy of the sort that kept the Mississippi and South Sea bubbles afloat. Rest assured, the great American housing bubble would not be lacking that policy for long.

twenty-eight

Babel

IN JUNE 2000, A MONTH AFTER THE NASDAQ CRASH SIGNALED THE end of the dot-com boom, an obscure Egyptian named Mohamed Atta casually entered the United States and began plotting his evil mischief. As would soon become evident, peace was about to go the way of prosperity.

Even before the 9/11 attacks, chief bubble monitor Alan Greenspan had persuaded the Fed's Open Market Committee (FOMC) to lower the federal funds rate. He was responding to the recession that had officially begun in March 2001. After September 11, the Fed ratcheted the rate down to 1.75 in four quick steps and kept pushing it down until it reached 1 percent in mid-2003, the lowest rate since 1954.

Despite a surge in the economy in the second half of 2003, the Fed kept the interest rate at 1 percent for another year. "That is the Greenspan 'Put,'" observed veteran financial writer Charles Morris. "No matter what goes wrong, the Fed will rescue you by creating enough cheap money to buy you out of your troubles."[1]

Out in Calabasas, Angelo Mozilo was not about to complain. "It was the Roaring Twenties all over again,"[2] writes Adam Michelson of the atmosphere at Countrywide. This full-service mortgage company, the nation's largest, was getting larger every day. It could barely hire enough staff to keep up with the consumer demand to buy new homes or refinance old ones. For Mozilo, this meant more than mere profit. He and his key staff saw universal home owner-ship as America's destiny and Countrywide's mission. "I have never believed more in what I'm doing, Adam," one Countrywide exec told Michelson. "What could be more wonderful than helping someone get a home, really?"[3]

One other cultural trend deserves mention, and that is the public embrace of "sustainability." The charmed inhabitants of coastal California all but invented the concept, and the public officials of San Mateo County, due south of San Francisco, have labored like Hammurabi to codify it. For a dozen years now, San Mateo has been producing an entertaining document called "Indicators for a Sustainable San Mateo County," which purports to evaluate thirty-one trends "that form a snapshot of sustainability."[4]

On the first page of the 2005 tenth-anniversary document, when the housing bubble was at its most ebullient, the county congratulated itself for "increased use of solar," "fewer contaminated sites," "more transit oriented development" and even "improved academic performance."[5] Not until page two did the county bother its citizens with the unfortunate factoid that if theirs was a family of median income, they could afford to buy only 12 per-cent of the homes in the county. Nor was there any admission that certain sustainability measures—particularly restraints on land use—were pricing the middle class out of the county. San Mateo was not unique. "The affordability of housing is overwhelmingly a function of just one thing," reports a recent international study of home prices, "the extent to which governments place artificial restrictions on the supply of residential lands."[6]

Mozilo saw these changes in the culture up close. Countrywide head-quarters, after all, were located in Calabasas, an L.A. County enclave so environmentally prissy that in 2006 it made news by banning smoking out-doors. Nearly half of Countrywide's loans originated in California. Mozilo, however, failed to recognize the ramifications of the changes underfoot, and the wonkish Greenspan did not even see them. This collective blindness would cost everyone.

As the mortgage market heated up, the true believers at Countrywide began to think that Mozilo's vision of a "loan for every customer" might actually be within reach. To realize this vision, Countrywide had created a subsidiary brand called Full Spectrum Lending. For decades, subprime applicants had been treated like pariahs within the lending industry, but FSL sent out truck-loads of mail each month to solicit just such borrowers. Countrywide, says Michelson, took to heart its goal of "'lowering the barriers to homeowner-ship' for African Americans, Latinos, and other minority groups who could face potential challenges within the existing lending system."[7]

Things were equally busy in Wilton, Connecticut, home of AIG's Financial Products division. In 2001, Hank Greenberg had appointed the son of a Brooklyn cop, Joe Cassano, to run AIGFP. Greenberg made the move not to fulfill any Jewish-Italian cultural destiny, but to keep this cash cow under his control. By all accounts, Cassano, a Brooklyn College political science grad, mirrored his boss's bullying style but without the compensat-ing talent.[8] He was indebted to Greenberg, and he knew it. Under Cassano, AIGFP had expanded the kinds of debt it insured. In addition to loans to major corporations, Cassano's unit was now insuring just about any kind of debt that generated a cash flow—student loans, auto loans, credit-card debt, and especially home mortgages, almost all of them, at least at this stage, to prime borrowers.

Back in New York, things were going swimmingly for Bear Stearns, still the big dog in the mortgage-backed securities market. In 2002, *Fortune Magazine* named Bear the "most admired securities firm"[9] on Wall Street. For eighty uninterrupted years, the firm had not had a losing quarter. In 2003, looking for growth opportunities, the firm staked millions of its own money on an in-house hedge fund. Chosen to direct the fund was Bear Stearns veteran Ralph Cioffi, still another Italian in a Jewish enterprise. Although known to be an indifferent, if not careless, manager, Cioffi made up for it with his smarts and market savvy. The firm rewarded him soon enough with a reported eight-figure compensation package.

The market was ready for a fund like Cioffi's. With equities stable and the return on Treasury bonds slight due to depressed interest rates, investors were clamoring for action. "Two things happened," one market analyst observed. "They took [on] more and more leverage, and they reached for riskier asset classes. Give me yield, give me leverage, give me return."[10]

The big ratings agencies—Moody's, Standard & Poor's, Fitch—helped pump air into the bubble. As the bond market expanded, so did their business. Keeping up was not easy, especially since the new securities were so complex that even their creators were hard-pressed to explain them.[11] Then, too, the people doing the explaining were the same investment banking houses paying their bills. The result was a whole lot of negotiated triple-As.

Government regulators, meanwhile, told commercial banks that if the rating agencies assigned triple-A ratings to certain assets, the banks could reduce the amount of capital held against them. This put all the more pressure on rating agencies to upgrade the rating of various asset packages and on banks to structure such packages to maximize leverage and, ideally, profits. Fractional reserve banking was getting progressively more fractional.

In Washington, the Bush administration picked up where Clinton had left off. In 2003, at President Bush's urging, Congress passed the American Dream Downpayment Act. Said Federal Housing Commissioner John Weicher, "The White House doesn't think those who can afford the monthly payment but have been unable to save for a down payment should be deprived from owning a home."[12] Conservatives would argue that the inability to save for a home suggests an inability to own one, but "compassionate conservatives" had moved beyond such narrow thinking. The spirit of Herbert Hoover was alive and well in Washington.

The year before, Bush had signed into law the Single-Family Affordable Housing Tax Credit Act. The program promised more than $2 billion in tax credits to those who would develop affordable single-family housing in economically challenged neighborhoods. Although the White House over-packaged the program as Renewing the Dream, Angelo Mozilo had to like the sound of it. In that same time frame, Countrywide was launching a new ad campaign with the theme Realize Your Dreams. That theme would become the company's new slogan.[13]

The biblically literate might hear in this home-building mantra an echo of building projects past. "And they said one to another, Go to, let us make brick, and burn them thoroughly. And they had brick for stone, and slime had they for mortar. And they said, Go to, let us build us a city and a tower, whose top may reach unto heaven" (Genesis 11:3–4). In the first years of the twenty-first century, this Babel-like effort would promise affordable housing for all people, regardless of income or character. Their debt obligations, should they choose to honor them, would be packaged, insured, and sold without risk. All would prosper and be like gods. This was not greed so much as hubris but, as its architects would soon understand, hubris can only take one so high, especially since, like the folks at Babel, their language had been confounded, and they did not understand one another's speech.

In August 2003, in the midst of all this mounting euphoria, the *New York Times* sounded a warning about the nation's second-largest financial company, Fannie Mae. The company had ramped up its business of buying mortgages from lenders and selling those mortgages or its own bonds to investors around the world, but it had become highly leveraged in the process, meaning it was carrying much more debt than equity.

What prompted the article were the results of internal Fannie Mae computer modeling on the question of company debt. The *Times* had acquired this information from a former employee concerned that Fannie Mae "was becoming a risk to taxpayers and the financial system."[14] The documents showed that if interest rates were to rise immediately by 1.5 percentage points, Fannie Mae's portfolio would lose $7.5 billion in value. "There is no reason for anybody to be worried about the company," executive vice president Peter Niculescu assured *Times* readers. "We are very happy, comfortable, and proud of our performance this year in what has turned out to be a very volatile interest rate environment."[15]

Fannie Mae's CEO Franklin Raines deflected criticism by focusing on Fannie Mae's success at social engineering. "We have met or exceeded our affordable housing goals, even as they have increased," he told the Congressional Finance Committee in late 2003. He also shared the company's "voluntary goal," namely, to "lead the market in serving minority families."[16] Through its energetic lobbying and strategic campaign donations, Fannie Mae had won many friends in Congress. At that same hearing, Congresswoman Maxine Waters commended "the outstanding leadership of Frank Raines" and insisted that regulatory reform not impede Fannie Mae's "affordable housing mission, a mission that has seen innovation flourish from desktop underwriting to 100 percent loans."[17]

When President Bush expressed concern about the precarious state of Fannie and Freddie in June 2004, seventy-six Democrats in Congress signed a letter warning that "an exclusive focus on safety and soundness is likely to come, in practice, at the expense of affordable housing."[18] Raines had long since transcended safety and soundness. Later in that same year, he took early retirement after the Office of Federal Housing Enterprise Oversight caught him cooking the books to the tune of six billion dollars to justify his own ninety million dollars in compensation.

In the summer of 2004, Countrywide rolled out an adjustable-rate product called the PayOption loan. This timely creation enabled borrowers to mix and match their mortgage payments as suited their fancy. If things were going well, they could pay the interest and principal as their parents had to do. If money were tight, they could make a minimum payment just as they did on their credit cards.[19] The negative amortization potential built into this loan actually allowed the principal to grow over time, a novel way of repaying a loan, to be sure.

Author Adam Michelson, who attended the rollout meeting for PayOption, was shocked out of his Countrywide loyalty. The concept flew in the face of "every bit of interpersonal, ethical, academic, and moral teaching" he had ever learned. At Countrywide, management had dressed up customer service and passed it off as ethics, and Countrywide was more sincere than most. "What if housing values *do* come down?" Michelson summoned the courage to ask. "Isn't it possible that *half the country* could be upside down on these loans?"[20] He was told that the chances of such a scenario were slim.

In 2004, chances must indeed have seemed slim. According to the Case-Shiller Index, arguably the most sophisticated of such indices, home prices had risen nationally every year for the previous thirteen years and sharply for the previous seven. In the previous four years alone, prices had increased 63 percent. Even when prices fell in 1991, the last down year, the dip was shallow and short-lived.[21] As long as home prices continued to grow, default would not be much of a threat for lenders or borrowers. The borrower could recoup his money by reselling, and if the borrower defaulted, the lender could recoup his loan by selling the home.

Besides, PayOption was precisely the kind of "innovative loan" Congress and the media had been championing. At the time, such loans made a certain amount of short-term sense. In the summer of 2004, the federal funds rate remained almost inexplicably low at 1.25 percent. As a consequence, the prime rate—the rate at which banks lend to trusted customers, typically three hundred basis points above the fed rate—stood at a seductive 4.25 percent. In 2004, the home ownership rate reached 69 percent.

"Stop! We're at 69 percent home ownership. We should go no further. These are people who should remain renters." Former HUD secretary Henry Cisneros wished someone had said this at the time, adding that it was "impossible to know in the beginning that the federal push to increase homeownership would end so badly."[22] In 1995, it was Henry Cisneros who had first used his authority as HUD chief to mandate that Fannie and Freddie's mortgages serve a fixed percentage of low- and moderate-income families—at that time 42 percent.

Low interest rates, easy credit, and the steady increase in home prices inevitably attracted speculators. If they could buy a home in a hot market for $500,000, spruce it up a bit, and sell it for $600,000 a year later, it is hard to fault them. This model worked well until June 2004, when the Fed finally began to raise the interest rate. There would be sixteen consecutive rate hikes by June 2006. Typically, when interest rates increase, the demand for home loans decrease. Prime borrowers took the cue. From June 2004 to June 2005, their borrowing fell by half. Subprime borrowers paid little heed to the rise in rates, however; in that same time frame, their borrowing doubled. It would double again.

To keep the supply flowing through a narrowing pipeline, Countrywide and other lenders had resorted to all manner of innovative and flexible home loans. The most popular loan for the subprime crowd—78 percent of all subprime loans in 2006—was commonly known as the 2-28.[23] A 2-28 adjustable rate mortgage (ARM) would have a low fixed rate for the first two years, often interest only. After two years, the loan would reset, typically at the prevailing interest rate. In a real-world scenario, a person who took out a 2-28 ARM mortgage in June 2004, when the prime rate was at 4.25 percent, would have found herself in a world of hurt in June 2006, when the remaining twenty-eight years reset with the prime at 8.25 percent.

A "predatory" loan only seems so in retrospect. At the peak of the bubble, many borrowers expected to accrue enough equity gain in the first two years to pay for the refinancing differential or to bail out altogether. What made this strategy possible was the euphemistically titled "stated income" loan, or, as they were more cynically known, liar loans. As originally intended, these loans allowed the self-employed a way around having to show a W-2. As the pool of new borrowers ran dry, however, lenders began to accept the word of just about anyone. Some lenders no longer asked to see proof of income, ID, or even citizenship. By 2006, most subprime and nearly all Alt-A loans, a class characterized by a lack of documentation, were stated income.

For years, community groups like ACORN had been pressing for the relaxation of income and identity standards. "No one who gets a mortgage ever has to go beyond [the Philadelphia ACORN] office,"[24] reported the 1992 *New York Times* article cited earlier. The *Times* benignly highlights ACORN-assisted borrowers who did not speak English, had no credit history, or had to "sign 'X' for their name."[25] To keep the bubble from bursting, lenders grew increasingly willing to take borrowers at their word. As Reuters reported, "Illegal immigrants were able to buy U.S. homes during the boom years, either by showing evidence that they pay taxes or by simply presenting false documents."[26] Almost half of the mortgage loans taken out by Hispanics were subprime. Many of the *legal* immigrants were unable to read the documents. For that matter, regulatory requirements had so thickened the stack of documents a borrower had to sign that all borrowers had to trust the goodwill of their lenders.

Despite early signs of impending disaster, Congress kept the pressure on. On June 27, 2005, Barney Frank, the ranking Democrat on House Financial Services Committee, offered a resolution supporting a national home ownership month. On the House floor, he chided those who worried about a housing bubble. "You are not going to see the collapse that you see when people talk about a bubble," he lectured his colleagues. "So those on our committee in particular are going to continue to push for homeownership." And push they did.

By 2006, Countrywide was offering almost two hundred different loan products. Ironically, the most complex of these loans were being sold to the people least capable of understanding them. When adjustable rate mortgages and PayOption (negative amortization) loans began to play out, Countrywide turned increasingly to home equity loans, often used by borrowers to consolidate credit card debt. These held promise as long as the equity bubble continued to expand, which it did into 2006.

One easy way for lenders to keep the bubble inflated was to waive the traditional 20 percent down payment. And this they did too. Some borrowers, like Melonie Griffiths-Evans profiled in the opening chapter, took out 80/20 combo loans: that is, one loan for the down payment and another for the remainder of the mortgage. This kind of loan allowed the borrower to avoid the private mortgage insurance charged to those without a 20 percent down payment. By 2006, 46 percent of all home loans in the United States were made with a down payment of less than 5 percent.[27] And in that same year, the subprime borrower put down on average just 6 percent.

In certain areas, home prices were escalating more quickly than others, and nowhere more so than coastal California. In the eight years from 1996 to 2004, the average cost of a California home had outpaced the average California family income by a full 100 percent, and home prices would continue to soar for the next two years. While environmental concerns constricted supply, an influx of subprime home seekers, some of them illegal citizens, expanded demand. The combination put conventional fixed-rate mortgages beyond the reach of even the responsible middle class.

Wall Street was beginning to notice. Meredith Whitney, a research analyst at Oppenheimer, was sending out warnings as early as October 2005. "Since 1996," she observed, "sub-prime lending has grown 489% [$90 to $530 billion] largely through the extension of credit to first-time borrowers. We believe that at least 5% of the mortgage market is at risk due to the very low equity positions in homes."[28] Although Whitney cited Greenspan's own cautions on the subject, Greenspan had been curiously incautious in the recent past.

In a now notorious February 2004 speech, Greenspan had an Ayn Rand moment. Overlooking the forced flood of incompetent homeowners into the market, he made the perfectly reasonable theoretical argument that "homeowners might have saved tens of thousands of dollars had they held adjustable-rate mortgages rather than fixed-rate mortgages during the past decade." He added, "American consumers might benefit if lenders provided greater mortgage product alternatives to the traditional fixed-rate mortgage."[29] Observes Charles Morris, "In any scrapbook of bad advice from economic gurus, that [speech] should be near the top of the list."[30]

Subprime and so-called Alt-A borrowers were marching to their own drummer. They kept borrowing and Wall Street kept underwriting their loans—to the tune of $2.8 trillion from June 2004 until June 2007. If there was one man making this possible—writer Matt Taibbi would name him Patient Zero of the subprime epidemic—it was AIG's Joe Cassano. After the usually vigilant Hank Greenberg had been forced out in early 2005 as a result of an unrelated accounting scandal, Cassano was left largely to his own devices. With a frightening lack of oversight, Cassano had allowed the potpourri of loans that AIG was insuring to mutate from diversified consumer credit into a toxic stew whose major ingredients were funky home loans.[31] With their debt insured by a powerhouse like AIG, Wall Street kept packaging the loans and Countrywide and others kept sending them loans to package.

Although Michelson saw no evidence of outright predatory lending or mortgage fraud at Countrywide, other lenders knowingly put people into loans they knew the borrowers could not hope to repay. Typically, the lender would pocket the origination and servicing fees and sell the loan into the secondary mortgage market. Greed might explain the motive here, but then, too, so might fear—the fear that without new customers the business would collapse.

As a way of personalizing the problem, Michelson peppers his book with profiles of borrowers who have gone awry. Most concede "partial responsibility" but no more than that. Typical is Susan, whose husband made more than a million a year and indulged her and her two daughters in a nicely affluent Santa Monica lifestyle. Then the marriage fell apart, as they tend to do in California. "With grit and guts," Michelson relates, "[Susan] set out again as a single woman with children to rebuild her life."[32]

Although the average American home price at the time was $165,000, Susan found a "charming cottage" that cost a little bit more, nearly $800,000 more in fact. To be fair, the home was in Santa Monica, whose eco-fussy residents had conspired to make it the least affordable city of its size in the world. Thanks to two loans from Countrywide, one a thirty-year fixed and another a piggyback loan to cover the spread between the cost of a home and the limits of a conventional first loan, Susan was able to buy a $950,000 house with no down payment. Only after she had moved in did Susan discover that she had to repay both loans. Alas, the combined $6,100 a month exceeded the budget of this newly single mom.

Meanwhile, the divorce proceedings had derailed, and her embittered husband stopped making child support payments. For six months Susan used her credit cards to make her house payments before maxing out. Upon calling Countrywide for help, she sensed that there would be no dreams realized in its nightmare bureaucracy. In the meantime, with her fabled grit and guts, she filed for bankruptcy. Once she had purged all her credit card debts—*mirabile dictu!*—the child support payments began flowing again, and she was able to resume paying her monthly mortgage bill. Although Michelson's is a generally fair-minded book, he shares the social puritan's eagerness to absolve the consumer. All he pulls from this story is that Countrywide had such confused customer service that Susan was able to miss thirty thousand dollars' worth of payments without the company either helping her or asking for it back.

In late 2005, Joe Cassano promoted the executive who had served as liaison to Wall Street's mortgage desks and asked a sharp AIG quant named Gene Park to replace him.[33] Park had misgivings. Earlier that year he had thought about personally investing in mortgage giant New Century but balked when he discovered how infected the firm was with subprime loans. Soon after, he had heard from a jobless friend whose newfound poverty did not dissuade a lender from laying a huge loan on him for a house he could not afford.

Upon being offered the job, Park did some serious snooping into AIG's risk. What he discovered scared the ambition out of him. Those most involved in insuring the debt packages at AIG had no idea just how much subprime junk they were insuring. All of them dramatically underestimated the percentage. During his final interview with Cassano, Park told him that if he had to take the job he would quit AIG. Cassano initially blew off his concerns. He told Park that, subprime or not, the only way the bonds could default was if housing prices fell everywhere all at once, and that, of course, was not possible.

Still, the interview had sufficiently unsettled Cassano that he sought out meetings with the major Wall Street firms whose debt packages AIG was insuring. "They all said the same thing," said one of the AIG execs present. "They'd go back to historical real-estate prices over 60 years and say they had never fallen all at once."[34] The shockingly slapdash nature of Wall Street's analysis convinced Cassano it was past time to stop insuring subprime bonds.

The damage, alas, had already been done. Throughout 2004 and 2005, Cassano had allowed AIG to assume enough risk to keep the connecting gears of the subprime machinery grinding away even in the face of federal rate hikes. "I'm convinced that our input into the system led to a substantial portion of the increase in housing prices in the U.S.," one AIG trader told writer Michael Lewis. "We facilitated a trillion dollars in mortgages. Just us."[35] By "us" he meant not AIG, not even AIGFP, but the credit default swaps unit within the four-hundred employee AIGFP.

The lending industry kept the gears of the mortgage machinery fluid throughout 2006 by lowering lending standards. When AIG declined to absorb the risk going forward, the major Wall Street firms—Merrill Lynch, Morgan Stanley, Lehman Brothers, Bear Stearns—had little choice in 2006 and 2007 but to absorb the risk themselves, lest the whole apparatus break down. It was not greed that was prompting this spontaneous cooperation across a wide range of financial sectors, but fear.

At Countrywide, the stock price held up through 2006, but those on the inside could hear the bells tolling. "It seems like the harder we try, the worse the numbers get," one mortgage executive told Michelson. "It's almost like we're running out of prospects out there."[36]

Countrywide *was* running out of prospects, especially in California. In 2006, anyone who looked closely at the California Association of Realtors' housing affordability index would have seen a bubble inflated to the bursting point. The figures refer to the percentage of homes in the marketplace that a family of median income could reasonably afford to buy.

City	1995	2006
San Francisco/ San Mateo	20.8	7.8
Los Angeles/ Long Beach	46.3	1.9
Santa Barbara	47.5	3.2
Modesto	70.9	3.9
San Diego	40.6	5.2
Riverside	52.3	8.4
Salinas	25.1	12.7
Bakersfield	75.4	16.5
Redding	52.3	14.6[37]

In 1995, a median income family could have afforded to buy nearly 50 percent of the homes in the L.A. metropolitan area. By mid-2006, it was down to one in fifty. Once affordable Central Valley cities like Modesto and Bakersfield had become no more affordable than Washington or New York. The executives at Countrywide, headquartered as they were in Los Angeles County, could see the problem on the drive in to work. They were exhausting their customer pool, and they knew it.

At Bear Stearns, meanwhile, almost no one had a clue just how weird things were getting in their own mortgage-related business. On January 17,

2007, its stock reached $172.69, its highest point ever. The following month, Bear Stearns released its 2006 annual report, which celebrated "83 years of profitability."[38] The most profitable of those years had been 2006. On revenues of $9.2 billion, the firm had recorded a net income of $2.05 billion, a 40 percent increase in profit from 2005.

That same month, however, Lewie Ranieri, the godfather of the mortgage-backed security and now semiretired, shared a deeply cautionary message with the readers of the *Wall Street Journal*. "I don't know how to understand the ripple effects throughout the system today," he said. It troubled him that 40 percent of the subprime borrowers in 2006 were not required to produce pay stubs or any proof of net worth (and here he underestimated the number). "We're not really sure what the guy's income is and . . . we're not sure what the home is worth," Ranieri added. "So you can understand why some of us become a little nervous."[39]

Bear Stearns execs should have been more nervous than they were. Their calm was due largely to a self-imposed ignorance. Ralph Cioffi's semiautonomous hedge fund had been routinely failing to get the approval of the fund's independent directors before trading with Bear Stearns. Although a technicality, Bear Stearns placed a moratorium on trading with its own affiliate. "It's classic Ralph," colleague Paul Friedman opined. "Details were just not his best trick."[40] Once they stopped trading with Cioffi's hedge fund, Bear execs stopped paying regular attention to what Cioffi was doing.

Cioffi's High-Grade Fund had problems. In August 2006, it had started to lose money. Cioffi assured his investors that only 6 percent of the fund was invested specifically in subprime loans, which the smarter investors had begun to distrust. What Cioffi did not tell his investors was that the more generic "asset-backed securities" in his portfolio were also heavily laced with subprime loans.[41]

In sum, the hedge fund was composed not of 6 percent but of 60 percent subprime. Unaware of this, when Cioffi split the fund into two entities on August 1, 2006, the *Financial Times* applauded the move. Given Cioffi's "stellar reputation," the publication observed, "If anyone could clean up on rising turmoil in the mortgage market, sparked by an increase in defaults by high-risk borrowers, it would be Bear Stearns and Mr. Cioffi." At this date, Wall Street still hoped to "clean up on" the mess rather than to "clean up" the mess. That would change in a hurry.

Among the very few people to anticipate what the future held was Peter Schiff, president of Euro Pacific Capital and a sound-money supporter of the Austrian School. On December 22, 2006, Schiff went public with his analysis that subprime loans "represent the weakest links in the mortgage/housing chain. Once they break the entire chain falls apart."[42] On any number of subsequent talk shows, Schiff was shouted down, often literally. Few wanted to hear what he had to say.

On February 28, 2007, the new Fed chief Ben Bernanke assured Congress that a housing downturn was not a "broad financial concern or a major factor in assessing the state of the economy."[43] Back in Calabasas, Mozilo was not worried either. At least, he did not seem to be. In a CNBC interview in March, he shared his belief that Countrywide would likely prosper from the subprime virus spreading through the industry. "This will be great for Countrywide," he said, "because at the end of the day, all of the irrational competitors will be gone."[44] Mozilo, however, was not telling the whole story. Beginning in 2005, he had started unloading his own Countrywide stock.

Warren Spector, the copresident of Bear Stearns, conveyed much the same impression as Bernanke. At a March 29, 2007, investor day, Spector told his audience, "The big question is will [the subprime mess] have a broad impact on the housing market. I don't see it. We're very proud of the way we do risk management. It's an integral part of our culture. . . . We have a strong culture of no surprises."[45] Spector would soon be reminded of the proverbial Wall Street wisdom that "the real risk is the one you can't see."[46]

Ralph Cioffi had a surprise in store for Spector. His funds were tanking. "I'm sick to my stomach over our performance in March," he would tell anyone who wanted to listen. In April, he would get sicker still. An internal Bear report on collateralized debt obligations spelled doom. "If it is correct," said Cioffi's partner Matthew Tannin, "then the entire subprime market is toast." Tannin added, "If Triple-A bonds are systematically downgraded, then there is simply no way for us to make money ever."[47] With a triple-A rating these subprime-heavy CDOs could be sold with a relatively low-interest coupon. Once that rating was taken away, and the CDO was revealed to be shaky, no one would buy such a bond at or near par. The price had to plummet it, and it did.

The subprime epidemic was exposing the Potemkin ratings infrastructure for what it was. In September 2007, Wall Street veteran Kyle Bass testified at a Capitol Hill hearing in language that the congressmen could understand. "It would be like cattle ranchers paying the Department of Agriculture to rate the quality and safety of their beef," he explained. "But it is becoming increasingly clear as each month passes, subprime credit has become the mad cow disease of structured finance. Nobody knows who consumed the infected product and nobody has any real faith in the [rating agencies] that gave it a clean bill of health."[48]

As analyst Meredith Whitney had shrewdly observed, "A company is only as solvent as the perception of its solvency."[49] The perception problem was about to kill Bear Stearns. By late May 2007, Cioffi's investors were beginning to wise up to the vulnerability of his hedge funds, and they began to cash out. Cioffi had a genuine dilemma on his hands: he could tell his investors just how profound the problem was, or he could finesse the truth, stall for time, and hope for some miracle intervention. Had Cioffi opted for the truth, the investors would have rushed to redeem. The banks would have pulled their loans. Cioffi would have desperately tried to sell off his remaining collateral for liquidity sake, and their value would have collapsed overnight. A panic at Bear Stearns would likely have caused similar panics up and down Wall Street, and markets could have crashed hard all over the world—damned if you do and damned if you don't. Cioffi chose option B: damned if you don't. He was about to prove Charles Morris's general rule that "only the smartest people can make catastrophic mistakes."[50]

On June 5, 2007, Warren Spector, Bear Stearns's copresident, walked into colleague Paul Friedman's office and served up a classic Wall Street understatement: "I think Ralph's got a liquidity problem."[51] This was the first Spector really knew of the mess in which Cioffi was mired. "All of the grown-ups who were looking at him were pushed aside," Friedman remembers. "The guys who were managing him didn't know what a hedge fund was, certainly didn't know what a mortgage was, and so it was inevitable he would get to the point where his strategy—which was also a microcosm—of more and more leverage on more and more complicated stuff blew up."[52]

Later that month, the lenders who provided Cioffi his leverage decided that they wanted their money back. Cioffi froze redemption requests by investors and pleaded with the banks to give him time. His thinking was that these banks were all loaded up on subprime securities themselves. It would only drive their price down if he had to sell his into a locked-down marketplace to honor their margin calls. It was too late for logic. Cioffi's request for time scared the banks all the more. "It was like a pebble being tossed in the pond," says Friedman. "This was the beginning"[53]—the beginning, that is, of the end.

By July 2007, when the national unemployment rate was in the 4 percent range, close to 10 percent of the subprime loans that Countrywide serviced were delinquent by ninety days or more, nearly twice the rate of the year before.[54] By August 2007, the secondary mortgage market for anything except conventional triple-A rated conforming mortgages dried up completely. No one was trading, which meant that no one was buying the kind of mortgages that Countrywide most needed to sell.

On August 6, Countrywide reported to the SEC that "these conditions, which increase the cost and reduce the availability of debt, may continue or worsen in the future."[55] If they continued, Countrywide acknowledged, there could be no assurance that the company would be able "to operate at profitable levels."[56] On August 15, Merrill Lynch advised its clients to dump their Countrywide stock. The shares had already fallen 50 percent that year. They would fall more.

As late as August 2007, Joe Cassano and his colleagues at AIGFP were congratulating themselves for having gotten out of the game and avoided the 2006 and 2007 loans now heading south. "It is hard for us, without being flippant, to even see a scenario within any kind of realm of reason that would see us losing $1 on any of those transactions,"[57] Cassano assured AIG investors on a conference call, but Cassano had long since ceased to understand what he was hearing or reading.

"So the LORD scattered them abroad from thence upon the face of all the earth: and they left off to build the city" (Genesis 11:8).

twenty-nine

House on Fire

THE UNRAVELING HAPPENED AT UNIMAGINABLE SPEED. AFTER MUCH dithering, Bear Stearns tried to bail out Cioffi's funds, but the bailout ended up sinking Bear Stearns. In March 2008, only one enterprise on Wall Street had the wherewithal to save Bear Stearns, and this it did reluctantly and grudgingly. "Buying a house and buying a house on fire are two different things,"[1] said CEO Jamie Dimon. Yet for Dimon there seemed little choice. There was Wall Street's legacy to think of. People were telling him, "You have to save them, you're J. P. Morgan."

In 1999, President Clinton had signed into law the repeal of the Glass-Steagall act. This meant that a commercial bank like J. P. Morgan, which had had to shuck its investment banking arm sixty-five years earlier, could get back into the investment banking business. As a commercial bank, now officially J. P. Morgan Chase after its friendly 2000 acquisition by Chase Manhattan, it was eligible for something that an investment bank like Bear Stearns was not: namely, a loan from the Federal Reserve. That loan enabled it to do the Bear Stearns deal. In October 2007, Bear Stearns execs had refused to entertain buyout offers because at $115 they thought their stock was undervalued. Six months later, J. P. Morgan Chase bought them out at two dollars a share.[2]

Countrywide fared no better. In June 2008, the public learned the details of a deal known internally as FOA (Friends of Angelo). FOA waived points, lender fees, and company borrowing rules for politically useful allies, among them former Fannie Mae chairmen Franklin Raines and James Johnson, chairman of the Senate Banking Committee Christopher Dodd, chairman of the Senate Budget Committee Kent Conrad, and a host of other prominent politicians.[3] That same month, the attorney general of California sued the company for predatory lending practices. Illinois did the same. On July 1, 2008, Bank of America put the faltering giant out of its misery and bought it for $4.25 a share, one-tenth of its share price just eighteen months earlier. As a final insult, the SEC accused Mozilo "of remaining publicly upbeat about his company's prospects during a period when he knew things weren't going well for the firm."[4] The nerve!

Connecticut Senator Christopher Dodd had another friend in AIG's Joe Cassano. Cassano had donated heavily to Dodd's senate campaigns as well as to his absurd run for president in 2008 and had personally solicited contributions for Dodd from his employees.[5] Hedging his bets, Cassano contributed to Barack Obama's primary fund and maxed out in the general election for Obama. By this time, though, Cassano was investing only to save his skin. AIG was on the chopping block.

As the subprime market collapsed, the major Wall Street firms, led by Goldman Sachs, demanded that AIG honor its insurance policies. AIG did not have nearly the capital to tame a tempest everyone had thought unthinkable. Goldman Sachs, however, did not despair. The firm had another form of insurance: its former chief, Republican Henry "Hank" Paulson, was now secretary of the treasury. Another former Goldman Sachs chief, Democrat Robert Rubin, had held the same position under Bill Clinton. Still another ex-chief, Democrat Jon Corzine, had served in the U.S. Senate and was now governor of New Jersey. Paulson convinced the leadership of both parties to cover AIG's losses at the swaps table, $182 billion and counting, and pay its creditors one hundred cents on the dollar. If Wall Street breathed a little easier, Andrew Jackson had to be urging the angels to remove his name from Jackson Days.

As to Congressman Barney Frank, in April 2009, he was denying that he had ever advocated home ownership for low- and middle-income people. Without breaking a grin, he told PBS's Tavis Smiley that he had long been an advocate for decent rental housing. "When people are making, frankly, $30,000 or $40,000 a year in much of this country, they're not going to be able to afford a home. And if you pretend that they can, you get them into trouble. The right kind of rental housing is appropriate." The housing crisis he attributed to the "conservative view that rental housing was a bad thing."[6] Christopher Dodd, meanwhile, was denouncing those who lent money to "lower-income and unsophisticated borrowers" as "unconscionable."[7]

In the search for scapegoats, many zeroed in on Alan Greenspan. In April 2008, an Economists Forum in the *Financial Times* enabled major players from all over the financial world to take a swat at a man who had morphed overnight from maestro to *piñata*. Paul De Grauwe, a prominent Belgian economist, called the Greenspan article that launched the forum "a smokescreen to hide his own responsibility in making the financial crisis possible."[8] De Grauwe voiced what seemed like a consensus opinion on Greenspan's two major failings: his prolonged suppression of interest rates, and his "religious optimism in the wondrous workings of the financial markets."[9]

Not a single one of the economists who weighed in on the subprime crisis mentioned the moral/cultural factors that contributed to it. Neither did Greenspan for that matter. There was nary a word about the erosion of religious restraints, the cultural embrace of credit, the breakdown in the family, the media support for profligates, the government imposition of race and gender quotas on lenders, the consequences of land restrictions, the political pressures to put people in homes, the overrepresentation of single women in housing defaults, the sanctioned waiving of documentation, and the easy purchase of Congressional support by financial institutions, especially the government-sponsored enterprises.

The reader had to go at least twenty deep in the posts on the Economists Forum, well below those of the prominent economists, to find the first mention of individual responsibility. "What's troubling is that the undertone of all this Greenspan bashing: a call for more government," wrote "Mladek," an American ex-pat living in Europe. "Instead of being afraid of government's suffocating embrace, they pine for the warm and fluffy security blanket that will protect them not only from international competition, but from their own stupidity."[10]

In the final analysis, Wall Street has proved much more honest in assigning guilt and accepting blame than Washington. In summing up the rise and fall of history's most calamitous bubble, Bear Stearns's Friedman gives a share of the blame to the investment banking houses for failing to decipher this novel and extraordinarily complex market moment and a share to "FHA and HUD and all those people saying, 'You better lend to those poor people.'"[11]

"But, in truth," says Friedman. "It was a team effort. We all f***ed up. Government. Rating agencies. Wall Street. Commercial banks. Regulators. Investors. Everybody."[12]

thirty

Restoration

ON A COOL MAY AFTERNOON IN 2009, SOME TEN THOUSAND GOOD souls, most of them couples, flood into Kemper Arena in Kansas City, Missouri, to begin their "Total Money Makeover." Hosting the event is a balding, goateed, forty-eight-year-old named Dave Ramsey. Dressed in jeans and a flannel shirt, no more or less formal than his audience, Ramsey struts back and forth across the stage, telling jokes, sharing stories, imparting wisdom in his honeyed Tennessee drawl. He will hold this audience spellbound for the next five hours.

Ramsey knows where his audience is coming from. He's "been there, done that, got the T-shirt." By the age of twenty-six, Ramsey, an aspiring real estate tycoon, had a four-million-dollar portfolio, as well as a loving wife, two babies, and a Jaguar in the driveway. And then, through bad business decisions and worse lifestyle choices, he blew it all. He was sued, foreclosed on, bankrupted. "*Scared* doesn't begin to cover it," he notes. "*Crushed* comes close."[1] This all led to a period of deep soul searching and investigation into the way money worked.

"My great-grandparents thought debt was sin," Ramsey tells his Kansas City audience, and after his own experiences in "financial hell," he had begun to think they were right. In examining his life, Ramsey had "discovered God's and Grandma's simple way of handling money." Their message was as simple as promised: "Live on less than you make."² The strategy was just as simple: avoid debt at all costs.

Ramsey began to share what he was learning. He spoke at church and with his friends, and they encouraged him to seek a bigger stage. In 1992, he launched a local radio show, which found an audience hungry for the basics. He started writing and found readers enough to put him on the *New York Times* best-seller list. By 2009, his show was being syndicated on four hundred stations nationwide. Along the way, he had not been afraid to reach into the Bible for wisdom; and in Kansas City he cites, by name and number, Proverbs 22:7: "The rich ruleth over the poor, and the borrower is servant to the lender." If anything, the unraveling of the previous year proved anew the timelessness of biblical teaching on debt.

Dave Ramsey is not the only media-wise financial evangelist. Equally visible is Suze Orman, who, though Jewish, lesbian, and liberal, preaches a common-sense message not unlike Ramsey's. Where they differ—a critical difference—is on the question of debt. Orman makes her peace with it. Ramsey refuses to. Orman encourages her fans to find out their FICO score as soon as they can. "Congratulations if your score falls into the 720–850 range," she tells them. "You are in the highest FICO range and that typically means you will be offered the best terms on loans and other financial products."³

Ramsey loathes FICO and all it stands for. He calls FICO results "your 'I love debt' score." In Kansas City, he lays the blame for the subprime mess at least in part on FICO and its consequences. From his perspective, there is no such thing as "good debt." He sees it merely as "a symptom of overspending and undersaving." Something as routine as a car payment, he calls "one of the dumbest things people do." And even a home mortgage, he tells the audience, should be avoided if possible and, if not, limited to a fixed fifteen-year term.

Ramsey has no more affection for the dispensers of credit than do the social puritans. "Debt is the most aggressively marketed product in our culture today,"⁴ he contends. He calls payday loans operations "legalized loan shark-ing."⁵ And he does not hesitate to label credit outreach to children as flat-out "immoral." Ramsey, however, gags on the social puritan gospel of victimiza-tion. "The challenge is you," he tells his audience. "You are the problem with your money."⁶ Like all traditionalists, Ramsey believes in sin. There are no victims in his world, only sinners; no pity, only the promise of redemption. The only regulation he asks for is self-regulation.

In May 2009, there was a new urgency to Ramsey's message. Both he and his audience had seen what happens when a population grows addicted to debt, when a government encourages that addiction, and when the markets conspire to feed it. Ramsey does not want to see this scary a scenario again. He envisions instead a nation free of debt and dreams of a national Total Money Makeover that would proceed one citizen at a time.

"Saving and investing would cause wealth to be built at an unprecedented level," he believes, "which would create more stability and spending. Giving would increase, and many social problems would be privatized; thus, the government could get out of the welfare business. Then taxes would come down, and we would have even more wealth."[7]

This is pretty much the way Moses saw the world—and Augustine and Aristotle and Aquinas and Andrew Jackson. Ramsey, however, is no monk. He enjoys his wealth and respects the system that has allowed him to achieve it. What that system needs, he believes, is not more regulation but a restoration of individual responsibility. Unlike so many of his academic betters, he understands the connection between the character of the individual and the success of the economy. The final word on the subject he gives to that esteemed social philosopher Austin Powers: "Capitalism, yeah baby!"

Notes

CHAPTER 1

1. W. D. Ross, translator, *Nicomachean Ethics* (Digireads.com Publishing: Stillwell, KS, 2005), available online at Google Books, http://books.google.com/books?id=Q0jjxC3t_XIC&printsec=frontcover&dq=W.D.+Ross#v=onepage&q=&f=false (accessed 10 October 2009).
2. David Koeppel, "Single Women Slammed by Housing Mess," MSN Money, MSN.com, articles.moneycentral.msn.com/Investing/StockInvestingTrading/SingleWomenHousingMess.aspx (accessed 21 September 2009).
3. Ibid.
4. Ibid.
5. Robert Pinsky, translator, *The Inferno of Dante* (NY: Farrar, Straus and Giroux, 2000).
6. Ibid.
7. Ibid., 87.
8. Ibid., 89.
9. Ibid., 91.
10. Ibid.
11. Ibid.
12. Ibid., 303.
13. Ibid., 57.
14. Ibid.
15. Edmund Burke, "Society Cannot Exist...," Tryon Edwards, editor, *A Dictionary of Thoughts* (Detroit: F.B. Dickerson Co., 1908), 204.
16. Koeppel, "Single Women."
17. Michael Novak, *The Spirit of Democratic Capitalism* (Lanham, MD: Madison Books, 2000), 103.

18. Binyamin Appelbaum, "Homeowner Gains a Reprieve from Eviction," *The Boston Globe*, 24 January 2008.

CHAPTER 2

1. John M. Houkes, *An Annotated Bibliography of the History of Usury and Interest from the Earliest Times Through the Eighteenth Century* (Lewiston, NY: Edwin Mellen Press, 2004), 11.
2. Calvin Elliott, *Usury* (Charleston, SC: BiblioBazaar, 2007), 11.
3. Ibid., 23.
4. Paul Johnson, *A History of the Jews* (NY: HarperPerennial, 2008), 133.
5. Elliott, *Usury*, 23.

CHAPTER 3

1. John T. Noonan, Jr., *A Church That Can and Cannot Change* (South Bend, IN: University of Notre Dame Press, 2005), 128.
2. Calvin Elliott, *Usury* (Charleston, SC: BiblioBazaar, 2007), 45.
3. Martin Luther, *A Treatise on Usury* (1524), available online at www.scribd.com/doc/10322491/Martin-Luther-A-Treatise-on-Usury- (accessed 21 September 2009).
4. Gary Anderson, "Faith & Finance," *First Things*, May 2009.
5. Ibid.
6. Ibid.
7. John M. Houkes, *An Annotated Bibliography of the History of Usury and Interest from the Earliest Times Through the Eighteenth Century* (Lewiston, NY: Edwin Mellen Press, 2004), 44.
8. Ibid.
9. Ibid., 46.
10. Robert Pinsky, translator, *The Inferno of Dante* (NY: Farrar, Straus and Giroux, 2000).
11. Houkes, *History of Usury*, 57.
12. Ibid., 48.
13. Ibid.
14. Ibid., 54.
15. Ibid., 56.
16. Ibid.
17. Paul Johnson, *A History of the Jews* (NY: HarperPerennial, 2008), 64.
18. Ibid., 164.

CHAPTER 4

1. Daniel J. Boorstin, *The Discoverers* (New York: Random House, 1985), 100.
2. Richard E. Rubenstein, *Aristotle's Children: How Christians, Muslims, and Jews Discovered Ancient Wisdom and Illuminated the Middle Ages* (New York: Harvest Books, 2004), 15.
3. Ibid., 35.
4. Ibid., 9.
5. Ibid.
6. Ibid., 283.
7. Robert Pinsky, translator, *The Inferno of Dante* (NY: Farrar, Straus and Giroux, 2000), 33.

8. Rubenstein, *Aristotle's Children*, 272.

9. Ibid., 102.

10. Robert B. Ekelund et al., *Sacred Trust: The Medieval Church as an Economic Firm* (NY: Oxford University Press, 1996), 182.

11. John M. Houkes, *An Annotated Bibliography of the History of Usury and Interest from the Earliest Times Through the Eighteenth Century* (Lewiston, NY: Edwin Mellen Press, 2004), 96–97.

12. Rubenstein, *Aristotle's Children*, 284.

13. "Thomas Aquinas," from the *Catholic Encyclopedia* online, available at New Advent.

14. Rubenstein, *Aristotle's Children*, 195.

15. Thomas Aquinas, "Volume 2, Question 78," *Summa Theologica*, translated by Fathers of the English Dominican Province, available online at Google Books.

16. Pinsky, *Inferno of Dante*.

17. Aristotle, *The Politics*, Trevor J. Saunders, ed., T. A. Sinclair, translator (NY: Penguin Classics, 1981), available online at Google Books.

18. Pinsky, *Inferno of Dante*, 87.

19. Ibid., 91.

20. Ezra Pound, "Canto VLV," *The Cantos of Ezra Pound*, available online at Google Books.

21. Aquinas, *Summa Theologica*, 197.

22. Ibid.

23. Thomas E. Woods Jr., *The Church and the Market: A Catholic Defense of the Free Economy* (Lanham, MD: Lexington Books, 2005), 112.

24. John T. Noonan Jr., *A Church That Can and Cannot Change* (South Bend, IN: University of Notre Dame Press, 2005), 205.

25. Houkes, *History of Usury*, 101.

26. Paul Johnson, *A History of the Jews* (NY: HarperPerennial, 2008), 170.

27. Dinesh D'Souza, *What's So Great about Christianity* (Washington, DC: Regnery Publishing), 108–10.

28. Edward Grant, *A History of Natural Philosophy: From the Ancient World to the Nineteenth Century* (Cambridge University Press, 2007), available online at Google Books.

29. Michael Novak, *The Spirit of Democratic Capitalism* (Lanham, MD: Madison Books, 2000), 8.

CHAPTER 5

1. Malcolm Barber, *The New Knighthood: A History of the Order of the Temple* (Cambridge University Press, 1996), 9.

2. Ibid., 63.

3. Ibid., 15.

4. Ibid., 16.

5. Ibid., 59.

6. Ibid., 67.

7. Ibid., 296.

8. Ibid., 277.

9. Ibid., 298.

10. Ibid., 299.

11. Ibid., 301.

12. Ibid., 312.

13. "Purgatorio, Canto XX: The Divine Comedy by Alighieri Dante," Classic Reader (©2008 Blackdog Media), www.classicreader.com/book/142/20/ (accessed 27 September 2009).

14. Ibid.

15. Christopher Knight, Robert Lomas, *The Second Messiah: Templars, the Turin Shroud, and the Great Secret of Freemasonry* (Beverly, MA: Fair Winds Press, 2001).

16. Sir Walter Scott, *Ivanhoe* (Mineola, NY: Dover Publications, 2004), 25.

17. Ibid., 34.

18. Ibid., 35.

19. Thomas Madden, "Inventing the Crusades," *First Things*, June/July 2009.

CHAPTER 6

1. J. M. Rigg, *The Decameron of Giovanni Boccaccio: Faithfully Translated by J. M. Rigg*, available online at Google Books, 25–30.

2. Ibid.

3. Tim Parks, *Medici Money: Banking, Metaphysics, and Art in Fifteenth-Century Florence* (New York: W. W. Norton, 2006), 22.

4. Ibid., 41–43.

5. Ibid., 46–47.

6. Niall Ferguson, *The House of Rothschild: The World's Bankers 1849–1999* (New York: Penguin Books, 2000), 64.

7. Parks, *Medici Money*, 49.

8. Ibid., 31.

9. Niall Ferguson, *The Ascent of Money: A Financial History of the World* (New York: Penguin Press, 2008), 46.

10. Parks, *Medici Money*, 234.

11. John M. Houkes, *An Annotated Bibliography of the History of Usury and Interest from the Earliest Times Through the Eighteenth Century* (Lewiston, NY: Edwin Mellen Press, 2004), 164.

12. Robert B. Ekelund et al., *Sacred Trust: The Medieval Church as an Economic Firm* (NY: Oxford University Press, 1996), 175.

13. John T. Noonan Jr., *A Church That Can and Cannot Change* (South Bend, IN: University of Notre Dame Press, 2005), 135–36.

14. Parks, *Medici Money*, 183.

15. Ibid., 185–88.

16. Ibid., 210.

17. Matthew Bunson, *OSV's Encyclopedia of Catholic History* (Huntington, IN: Our Sunday Visitor, 2004), available online at Google Books, 802–03.

18. Girolanio Savonarola, *New Advent Catholic Encyclopedia*, available online at http:www.newadvent.org/cathen/13490a.htm.

19. "Montes Pietatis," from the *Catholic Encyclopedia* online, available at New Advent, www.newadvent.org/cathen/10534d.htm (accessed 26 September 2009).

20. Montes Pietatis, "The Case upon Which Leo Ruled," *New Advent Catholic Encyclopedia*, available online at http://www.newadvent.org/cathen/10534d.htm.

21. Muhammad Yunus, *Banker to the Poor: Micro-Lending and the Battle against World Poverty* (New York: PublicAffairs, 2003), 117–30.

22. Houkes, *History of Usury*, 246.

CHAPTER 7

1. Max Weber, *The Protestant Ethic and the Spirit of Capitalism*, translated by Talcott Parsons (Cambridge: Harvard University Press, 1958), 64.
2. Ibid.
3. Thomas E. Woods Jr., *The Church and the Market: A Catholic Defense of the Free Economy* (Lanham, MD: Lexington Books, 2005), 114.
4. Martin Brecht, *Martin Luther*, translated by James L. Schaaf (Philadelphia: Fortress Press, 1993), 12–27.
5. "Martin Luther: On Trading and Usury," C. M. Jacobs, translator, *Works of Martin Luther* (Philadelphia: A. J. Holman Company, 1915), available online at www.godrules.net/library/luther/NEW1luther_d3.htm (accessed 26 September 2009).
6. Ibid.
7. Ibid.
8. Ibid.
9. Ibid.
10. Ibid.
11. Ibid.
12. Ibid.
13. "John Calvin: Letter on Usury," Franklin Le Van Baumer, ed., *Main Currents of Western Thought: Readings in Western European Intellectual History from the Middle Ages to the Present* (New York: Random House, 1970), 232–34.
14. Ibid.
15. Ibid.
16. Ibid.
17. Calvin Elliott, *Usury* (Charleston, SC: BiblioBazaar, 2007), 57.
18. Baumer, *Main Currents of Western Thought*.
19. Paul Johnson, *A History of the Jews* (NY: HarperPerennial, 2008), 242.
20. Martin Luther, "On the Jews and Their Lies," Martin H. Bertram, trans., *Luther's Works Volume 47*, (Minneapolis: Augsburg Fortress, 1971).
21. Ibid.
22. Johnson, *History of the Jews*.
23. Bertram, *Luther's Works*.
24. Ibid.
25. John M. Houkes, *An Annotated Bibliography of the History of Usury and Interest from the Earliest Times Through the Eighteenth Century* (Lewiston, NY: Edwin Mellen Press, 2004), 185.
26. "Historical Overview of Usury," Mission Islam.

CHAPTER 8

1. Paul Johnson, *A History of the Jews* (NY: HarperPerennial, 2008), 227.
2. John M. Houkes, *An Annotated Bibliography of the History of Usury and Interest from the Earliest Times Through the Eighteenth Century* (Lewiston, NY: Edwin Mellen Press, 2004), 187.
3. Act 1, scene 3.
4. John Gross, *Shylock: A Legend and Its Legacy* (New York: Touchstone, 1994), 15.
5. William Shakespeare, *The Merchant of Venice*, Act 1, scene 3.
6. Gross, *Shylock*, 36.
7. Ibid., 310.

8. Ibid., 108.
9. Ibid., 111.
10. Ibid., 139.
11. Ibid., 141.
12. Ibid., 158.

CHAPTER 9

1. Adam Smith, *An Inquiry into the Nature and Causes of the Wealth of Nations* (London, T. Nelson and Sons, 1852), 37–38.
2. Ibid., 143–44.
3. Ibid.
4. Ibid., 147.
5. Jeremy Bentham, *Defence of Usury*, available online at the Online Library of Liberty, http://www.econlib.org/library/Bentham/bnthUs1.html (accessed 15 September 2009).
6. Smith, *Wealth of Nations*, 147.
7. Ibid.
8. Jeremy Bentham, *An Introduction to the Principles of Morals and Legislation*, available at the Library of Economics and Liberty http://www.econlib.org/library/Bentham/bnthPML.html (accessed 15 September 2009).
9. Jeremy Bentham, *Defence of Usury*.
10. Ibid.
11. Ibid.
12. Ibid.
13. Ibid.
14. Ibid.
15. Ibid.
16. Ibid.
17. Ibid.
18. Ibid.
19. Ibid.
20. Ibid.
21. Ibid.
22. Ibid.
23. Ibid.
24. Ibid.
25. Ibid.
26. Adam Smith, *The Theory of Moral Sentiments* (Indianapolis: Liberty Fund, 1984), 165.
27. Ibid., 163.
28. Michael Novak, *The Spirit of Democratic Capitalism* (Lanham, MD: Madison Books, 2000), 79.

CHAPTER 10

1. Niall Ferguson, *The Ascent of Money: A Financial History of the World* (New York: Penguin Press, 2008), 70–74.
2. Ibid., 131.
3. Ibid., 48.

4. Peter M. Garber, *Famous First Bubbles: The Fundamentals of Early Manias* (Cambridge, MA: MIT Press, 2001), 38.
5. Garber, *Famous First Bubbles*, 24.
6. Ibid., 43.
7. Ibid., 44–45.
8. Ibid., 60–62.
9. Ibid., 75–81.
10. Ibid.

CHAPTER 11

1. Malcolm Balen, *The King, The Crook & The Gambler: The True Story of the South Sea Bubble and the Greatest Financial Scandal in History* (New York: Fourth Estate, 2003), 4–5.
2. Ibid., 15.
3. Ibid., 13–16.
4. Ibid., 17–19.
5. Ibid., 49–53.
6. Ibid., 54–57.
7. Ibid., 58.
8. Ibid., 60–65.
9. Peter M. Garber, *Famous First Bubbles: The Fundamentals of Early Manias* (Cambridge, MA: MIT Press, 2001), 94–96.
10. Balen, *The King, The Crook*, 60.
11. Ibid., 66.
12. Ibid., 23–24.
13. Ibid., 32–33.
14. Ibid., 77.
15. Ibid., 83.
16. Ibid., 113.
17. Ibid., 119.
18. Niall Ferguson, *The Ascent of Money: A Financial History of the World* (New York: Penguin Press, 2008), 150.
19. Balen, *The King, The Crook*, 120.
20. Ibid., 122.
21. Ibid., 124.
22. Ibid., 142.
23. Ibid., 146.
24. Ibid., 157.
25. Thomas E. Woods Jr., *Meltdown: A Free-Market Look at Why the Stock Market Collapsed, the Economy Tanked, and Government Bailouts Will Make Things Worse* (Washington, DC: Regnery Publishing, 2009), 85.

CHAPTER 12

1. Niall Ferguson, *The House of Rothschild: The World's Bankers 1849–1999* (New York: Penguin Books, 2000), 80.
2. "Martin Luther: On Trading and Usury," C. M. Jacobs, translator, *Works of Martin Luther* (Philadelphia: A. J. Holman Company, 1915), available online at www.godrules.net/library/luther/NEW1luther_d3.htm (accessed 26 September 2009).

3. Ferguson, *The House of Rothschild*, 35.
4. Ibid.
5. Ibid., 141.
6. Ibid., 40–41.
7. Ibid., 78.
8. Ibid., 50.
9. Ibid., 51.
10. Ibid., 77.
11. Niall Ferguson, *The Ascent of Money: A Financial History of the World* (New York: Penguin Press, 2008), 89.
12. Ferguson, *The House of Rothschild*, 83–85.
13. Ibid., 84.
14. Ibid., 96–99.
15. Ibid., 123.
16. Ibid., 77.
17. Ibid., 257.
18. Sir Walter Scott, *Ivanhoe* (Mineola, NY: Dover Publications, 2004), 88.
19. Ferguson, *Ascent of Money*, 93–96.
20. Ibid.
21. Ibid.
22. Ibid., 90.
23. Ibid., 94.
24. Ibid., 91.

CHAPTER 13

1. Paul Johnson, *A History of the Jews* (NY: HarperPerennial, 2008), 342.
2. Ibid., 349.
3. Ibid.
4. Ibid., 343–44.
5. Ibid.
6. Ibid., 347.
7. Lee Harris, "The Intellectual Origins of America Bashing," *Policy Review*, December 2002.
8. Georgi Marchinko, "Karl Marx," trans. Alexei Salapativ, *Predvestnik #2*, 1991, available online at atheismquotes.wordpress.com/marx/ (accessed 28 Septembr 2009).
9. Karl Marx, "On the Jewish Question" (Berlin: Deutsch-Franzosische Jahrbucher, 1844), available online at radioislam.org/marx/marxjew4.htm (accessed 28 September 2009).
10. Ibid.
11. Ibid.
12. Ibid.
13. Ibid.
14. Ibid.
15. Ibid.
16. Ibid.
17. Ibid.
18. Ibid.
19. Johnson, *History of the Jews*, 353.
20. Ibid.
21. Ibid., 350.

CHAPTER 14

1. Karl Marx, "On the Jewish Question" (Berlin: Deutsch-Franzosische Jahrbucher, 1844), available online at radioislam.org/marx/marxjew4.htm (accessed 28 September 2009).
2. Ibid.
3. "William Bradford: from History of Plymouth Plantation, circa 1650," Modern History Sourcebook, available online at www.fordham.edu/halsall/mod/1650bradford.html (accessed 28 September 2009).

CHAPTER 15

1. Lendol Calder, *Financing the American Dream: A Cultural History of Consumer Credit* (Princeton, NJ: Princeton University Press, 1999), 22.
2. Ibid., 27.
3. Ibid., 26.
4. Murray N. Rothbard, *A History of Money and Banking in the United States: The Colonial Era to World War II* (Auburn, AL: Ludwig von Mises Institute, 2005), 48.
5. Thomas E. Woods Jr., *The Church and the Market: A Catholic Defense of the Free Economy* (Lanham, MD: Lexington Books, 2005), 87–88.
6. Rothbard, *A History of Money*, 59.
7. Ibid., 57.
8. George Selgin, "Gresham's Law," EH.Net Encyclopedia, edited by Robert Whaples, 9 June 2003, available online at eh.net/encyclopedia/article/selgin.gresham.law (accessed 28 September 2009).
9. Benjamin Franklin, "Advice to a Young Tradesman, 1748," *Poor Richard's Almanack*, available online at Google Books.
10. Ibid.
11. Ibid.
12. Ibid.
13. Ibid.
14. Ibid.
15. Rothbard, *A History of Money*, 57.
16. Ibid., 58–58.
17. Franklin, "Advice to a Young Tradesman."
18. Ibid.
19. Rothbard, *A History of Money*, 59–60.
20. Ibid., 67.
21. "Thomas Jefferson on Politics & Government," Etext Center, University of Virginia Library.
22. Ibid.
23. Ibid.
24. Ibid.
25. Alan Pell Crawford, *Twilight at Monticello: The Final Years of Thomas Jefferson* (New York: Random House, 2008), 63.
26. Ibid., 177–79.
27. "Thomas Jefferson on Politics."
28. Ibid.
29. Crawford, *Twilight at Monticello*, 223.
30. Ibid., 230.
31. David McCullough, *Truman* (New York: Simon & Schuster, 1999), 963.

CHAPTER 16

1. "Thomas Jefferson on Politics & Government," Etext Center, University of Virginia Library.
2. Murray N. Rothbard, *A History of Money and Banking in the United States: The Colonial Era to World War II* (Auburn, AL: Ludwig von Mises Institute, 2005), 68–70.
3. Ibid., 73.
4. Ibid., 74–76.
5. "In Crisis, Opportunity for Obama," *Wall Street Journal*, 21 November 2008.
6. Rothbard, *A History of Money*, 75–86.
7. Ibid., 90.
8. John Lahr, "A Black 'Death of a Salesman,'" *New Yorker*, 21 May 2009.
9. Rothbard, *A History of Money*, 91.
10. Jon Meacham, *American Lion: Andrew Jackson in the White House* (New York: Random House Trade Paperbacks, 2009), 75.
11. Ibid., 103.
12. Ibid., 209.
13. Ibid., 212.
14. Ibid.
15. Ibid., 264.
16. Ibid., 270.
17. Ibid., 269.
18. Ibid., 165.
19. Ibid., 273.
20. Ibid., 276.
21. Ibid.
22. Ibid., 278.
23. Rothbard, *A History of Money*, 103–104.

CHAPTER 17

1. Alexis de Tocqueville, *Democracy in America* (trans. by Henry Reeve, 1899), Book I, chapter XIII, electronic edition deposited by the American Studies Program at the University of Virginia, June 1, 1997, available online at xroads.virginia.edu/~HYPER/DETOC/home.html (accessed 28 September 2009).
2. Ibid., Book I, chapter XVII.
3. Charles Dickens, *American Notes for General Circulation* (New York: Appleton and Company, 1868), 101.
4. Ibid.
5. Ibid.
6. Lendol Calder, *Financing the American Dream: A Cultural History of Consumer Credit* (Princeton, NJ: Princeton University Press, 1999), 37.
7. Ibid., 39.
8. Ibid., 43.
9. Ibid., 46.
10. Ibid., 54.
11. Ibid., 55.
12. Ibid., 58.
13. Ibid., 162–63.
14. Tocqueville, *Democracy in America*, Book II, chapter V.

15. Alexis de Tocqueville, excerpt from a letter to his sister-in-law, Mme. Edouard, 18 October 1831, "The Alexis de Tocqueville Tour," C-SPAN © 2009 National Cabel Satellite Corporation.
16. Calder, *Financing the American Dream*, 67.
17. Ibid.
18. Ibid., 73.
19. Tocqueville, *Democracy in America*, Book I, chapter XVII.
20. Ibid., Book II, chapter XI.
21. Calder, *Financing the American Dream*, 92.
22. Ibid., 37.

CHAPTER 18

1. William Jennings Bryan, "Cross of Gold" speech (1896), available online at History Matters, © 1998–2005 American Social History Productions, Inc., historymatters.gmu.edu/d/5354/ (accessed 29 September 2009).
2. Ibid.
3. Ibid.
4. Ron Chernow, *The House of Morgan: An American Banking Dynasty and the Rise of Modern Finance* (New York: Grove Press, 2001), 8–12.
5. Chernow, *House of Morgan*, 4–5.
6. Ibid., 6.
7. Ibid.
8. Ibid., 9–10.
9. Ibid., 12.
10. Ibid., 31–32.
11. Ibid., 58.
12. Ibid., 37.
13. Ibid., 67.
14. Murray N. Rothbard, *A History of Money and Banking in the United States: The Colonial Era to World War II* (Auburn, AL: Ludwig von Mises Institute, 2005), 161–62.
15. Ibid., 167.
16. Chernow, *House of Morgan*, 73.
17. Judith Ramsey Ehrlich and Barry J. Rehfeld, *The New Crowd: The Changing of the Jewish Guard on Wall Street* (New York: Harper Perennial, 1990), 23.
18. Chernow, *House of Morgan*, 71–72.
19. Ibid.
20. Ibid., 76.
21. Ibid.
22. Rothbard, *A History of Money*, 176.
23. Ibid., 171.
24. Chernow, *House of Morgan*, 122–26.
25. Ibid.

CHAPTER 19

1. Mitchell Zuckoff, *Ponzi's Scheme: The True Story of a Financial Legend* (New York: Random House Trade Paperbacks, 2006), 49–50.
2. Ibid., 45.

3. Ibid., 20–23.

4. Ibid., 53.

5. Ibid., 83–86.

6. Ibid., 98.

7. Ibid., 1134.

8. Jack Cashill, *Hoodwinked: How Intellectual Hucksters Hijacked American Culture* (Nashville, TN: Thomas Nelson, 2005), 18–19.

9. Zuckoff, *Ponzi's Scheme*, 246.

10. Ibid., 220.

11. Ibid., 187.

12. Ibid.

13. Zuckoff, *Ponzi's Scheme*, 98.

14. Ibid., 186.

15. Ibid., 248.

16. Ibid., 281–85.

17. Cashill, *Hoodwinked*, 23–25.

18. Zuckoff, *Ponzi's Scheme*, 294.

CHAPTER 20

1. Ron Chernow, *The House of Morgan: An American Banking Dynasty and the Rise of Modern Finance* (New York: Grove Press, 2001), 145.

2. Liaquat Ahamed, *Lords of Finance: The Bankers Who Broke the World* (New York: Penguin Press, 2009), 55–56.

3. Chernow, *House of Morgan*, 128.

4. Ibid.

5. Murray N. Rothbard, *A History of Money and Banking in the United States: The Colonial Era to World War II* (Auburn, AL: Ludwig von Mises Institute, 2005), 242–44.

6. Ibid., 250.

7. Ibid., 244.

8. Ibid., 245.

9. Ibid., 252–53.

10. Ahamed, *Lords of Finance*, 56.

11. Ibid.

12. Rothbard, *A History of Money*, 255–56.

13. Ibid., 254–57.

CHAPTER 21

1. "A Sensation at Saratoga," *New York Times*, 19 June 1877, http:query.nytimes.com/gst/abstract.html?res=9802EFD6123FE63BBC415DFB066838C669FDE (accessed 29 September 2009).

2. Stephen Birmingham, *Our Crowd: The Great Jewish Families of New York* (New York: Harper & Row, 1967), 33.

3. Lendol Calder, *Financing the American Dream: A Cultural History of Consumer Credit* (Princeton, NJ: Princeton University Press, 1999), 180.

4. Ibid., 171–72.

5. Ibid., 215–16.

6. Ibid., 230.
7. Ibid., 185.
8. Ibid., 186–91.
9. Ibid., 190.
10. Ibid., 192.
11. Ibid., 194.
12. Ibid., 227.
13. Ibid., 240.
14. Ibid., 238–45.
15. Ibid., 250.
16. Ibid., 254–57.
17. George Gilder, *The Israel Test* (Minneapolis: Richard Vigilante Books, 2009), 41.
18. Ibid.
19. "Henry Ford Invents a Jewish Conspiracy," Jewish Virtual Library, ©2009 The American-Israeli Cooperative Enterprise, www.jewishvirtuallibrary.org/jsource/anti-semitism/ford1.html (accessed 29 September 2009).
20. *Protocols of the Learned Elders of Zion*, Victor Marsden, translator (Escondido: The Book Tree, 1999), 216.
21. Calder, *Financing the American Dream*, 183.

CHAPTER 22

1. Jim Powell, *FDR's Folly: How Roosevelt and His New Deal Prolonged the Depression* (New York: Crown Forum, 2003), 71–72.
2. Amity Shlaes, *The Forgotten Man: A New History of the Great Depression* (New York: HarperCollins, 2007), 18.
3. Ibid., 19.
4. Liaquat Ahamed, *Lords of Finance: The Bankers Who Broke the World* (New York: Penguin Press, 2009), 298–99.
5. Ron Chernow, *The House of Morgan: An American Banking Dynasty and the Rise of Modern Finance* (New York: Grove Press, 2001), 313.
6. Ibid., 312.
7. Lendol Calder, *Financing the American Dream: A Cultural History of Consumer Credit* (Princeton, NJ: Princeton University Press, 1999), 218.
8. Ahamed, *Lords of Finance*, 318.
9. Shlaes, *The Forgotten Man*, 38.
10. Ibid., 31.
11. Ibid., 3.
12. Ibid., 92.
13. Powell, *FDR's Folly*, 37.
14. Murray N. Rothbard, *A History of Money and Banking in the United States: The Colonial Era to World War II* (Auburn, AL: Ludwig von Mises Institute, 2005), 275.
15. Shlaes, *The Forgotten Man*, 90.
16. Ahamed, *Lords of Finance*, 322.
17. "'The Only Thing We Have to Fear Is Fear Itself': FDR's First Inaugural Address," 4 March 1933, available online at History Matters, © 1998–2005 American Social History Productions, Inc., historymatters.gmu.edu/d/5057/ (accessed 29 September 2009).
18. Ibid.

19. Karl Marx, "On the Jewish Question" (Berlin: Deutsch-Franzosische Jahrbucher, 1844), available online at radioislam.org/marx/marxjew4.htm (accessed 28 September 2009).
20. "The Only Thing We Have to Fear Is Fear Itself."
21. Ibid.
22. Powell, FDR's Folly, 69–71.
23. "The Only Thing We Have to Fear Is Fear Itself."
24. Ibid.
25. Franklin Delano Roosevelt, "A Rendezvous with Destiny," speech before the 1936 Democratic National Convention, Philadelphia, June 27, 1936, available online at http:www2.austin.cc.tx.us/lpatrick/his2341/fdr36acceptancespeech.htm.
26. Powell, FDR's Folly, 31.
27. Michael Lewis, Liar's Poker: Rising Through the Wreckage on Wall Street (New York: W.W. Norton & Company, 1989), 27.
28. Chernow, House of Morgan, 375.
29. Ibid., 176.
30. Ibid., 379.
31. Ibid.
32. Ibid., 387.
33. William Beach and Ken McIntyre, "Get Over It: New Deal Didn't Do the Job," Human Events, 20 January 2009.

CHAPTER 23

1. Mark Skousen, "Saving the Depression: A New Look at World War II," The Review of Austrian Economics, December 1988.
2. D. J. Waldie, Holy Land: A Suburban Memoir (New York: St. Martin's Press, 1996), 49.
3. Jim Powell, FDR's Folly: How Roosevelt and His New Deal Prolonged the Depression (New York: Crown Forum, 2003), 45.
4. Ibid.
5. Lendol Calder, Financing the American Dream: A Cultural History of Consumer Credit (Princeton, NJ: Princeton University Press, 1999), 289.
6. Powell, FDR's Folly, 46.
7. Steven Malanga, "Obsessive Housing Disorder," City Journal, Spring 2009.
8. William J. Collins and Robert A. Margo, "Race and Home Ownership: A Century Long View," May 2000, Department of Economics, Vanderbilt University.
9. Malanga, "Obsessive Housing."
10. Ibid.
11. Waldie, Holy Land, 102.
12. California's historical divorce statistics are available online at www.christianparty.net/divorcecalifornia.htm.

CHAPTER 24

1. Michael Lewis, Liar's Poker: Rising Through the Wreckage on Wall Street (New York: W.W. Norton & Company, 1989), 35–36.
2. Ibid., 83–84.
3. Ibid., 100.
4. Charles R. Morris, The Two Trillion Dollar Meltdown: Easy Money, High Rollers, and the Great Credit Crash (New York: PublicAffairs, 2008), 140.

5. Lewis, *Liar's Poker*, 36.

6. Henry Kaufman, *On Money and Markets: A Wall Street Memoir* (New York, McGraw-Hill, 2000), 87–88.

7. Lewis, *Liar's Poker*, 47.

8. Ibid., 83.

9. Ibid.

10. Ibid., 86–88.

11. Ibid., 91–94.

12. Ibid., 88.

13. Ibid., 104.

14. Ibid., 114.

15. Bob Woodward, *Maestro: Greenspan's Fed and the American Boom* (New York: Simon & Schuster, 2000), 65.

16. Kaufman, *On Money and Markets*, 97.

17. Lewis, *Liar's Poker*, 203.

18. Tom Wolfe, *Bonfire of the Vanities* (New York: Farrar, Straus and Giroux, 1987), 60.

19. Kaufman, *On Money and Markets*, 85.

20. Lawrence Roberts, *The Great Housing Bubble: Why Did House Prices Fall?* (Las Vegas: Monterey Cypress Publishing, 2008), 60–62.

21. Kaufman, *On Money and Markets*, 82.

22. Michael Lewis, "What Wall Street's CEOs Don't Know Can Kill You," *Bloomberg News*, 26 March 2008.

23. Roger Lowenstein, "Triple-A Failure," *New York Times*, 27 April 2008.

24. Roberts, *Great Housing Bubble*, 60–61.

25. Morris, *Two Trillion Dollar Meltdown*, 118–19.

26. Lewis, *Liar's Poker*, 139–142.

27. Ibid., 148–49.

CHAPTER 25

1. Robert Manning, *Credit Card Nation: The Consequences of America's Addiction to Credit* (New York: Basic Books, 2000), 11.

2. James D. Scurlock, *Maxed Out: Hard Times, Easy Credit, and the Era of Predatory Lenders* (New York: Scribner, 2007), 42–55.

3. Calvin Elliott, *Usury* (Charleston, SC: BiblioBazaar, 2007), 11.

4. Manning, *Credit Card Nation*, 145–49.

5. Ibid.

6. Ibid.

7. Ibid.

8. Ibid.

9. Ibid.

10. Ibid.

11. Ibid.

12. Ibid., 128–29.

13. Ibid.

14. Ibid., 45.

15. Ibid., 19.

16. Ibid., 125–27.

17. Ibid.

18. "In Profile: Rev. Robert Trache of St. Mark the Evangelist Episcopal Church," *Daily Press*, January 4, 2009.

19. Ibid.

20. Manning, *Credit Card Nation*, 119.

21. Ibid., 24.

22. Scurlock, *Maxed Out*, 48.

23. Ibid., 158–61.

24. Ibid., 134.

25. Michael Novak, *Business as a Calling: Work and the Examined Life* (New York: The Free Press, 1996), 117.

CHAPTER 26

1. James Stewart, *Den of Thieves* (New York: Simon & Schuster Paperbacks, 1992), 264–65.

2. "Stu's Greatest Parties," Le Clique Entertainment, © 2009 Stu Feinstein, www.party-buzz.net/stuGreatestParties.shtml (accessed 30 September 2009).

3. James Stewart, *Den of Thieves*, 265.

4. Ibid.

5. Judith Ramsey Ehrlich and Barry J. Rehfeld, *The New Crowd: The Changing of the Jewish Guard on Wall Street* (New York: Harper Perennial, 1990), 342.

6. Ibid., 345.

7. Ibid.

8. Stewart, *Den of Thieves*, 226–27.

9. Ibid., 171.

10. Ibid., 41–43.

11. Ehrlich and Rehfeld, *The New Crowd*, 13.

12. Stewart, *Den of Thieves*, 28–31.

13. Ibid., 29.

14. Ibid.

15. Ibid., 68–70.

16. Ibid., 68.

17. Connie Bruck, *Predator's Ball: The Inside Story of Drexel Burnham and the Rise of the Junk Bond Raiders* (New York: Penguin Books, 1988), 24–25.

18. Ibid., 27–28.

19. Ibid., 30–32.

20. Connie Bruck, *Predator's Ball: The Inside Story of Drexel Burnham and the Rise of the Junk Bond Raiders* (New York: Penguin Books, 1988), 31.

21. Stewart, *Den of Thieves*, 82–83.

22. Bruck, *Predator's Ball*, 25.

23. Ibid., 57.

24. Ibid., 88.

25. Ibid., 86–87.

26. Ibid., 39.

27. Stewart, *Den of Thieves*, 60.

28. Bruck, *Predator's Ball*, 84.

29. Ibid., 84.

30. Stewart, *Den of Thieves*, 343.

31. Ibid., 289.

32. Ibid., 319.
33. Stewart, *Den of Thieves*, 379.
34. Gilder, *The Israel Test*, 40.
35. Stewart, *Den of Thieves*, 518.
36. Ibid., 317.
37. Ibid., 351.
38. *Aristotle's Politics*, Benjamin Jowett, trans. (Stilwell, KS: Digireads.com Publishing, 2005), 25.
39. Jerry Oppenheimer, *Madoff with the Money* (Hoboken, NJ: John Wiley & Sons, 2009), 23–30.
40. Ibid., 62.
41. Mark Seal, "Madoff's World," *Vanity Fair*, April 2009.
42. Ibid.
43. Ibid.
44. Ibid.
45. Ibid.
46. Mitchell Zuckoff, *Ponzi's Scheme: The True Story of a Financial Legend* (New York: Random House Trade Paperbacks, 2006), 294.
47. Erin Arvedlund, "Don't Ask, Don't Tell: Bernie Madoff Is So Secretive, He Even Asks Investors to Keep Mum," *Barron's*, 7 May, 2001.
48. Ibid.
49. Seal, "Madoff's World."
50. Ibid.
51. Ibid.
52. Ibid.

CHAPTER 27

1. Rupert Cornwell, "Greenspan steps down as Fed chief with his reputation at its zenith," *The Independent* (London), 1 February 2006.
2. Bob Woodward, *Maestro: Greenspan's Fed and the American Boom* (New York: Simon & Schuster, 2000), 55–56.
3. Adam Michelson, *The Foreclosure of America: The Inside Story of the Rise and Fall of Countrywide Homes, the Mortgage Crisis, and the Default of the American Dream* (New York: Berkley Books, 2009), 54.
4. Tom Wolfe, *Bonfire of the Vanities* (New York: Farrar, Straus and Giroux, 1987), 61.
5. Michael Lewis, "What Wall Street's CEOs Don't Know Can Kill You," *Bloomberg News*, 26 March 2008.
6. "Family and Living Arrangements—Fewer 'traditional' Families," www.libraryindex.com
7. "Non-traditional Families More Common," *Associated Press*, 28 July 2003.
8. "Children Suffer As Single-Parenting Rates Soar in Chicago and Across the U.S.," Smart Library on Urban Poverty available online at www.poverty.smartlibrary.org (accessed 15 September 2009).
9. Thomas Sowell, *The Housing Boom and Bust* (New York: Basic Books, 2009), 97–99.
10. Ibid.
11. Ibid., 99.
12. Ibid.

13. "Analysis of FHA Single-Family Default and Loss Rates," *HUD User Publications*, March 2004.

14. Jonathan Fisher and Angela Lyons, "The Ability of Women to Repay Debt After Divorce," presented at Women Working to Make a Difference, the seventh International Women's Policy Research Conference, June 2003.

15. Charles R. Morris, *The Two Trillion Dollar Meltdown: Easy Money, High Rollers, and the Great Credit Crash* (New York: PublicAffairs, 2008), 44–47.

16. Woodward, *Maestro*, 47.

17. Ibid.

18. *2001: A Space Odyssey*, screenplay by Stanley Kubrick and Arthur C. Clarke, 1968.

19. Woodward, *Maestro*, 151.

20. Ibid., 126.

21. Housing and Community Development Act of 1977—Title VIII (Community Reinvestment), http://www.fdic.gov/regulations/laws/rules/6500-2515.html.

22. Leslie Wayne, "Fading Red Line; A Special Report; New Hope in Inner Cities: Banks Offering Mortgages," *New York Times*, 14 March 1992.

23. Ibid.

24. Ibid.

25. Sowell, *The Housing Boom*, 38–43.

26. Steven Holmes, "Fannie Mae Eases Credit to Aid Mortgage Lending," *New York Times*, 30 September 1999.

27. Ibid.

28. Ibid.

29. Michelson, *Foreclosure of America*, 86.

30. Ibid., 89.

31. "First Union Capital Markets Corp., Bear, Stearns & Co. Price Securities Offering Backed by Affordable Mortgages," press release, 20 October 1997.

32. Michael Lewis, "A Wall Street Trader Draws Some Subprime Lessons," *Bloomberg News*, 5 September 2007.

33. William D. Cohan, *House of Cards: A Tale of Hubris and Wretched Excess on Wall Street* (New York: Doubleday, 2009), 153–60.

34. Ibid. 197.

35. Ibid., 208–11.

36. Michael Lewis, "The Man Who Crashed the World," *Vanity Fair*, August 2009.

37. "HUD Announces New Regulations to Provide $2.4 Trillion in Mortgages for Affordable Housing for 28.1 Million Families," HUD news press release, 31 October 2000.

38. Wayne Barrett, "Andrew Cuomo and Fannie and Freddie: How the youngest Housing and Urban Development secretary in history gave birth to the mortgage crisis," *Village Voice*, 5 August 2008.

CHAPTER 28

1. Charles R. Morris, *The Two Trillion Dollar Meltdown: Easy Money, High Rollers, and the Great Credit Crash* (New York: PublicAffairs, 2008), 65.

2. Adam Michelson, *The Foreclosure of America: The Inside Story of the Rise and Fall of Countrywide Homes, the Mortgage Crisis, and the Default of the American Dream* (New York: Berkley Books, 2009).

3. Ibid., 55.

4. "2005 Indicators Report," Sustainable San Mateo County, © 2007, www.sustainable-sanmateo.org/indicators-report/reports/the-indicators-project-may-2005/ (accessed 30 September 2009).

5. Ibid.

6. Thomas Sowell, *The Housing Boom and Bust* (New York: Basic Books, 2009), 13.

7. Michelson, *Foreclosure of America*, 136.

8. Michael Lewis, "The Man Who Crashed the World," *Vanity Fair*, August 2009.

9. William D. Cohan, *House of Cards: A Tale of Hubris and Wretched Excess on Wall Street* (New York: Doubleday, 2009), 275.

10. Ibid., 277.

11. Morris, *Two Trillion Dollar Meltdown*, 77.

12. Sowell, *The Housing Boom*, 41–42.

13. Michelson, *Foreclosure of America*, 125.

14. Alex Berenson, "Fannie Mae's Loss Risk Is Larger, Computer Models Show," *New York Times*, 7 August 2003.

15. Ibid.

16. Sowell, *The Housing Boom*, 53.

17. Ibid., 50–51.

18. Ibid.

19. Michelson, *Foreclosure of America*, 15.

20. Ibid., 21.

21. The S&P/Case-Shiller Index is a composite index of the home price index for the top 10 metropolitan areas in the United States. The index is published monthly by Standard & Poor's and uses the Karl Case and Robert Shiller method. For actual numbers: http://www2.standardandpoors.com/spf/pdf/index/csnational_value_052619.xls.

22. Cohan, *House of Cards*, 300.

23. Lawrence Roberts, *The Great Housing Bubble: Why Did House Prices Fall?* (Las Vegas: Monterey Cypress Publishing, 2008), 16–18.

24. Leslie Wayne, "Fading Red Line; A Special Report; New Hope in Inner Cities: Banks Offering Mortgages," *New York Times*, 14 March 1992.

25. Ibid.

26. "Illegal Immigration and the Subprime Mortgage Crisis," *Reuters*, 30 January 2008.

27. Roberts, *Great Housing Bubble*, 18–20.

28. Cohan, *House of Cards*, 300.

29. "Economic Outlook and Current Fiscal Issues," testimony of Chairman Alan Greenspan before the Committee on the Budget, U.S. House of Representatives, 25 February 2004.

30. Morris, *Two Trillion Dollar Meltdown*, 69.

31. Lewis, "The Man Who Crashed."

32. Michelson, *Foreclosure of America*, 134–35.

33. Lewis, "The Man Who Crashed."

34. Ibid.

35. Ibid.

36. Michelson, *Foreclosure of America*, 232.

37. "Traditional Housing Affordability Index," © 2009 California Association of Realtors, www.car.org/economics/marketdata/haitraditional/ (accessed 30 September 2009).

38. Cohan, *House of Cards*, 315–20.

39. Ibid., 318.

40. Ibid., 302.
41. Ibid., 306–07.
42. Peter Schiff, "Sub-Prime Disaster in the Making," *SafeHaven*, 22 December 2006.
43. Cohan, *House of Cards*, 323.
44. Gretchen Morgenson, "Inside the Countrywide Lending Spree," *New York Times*, 26 August 2007.
45. Cohan, *House of Cards*, 326.
46. Richard Bookstaber, *A Demon of Our Own Design: Markets, Hedge Funds, and the Perils of Financial Innovation* (Hoboken: John Wiley & Sons, 2007), 50.
47. Cohan, *House of Cards*, 328.
48. Ibid., 332.
49. Ibid., 75.
50. Morris, *Two Trillion Dollar Meltdown*, 49.
51. Cohan, *House of Cards*, 344–45.
52. Ibid.
53. Ibid., 349–50.
54. Michelson, *Foreclosure of America*, 257.
55. Ibid.
56. Ibid.
57. Lewis, "The Man Who Crashed."

CHAPTER 29

1. William D. Cohan, *House of Cards: A Tale of Hubris and Wretched Excess on Wall Street* (New York: Doubleday, 2009), 98.
2. Ibid., 398.
3. Adam Michelson, *The Foreclosure of America: The Inside Story of the Rise and Fall of Countrywide Homes, the Mortgage Crisis, and the Default of the American Dream* (New York: Berkley Books, 2009), 270–72.
4. Ibid., 284.
5. Michael Lewis, "The Man Who Crashed the World," *Vanity Fair*, August 2009.
6. *Tavis Smiley Show*, April 20, 2009, available online at http://www.pbs.org/kcet/tavissmiley/archive/200904/20090420_frank.html.
7. Christopher Dodd, "Mortgage Market Turmoil: Causes and Consequences," opening statement by Chairman Christopher Dodd at the U.S. Senate Committee on Banking, Housing and Urban Affairs, 22 March 2007.
8. Alan Greenspan, "A Response to My Critics," Financial Times Economists' Forum, April 6, 2008, available online at http://blogs.ft.com/economistsforum/2008/04/alan-greenspan-a-response-to-my-critics/.
9. Ibid.
10. Ibid.
11. Cohan, *House of Cards*, 450.
12. Ibid.

CHAPTER 30

1. Dave Ramsey, *The Total Money Makeover: A Proven Plan for Financial Fitness* (Nashville, TN: Thomas Nelson, 2007), 3.

2. Ibid.

3. Suze Orman, *The 9 Steps to Financial Freedom: Practical and Spiritual Steps So You Can Stop Worrying* (New York: Three Rivers Press, 2000), 181–82.

4. Ramsey, *Total Money Makeover*, 26.

5. Ibid., 29.

6. Ibid., 4.

7. Ibid., 50.

Acknowledgments

I WOULD LIKE TO THANK JOEL MILLER OF THOMAS NELSON BOTH FOR the idea and the opportunity to pursue it; my agent, Alex Hoyt, for his unstinting labor on my behalf; my wife, Joan Dean, for her editorial assistance and general understanding; Merrill Lynch financial advisor Clint Anderson for his technical review; my editor, Kristen Parrish, for her smart and good-spirited work; and fellow boiler John M. Houkes for his masterful, old-school scholarship on the history of usury.

About the Author

JACK CASHILL HAS PRODUCED A SCORE OF DOCUMENTARIES, MOST RECENTLY *Thine Eyes: A Witness to the March for Life* with Jennifer O'Neill. His writing has appeared in *Fortune, The Wall Street Journal, Washington Post,* and *Weekly Standard,* and he also writes regularly for the *American Thinker* and *WorldNetDaily.* His recent books include *Hoodwinked, Sucker Punch,* and *What's the Matter with California?* Jack has a PhD in American studies from Purdue University.